You Owe
Yourself a Drunk

You Owe
Yourself a Drunk

An
Ethnography
of Urban Nomads

JAMES P. SPRADLEY

Prospect Heights, Illinois

For information about this book, write or call:
Waveland Press, Inc.
P.O. Box 400
Prospect Heights, Illinois 60070
847/634-0081

To *my friend,* the Tramp

He was genuinely puzzled by frenzy and by hate because he was incapable of it himself. He could never quite understand it in others. The last time I saw him that was what he talked about. He was puzzled by the hatred he had seen in our times. And he said the thing the world needs most today is understanding and an ability to see the other person's point of view and not to hate him because he disagrees. That was Dwight Eisenhower.

President Richard M. Nixon

Praise for YOU OWE YOURSELF A DRUNK

"Spradley's *You Owe Yourself a Drunk* stands the test of time, combining as it does careful scholarship, a concern for social policy, and a palpable compassion for the human beings whose lives are depicted in such rich ethnographic detail."
    Michael V. Angrosino, *University of South Florida*

"Spradley's respect for the complex cognitive worlds and textured social relations of urban nomads, his outrage at the criminal justice system that oppresses them, and his respectfully rendered ethnography always inspire many students."
    Brett Williams, *American University*

"Both sound ethnographic reporting and quintessentially relevant applied social science, this book reflects how Spradley's investment of time and effort in sensitively portraying the way of life of a marginal population (long before "the homeless" became a fashionable cause), resulted in realistic and humanitarian adjustments in the criminal justice system of some major cities."
    Dwight B. Heath, *Brown University*

"In the years since Spradley's classic study of urban nomads first appeared, the anthropology of alcohol and drug studies has come of age, applied anthropology has grown enormously, and medical anthropologists increasingly have engaged in public health and social justice issues. Many of the matters that Spradley addresses remain with us today in only slightly altered form, e.g., the high rates of alcohol and other substance abuse among contemporary homeless populations in America and the ways these are handled by the police and other law enforcement agencies. It is wonderful to once more have this book available for classroom use."
    Mac Marshall, *University of Iowa*

"While some of the data may have changed since the research was conducted thirty years ago, Spradley's superb combination of ethnographic method, analytical skill, and personal empathy continues to shine through this pioneering study of life on one of the margins of urban America. *You Owe Yourself a Drunk* reminds us of the sense and understanding that anthropology can bring to the study of contemporary issues."
    Lawrence B. Breitborde, *Knox College*

"Thirty years ago, James Spradley shook us from our sleep. Now we cheer the reavailability of *You Owe Yourself a Drunk* in these complacent times. A classic and a wake-up call!"
    Alisse Waterston, author of *Love, Sorrow and Rage:*
        Destitute Women in a Manhattan Residence

Contents

Acknowledgements

This book would not have been possible without the generous cooperation of men like Bill, Harry, James, Ed, Jesse, Joe, and Ralph who live by the culture of urban nomads. They patiently endured the invasion of their lives and freely answered my questions, often at great personal risk. Their humor, spontaneity, honesty, interest, and acceptance made this study a most enjoyable experience.

This study was made possible by the support provided by the Departments of Psychiatry and Anthropology, University of Washington. Partial support was also received from the U.S. Public Health Service Undergraduate Training in Human Behavior Grant, No. 5-T2-MH-7871-06 from the Institute of Mental Health and the State of Washington Initiative 171 Funds for Research in Biology and Medicine. I owe a special debt of gratitude to Thomas H. Holmes, who not only read the manuscript and made important suggestions, but also provided a stimulating and congenial research environment in the Department of Psychiatry at the University of Washington. I wish to thank Ron Fagan, Director of the Cedar Hills Alcoholism Treatment Center, as well as other members of that organization, for their interest and cooperation during this project. The staff of the Municipal Criminal Court, Department No. 2, Seattle, Washington, were most helpful and made my research in their court a pleasant experience.

Mary Jahn worked as my personal editor and made invaluable contributions to this study. The content and organization of the book were influenced at every stage by discussions with her. By careful editing of numerous drafts of the manuscript she added clarity and style to the final product. She taught me that all colleagues are not professional social scientists. Throughout the project, her compassionate understanding of the men of this book was a constant reminder that they were not simply subjects for anthropological scrutiny, but fellow human beings worthy of respect.

I wish to acknowledge the assistance of Pere Hage who introduced me to ethnoscience and while a student became my teacher; John Atkins who contributed many insights on the theoretical problems of ethnography; Joy Sullivan who typed many drafts of the manuscript and made frequent suggestions for its improvement; Seattle Councilman Tim Hill and Judge James Noe, who not only read parts of the manuscript but were an inspiration because of their desire to provide social justice for the Skid Road Alcoholic. Many individuals made suggestions about the research and made critical comments on earlier drafts of the manuscript including Paula Johnson, Paul Kay, Robert Rhodes, Linda Rodgers, William Rodgers, Tom Weaver, Mike Lieber, Tom Hill, John Junker, Luverne Rieke, Leon Arksey, Laura Arksey, James Oakland, Jim Coughlin, and Frank Johnson. To these, and also those I may have omitted, I am grateful.

Most of all, I am indebted to my wife, Barbara, whose insights, interest, and advice cannot be measured.

YOU OWE YOURSELF A DRUNK
James P. Spradley's Enduring Perspective

MERRILL SINGER
Hispanic Health Council

You Owe Yourself a Drunk is a challenge! Its widely recognized status as an anthropological model, in fact, rests on its success in weaving together several cogent challenges, all of them as relevant today as when James Spradley began the research for this book on the streets of Seattle, Washington, in August 1968.

First, *You Owe Yourself a Drunk* presents a poignant challenge to society about our capacity to endure and accept nonconformity and social diversity. The people Spradley studied and writes about in this volume, those he sensitively referred to as "urban nomads" (or tramps, their self-selected designation) but whom society usually dismisses as good-for-nothing skid row bums, winos, derelicts, and beggars, do not fit neatly into conventional social roles nor adhere to established social standards. They talk differently. They dress differently. They live their lives in ways that are routinely held up to ridicule and dismissal. They are, in many people's eyes, social failures. As Spradley once pointed out on paper about the ways urban nomads attempt to limit their time in jail when arrested for public inebriation:

> The values our culture places upon privacy, materialism, moralism, and work are not the ones affecting the lives of tramps. These are men who live in a society that holds no place for them. Their lifestyle is offensive to most Americans, and for this reason they are arrested, jailed, and punished by standards that do not apply to the rest of society.[1]

It is significant, therefore, that even readers who hold such views of urban nomads find it hard to complete this book without gaining a new awareness of the fundamental importance of learning the other person's point of view, especially when that person is someone who, it is assumed, does not have a coherent view of life, to say nothing of a unique cultural tradition and a set of penetrating and often unflattering insights about the peculiar ways of the dominant society. As a result, many readers of this book are challenged to rethink their view of tramps and, perhaps, to begin questioning various taken-for-granted assumptions about other culturally different people as well.

Second, this book is a sharp challenge to politicians, policy-makers, judges, the police, and others who are inclined to punish people "for the crime of poverty."[2] It is Spradley's assertion, in fact, that many of our urban ills, those that first began to be noticed at the time this book was originally published in 1970, have their roots in policies of intolerance. He argues, "If we continue to make poverty and lifestyles, which threaten us because they are different, the basis for justice and punishment, then the urban crisis will continue."[3] Without doubt, America's urban crisis has continued! Central to the problems of the city today are poverty, homelessness, police-community relations, and substance abuse—issues that are closely examined in this volume. One of the goals of this book is to demonstrate the utility of anthropology's ethnographic method and cultural perspective in addressing these issues. As Spradley and his long-time colleague David McCurdy have observed:

> More than anything else, the study of culture separates anthropologists from other social scientists. Other scholars do not ignore culture, they assume their subjects have it, but their main interest is to account for human behavior by plotting correlations among variables. . . [By contrast] . . . almost every anthropologist starts with ethnography, the description of a peculiar culture, and such studies are required to understand the complexity and conflict within American society.[4]

Sadly, it has taken the AIDS epidemic, with its horrible toll on human life and well-being, for the contributions of ethnographic research and a culturally sensitive approach to addressing human social issues to gain a degree of acceptance among policymakers.

This book urges that far bigger steps are needed, and it provides a methodology for harnessing ethnography and a cultural perspective in responding to pressing social problems.

Third, in adopting such a focus, this book is a challenge to social scientists to move beyond a narrow concern with purely intellectual issues and to jump into the trenches of applied research. Spradley's goal in writing this book, in part, was to summon his fellow anthropologists to choose "the risk of making a mistake to the danger of inaction."[5] This challenge remains an important one. In some ways, in fact, it is more timely today than when Spradley completed this study and the accompanying applied work he undertook to change the public treatment of urban nomads in Seattle. But much has changed since then.

In the years since *You Owe Yourself a Drunk* originally was published, anthropology has undergone a crisis of confidence concerning its ability to accurately describe the cultures of other peoples. This dilemma has its roots in the postmodern transition that began to be felt in the aftermath of the Vietnam War. Prior to this period, anthropologists had headed into the field nervous about their ability to endure life in another culture or their acceptance by the people they intended to study but buoyed by a sense of confidence in their capacity not only to understand but to represent accurately the complexities, the insider understandings, and the experiences of other ways of life. These were the heady days of what has been termed "ethnographic realism," an allusion to the literary genre of nineteenth-century realist fiction. Whereas realist novelists, like Charles Dickens, sought to describe the whole social reality of the characters in their books through the creative presentation of abundant detail, realist ethnography is characterized by a strong sense of authorial control of extensive knowledge garnered through direct personal involvement in the culture of concern. The resulting text, the traditional ethnography (like the one you are holding), stands as a holistic representation of another way of life. The realist ethnography is of importance because it claims to be an accurate and full account of a social reality that was previously unknown or only minimally known to the reader.

However, during the days that Spradley sat for hours at his typewriter crafting the elegant and impassioned sentences that comprise this book, the social foundations upon which the realist ethnography and the whole anthropological enterprise are based began to shift. Before long, college campuses, insulated retreats where careful reflection and thoughtful composition about the wider world were possible, had become flashpoints of social unrest and testing grounds for alternative lifestyles. The antiwar movement and its condemnation of the Vietnam War as an unjust and indefensible act of aggression by an industrial giant against a largely peasant society swept across America causing intense questioning of conventional wisdom and acceptable behavior. When America lost the war in Vietnam, a defeat that is still difficult for most Americans to admit or accept, dominant values and conceptions were further shaken. In the aftermath of the war, Third World and marginalized peoples long spoken for by others began to demand to speak for themselves (with telling implications for anthropology's claims to special authority and to a privileged voice about the ethnographic Other). At the same time, the Civil Rights movement, and other social upheavals that it helped to spark, such as feminism or the gay movement, generated sharp debate about America's commitment to its own oft expressed values of freedom and equality. Significant as they were, these were not the only changes that helped to reshape the contemporary world. When this book first appeared on bookstore shelves, computers were monstrous plotting contraptions hidden away on college campuses, while the idea of personal computers (and the dramatic ways in which our lives would be influenced by and come to depend upon them) or the existence of a global "information super highway" was the stuff of science fiction. Other technologies that are commonplace today, like video cameras, VCRs, microwave ovens, pay-per-view movie channels, cell phones and the like, could not be found in even the wealthiest American homes. Importantly, these transformations are not limited to highly industrialized societies, they have, to varying degrees, restructured human experience and social relations everywhere. As a result, the older anthropological conception of distinct peoples and cultures, isolated and understandable in their own terms, has given way to a fast-paced world of migrant populations and mobile ideas, a world in which an increasingly intense kaleidoscopic juxtaposition of cultural meanings, objects, and identities unfolds on a global scale.

These dramatic social and technological changes have important implications for the human sciences, including anthropology. One telling consequence has been a thorough-going shift in thinking about the nature of anthropological writing. While Spradley and his peers—as evidenced, for example, by the strong taxonomic orientation of this book—were greatly influenced by theoretical and methodological developments in linguistics (which appeared to offer more systematic methods for understanding culturally patterned knowledge), in subsequent years literary criticism, as well as the fields of rhetoric and poetics, became increasingly important sources of new ideas in anthropology. In the process, anthropological writing of the sort found in *You Owe Yourself a Drunk* was subject to evermore critical assessment. In time, the cognitive approach in anthropology—one that views culture, as Spradley did, as a set of categories, rules, maps, and plans used to generate and interpret behavior—began to loose its currency among anthropologists influenced by the postmodern rejection of epistemic approaches that appear to privilege the rational foundations of Western cultures. Cognitive anthropology was criticized specifically on the grounds that the cultural models it produces, such as Spradley's elaborate taxonomy of the kinds of "flops" (places to sleep) used by urban nomads or the componential definitions of the types of tramps that comprise the urban nomad population, are heavily burdened by the weight of the researcher's own cultural categories and assumptions.

Significantly, also under assault during the academic reign of postmodernist ideas was the direct involvement of anthropologists (as anthropologists) in applied work, including the types of initiatives undertaken very effectively by Spradley. For example, as he followed often-arrested urban nomads through their encounters with the police, the judicial system, and city jails—an arduous trail that is fervidity described in this volume—Spradley began to draw conclusions about the urgent policy implications of his findings. Indeed, the very title of this book, which is based on a common saying among urban nomads when they are released from jail after a prolonged incarceration, was specifically chosen to reflect a way in which public policies contribute to alcohol abuse among homeless people. When he subsequently was asked to participate in efforts to design a more effective drug treatment system for homeless men, he avidly agreed. As Spradley's wife, Barbara, has written of him, "Jim had a strong interest in conducting research that made a difference in people's lives, in bettering the human condition."[6]

Based on his growing insights about the daily lives, world-views, and heartfelt concerns of the urban nomads he was studying, Spradley was able to make a number of useful recommendations, such as calling for changes in the required length of stay in the treatment facility (six months), a period he found was causing the men "considerable anxiety and detracting from the effectiveness of the therapy programs."[7] Additionally, because their enforced social disempowerment made it impossible for the men Spradley studied to organize effectively on their own behalf, he also, at times, assumed the role of advocate for urban nomads. Working with an ad hoc committee of concerned citizens, he wrote a detailed report about the deplorable and exploitive ways that men arrested for public inebriation are treated while in custody. The report was delivered to a local judge, members of the city council of Seattle, the mayor's office, the police department, and to various other public policy and health care professionals. Although some people were angered by Spradley's indictment of the police, his work began to receive a great deal of media attention. For a solid week, Spradley's report was featured in front-page local newspaper coverage. As a result, within six months the city passed an ordinance establishing an alcohol detoxification program. Over the next few years, the state of Washington and other states as well decriminalized public drunkenness. Increasingly, public policy nationally began to emphasize detoxification rather than imprisonment for people stopped by the police for being under the influence of alcohol in a public place.

Despite the evident success of Spradley's efforts in advocating humane changes in social policies, the involvement of anthropologists in social intervention raises thorny questions given the traditional relativist concern of the discipline with understanding other societies on their own terms. A further basis for uneasiness with anthropological involvement in planned social change emerges from the postmodern understanding of culture. From the postmodern perspective, there are no enduring cultural truths and hence no objectively identifiable culture to be inscribed in fieldworkers' notebooks. Rather, people are constantly reinventing their culture under changing historic circumstances. What anthropologists encounter in the field, argue processually influenced postmodernist thinkers, is not culture writ large but rather situational responses that reflect the self-interested and contested positions of specific individuals or subgroups within a broader historic framework of relations and symbols. Culture, in other words, is the messy process of negotiated meaning in social context. Thus, postmodernist anthropology argues that culture does not exist outside the lived reality of day-to-day thought and action. The role of the anthropologist, as a consequence, cannot be to intervene on behalf of one or another subgroup or in support of a particular conception of reality in a contested social field, and hence it can never include endorsing one or another course of action. The anthropologist's job, instead, is to stand apart, to observe, to describe and to produce a detailed ethnographic account of unfolding events and interactions in all their complexity.

In light of the sweeping nature of the postmodern critique, it bears emphasizing that the primary alternative approach postmodernists have offered involves modifying the conventions of ethnographic writing to allow for multivocal texts that have study participants speak in their own words as co-producers of anthropological publications. Interestingly, this, in part, is precisely the strategy that Spradley employs at the beginning of this book when he opens the text to William R. Tanner, a 49-year-old urban nomad, and allows him to tell his own life story and recent experiences in his own words. However, it has come to be realized with increasing ire that this experimental twist strongly advocated by postmodernist anthropologists fails to overcome the fact that all ethnographic descriptions ultimately are authored by social scientists not by the people they study. In the end, it is still the anthropologist who exercises authority over textual content and style. Therefore, it is the anthropologist who constructs the social worlds of study participants even if the building blocks are their own words. As such, there is no real collaboration in the postmodern text; as with traditional realist texts, there is only the anthropologist as writer serving as final arbiter of what goes into and what stays out of published works.

Increasingly, as anthropologists have been called to the front to address human suffering and pressing social problems, like AIDS, homelessness, substance abuse, violence, shrinking natural resources, and the like, they have come to feel that the goal of research should not be the production of sanitized texts devoid of any hint of dominant culture influences nor descriptions that achieve ultimate "truth" about other ways of life. Instead, a quite satisfactory goal is the production of "good enough" descriptions that serve the practical ends of making useful contributions both to human knowledge as well as to the establishment of social programs that address unmet human needs. Moreover, in recent years anthropologists have come to recognize the core irony of postmodernism: it so doggedly promoted the production of collaborative, negotiated texts yet balked at collaborative, negotiated social action. Involvement in praxis, of course, as shown repeatedly throughout Spradley's study, is predicated on a sense of hope (that things can be made better), which was never a primary postmodern value.

In a sense, the discipline of anthropology has come full-circle. Ethnography remains its central methodology, and direct work on difficult social problems and other social applications is the arena that employs the majority of its college graduates. Even cognitive approaches have found new adherents, as applied anthropologists have explored effective methods for assessing insider understandings and associated behaviors. In short, the challenge of *You Owe Yourself a Drunk* for anthropology has grown anew in recent years, making its republication especially timely.

As applied anthropology has moved from the wings to occupy a more central location in the anthropological drama, a number of questions continue to be raised within the field that have direct bearing on this book: (1) In their work, do applied anthropologists actually apply anthropology or are they anthropologists in name and social technicians in practice? (2) Do their efforts have any detectable impact on the wider world; do they contribute to making changes that matter? (3) As anthropologists, are they taken seriously by those who formulate and enforce the social policies that shape our lives; does the discipline have credibility beyond the ivory towers? (4) How can applied anthropologists inject issues, understandings, and methods that make sense anthropologically into interdisciplinary settings that often are innocent of a clear appreciation of the discipline? and (5) What is the enduring place of applied work in an encompassing anthropological discipline steeped in a cultural relativist perspective that has long questioned the appropriateness of intervention in local settings?

In response to the first of the questions listed above, there is general agreement among applied anthropologists, especially those working in the fields of homelessness and substance abuse, that *You Owe Yourself a Drunk* stands as a shining example of the direct application of distinctly anthropological concepts (e.g., the cognitive mapping of the urban nomad subculture) and methods (e.g., ethnosemantic elicitation of cognitive categories) to address real-world problems. Relative to the issue of homelessness, for example, this volume was ahead of its time in calling attention to the problem prior to the significant upsurge in popular concern (including distress about rising rates of homelessness among whole families, women, and children) that developed in the late 1970s and early 1980s. It is estimated that on any given night over 700,000 individuals in America are homeless and, over the course of the year, as many as 2,000,000 people suffer from homelessness in the United States. Yet discerning the causes of homelessness remains a controversial issue. Some have asserted that people tend to become or remain homeless because of their mental health problems, because of alcoholism or drug addiction, or because of learned behavior patterns. By contrast, a number of ethnographers, beginning with Spradley, have found that homelessness is rooted in issues of poverty, institutions of social control (e.g., the police, courts, and jails), and the lack of available, affordable housing. In other words, while many policymakers, sectors of the media, and to a degree the general public portray homelessness as a product of individual traits or decisions, ethnographies like *You Owe Yourself a Drunk*, which are based on firsthand, close-up examinations of the day-to-day lives and experiences of homeless people, have tended to draw attention instead to social structural factors that perpetuate the problem. For Spradley, homelessness among the urban nomads is not an expression of personal shortcomings but rather a consequence of social alienation and the way these men are treated by societal institutions of law enforcement.

Relative to the second question noted above, it is evident from the prior discussion that *You Owe Yourself a Drunk* had an important impact on the way public intoxication is handled in Seattle and beyond. Without doubt, however, the broader issue of how society should respond to the problem of alcohol dependence remains unresolved. Currently, the National Institute on Alcohol Abuse and Alcoholism estimates that the cost to society for alcohol abuse is approximately $150 billion a year. With the AIDS epidemic, substance abuse among the homeless has emerged as a major public health crisis. Prior to Spradley's study, however, the anthropological voice on this issue was small indeed. Most anthropological research that touched on the issue of drinking behavior did so only in passing as a subtopic in the study of other subject matter. Following Spradley's lead, the number of anthropologists involved in applied research on drinking (and illicit drug use) has grown steadily in recent years. So too, the sociocultural model employed by Spradley, one that examines problem drinking in the context of general drinking patterns and general drinking patterns within a broader account of social conditions, structural relations, and cultural organization, has gained in importance. While debates rage over the relative contributions of genetic, psychosocial, familial, social structural, historic, and cultural factors in alcohol use and abuse, anthropology as a discipline has had a somewhat modest but growing level of influence on the way drinking and its health and social consequences are understood and addressed in American society and elsewhere. This volume deserves an important share of the credit for this achievement.

The third question concerns the level of credibility that applied anthropology has achieved, in this case, in the field of alcohol-related social intervention, including both prevention and treatment. On the one hand, this question reflects the experience of many anthropologists that their methods often are critiqued as being "soft" (i.e., impressionistic), for relying on small samples, and, because they are so dependent on the skills of the individual researcher, for producing findings that are hard to duplicate. Consequently, anthropological approaches are not always accorded full legitimacy, especially in health domains strongly influenced by quantitative methodologies and experimental research designs. On the other hand, anthropologists who, like Spradley, focus their research on urban populations in highly industrialized societies or on contemporary social problems, often encounter puzzled responses from people outside of the discipline, including students. As Spradley and McCurdy have written:

> Many students associate cultural anthropology with the study of primitive peoples. They picture the anthropologist as that slightly peculiar person who, dressed in khaki shorts and pith helmet, lives among some exotic tribe in order to record the group's bizarre and not altogether pleasant customs.[8]

Breaking these stereotypes and misconceptions is not easy, not just among students but among health care providers, drug treatment professionals, substance abuse prevention experts, and other kinds of caregivers as well.

One of the primary strengths of this book, in fact, is its productive anthropological examination of seemingly unremarkable people who dwell in the interstitial arenas of contemporary urban life. By focusing on a familiar population, although one that is often seen but rarely understood (in effect, hidden in plain sight), Spradley was able to spark a reexamination of taken-for-granted assumptions about the inner-city poor. Consequently, as the earlier discussion of his applied work indicates, the insights Spradley gained ultimately were seen as highly significant in the treatment of recidivist alcoholics as well as in creating a more appropriate and humane response to public drunkenness.

In this light, it is of interest to note that in his teaching Spradley often used very mundane behaviors and everyday experiences to demonstrate the value of the anthropological approach. For example, while attending college, Spradley supported himself by working nights in an egg company, unloading large boxes of eggs brought in from farms for sorting by size and other traits into marketable packages. In one of his articles,[9] he employed the distinctly anthropological analytic method (domain analysis) used in this book to examine this routine work setting. His goal: to demonstrate that culture is everywhere and that even the most ordinary, taken-for-granted, and outwardly natural behaviors are, in fact, culturally created (and thus not so simple, automatic, or self-evident after all). It has been said that the best ethnography makes the exotic familiar (by showing its very human character) while exoticizing the familiar (by revealing the incredible complexity of even very commonplace and prosaic behaviors). In this very tough assignment, *You Owe Yourself a Drunk* achieves unparalleled success.

You Owe Yourself a Drunk is significant in another way as well. It examines a subgroup within American society. Historically, anthropology emerged as the study of foreign peoples, including the indigenous populations of North America, who had been encountered by the imperial expansion of European society.[10] Anthropology, in short, came into being with a colonial mission to study conquered peoples dispersed around the globe. While there has been considerable debate within anthropology about the degree to which colonial administrators actually took anthropological insights into account in formulating colonial policies as well as admirable effort to make a clear break with its past, it is undeniably true that anthropology began in the West with the explicit goal of understanding the rest (i.e., non-European peoples). While *You Owe Yourself a Drunk* was far from the first anthropological study of a non-native population in North America, its appearance marked an early stage in an increasingly evident shift toward "bringing anthropology home." Spradley also contributed to this turn with a subsequent ethnography written with Brenda Mann entitled *The Cocktail Waitress: Women's Work in a Man's World.* Interestingly, it was not until 1990, twenty years after this book was first published, that a professional group devoted to furthering the anthropology of North America finally formed within the American Anthropological Association, an entity that itself was formed in 1901. The acceptance of North American anthropology within the wider discipline, however, still has not been fully achieved.

The fourth query directed at applied anthropology concerns its contributions to interdisciplinary work: are applied anthropologists accepted as collaborators and sought out for assistance by applied researchers from other disciplines? Interestingly, if there is a field in which interdisciplinary collaboration involving anthropologists is now well developed it is in applied research on substance use and abuse. Books like Spradley's *You Owe Yourself a Drunk*, Michael Agar's *Ripping and Running*, Catherine Allen's *The Hold Life Has: Coca and Cultural Identity*, Christine Eber's *Women and Alcohol in a Highland Maya Town*, Mac Marshall's *Weekend Warriors: Alcohol in a Micronesian Culture*, Philippe Bourgois' *In Search of Respect: Selling Crack in El Barrio*, and Claire Sterk's *Fast Lives: Women Who Use Crack Cocaine* are among a growing number of outstanding ethnographic studies that have contributed to this acceptance. In some areas, such as the ethnography of AIDS-risk among drug users, collaboration between ethnographers and epidemiological and public health researchers is now standard operating procedure. Moreover, anthropologists regularly are invited to sit on review panels for the National Institutes of Health to assess grant applications in the arena of substance abuse research.

The final question asked of applied anthropology concerns its impact on the wider field of anthropology. For example, what influence has *You Owe Yourself a Drunk* had on increasing the acceptance of applied anthropology within the wider discipline? Also, what effect has the book had on bringing issues like homelessness and substance abuse into the fold as accepted and valued topics of anthropological concern? These questions draw attention to the difficult time applied anthropologists have had in gaining full acceptance for their work among so-called theoretical anthropologists (those involved in basic research who normally do not use anthropology to address contemporary social issues). Historically, there has been a fair degree of animosity between the more theoretical and more applied camps within anthropology. Theoretical anthropologists criticized applied work on the grounds that it is atheoretical, it is a violation of the nonjudgmental, relativist stance traditional to the discipline, and it can involve sidetaking in contested areas of social life. Applied anthropologists counter that applied work both is guided by existing anthropological theories and contributes to new theory development within the discipline, that the relativist, value-free claim of theoretical anthropology is a chimera, and that lack of action under conditions of structural violence or social suffering is a kind of sidetaking on behalf of the status quo. *You Owe Yourself a Drunk* reflects the position of applied anthropology in all three of these disputes.

As noted, the theoretical stance of this book is rooted in the perspective of cognitive anthropology. This perspective sees culture as a set of cognitive structures that children learn as they grow up in a particular community and that they use to make decisions about their own behavior and to interpret the behaviors of the people around them. For example, Spradley shows how the cognitive frames about urban nomads and about acceptable social behavior that are held by members of the police force and the judicial system shape the harsh ways in which tramps are often treated in society. These frames, however, are not the ones held by urban nomads, who, in effect, have come to be resocialized into an alternative subculture that rationalizes and supports alternative ways of being and acting. Discovery of these alternative frames, analysis of their structure and logic, and assessment of the social consequences of conflicted social rules (e.g., between urban nomads and others, like mission workers or judges, who inhabit common social space) are the theoretical aims of this book. While culturalist explanations have been criticized for failing to move beyond the construction of cognitive frames to assess the ways societal inequality and power shape insider cultural understandings, this criticism does not apply to Spradley's work. He explicitly employed a cognitive model of culture to explicate rather than to obscure the role of political and economic factors in the creation of cultural worlds. This sophisticated theoretical model, in turn, guided the applied work that Spradley carried out in his effort to improve the lot of urban nomads and to change the ways they are treated by representatives of mainstream institutions.

In deciding to write and widely distribute his report on the conditions faced by urban nomads in jail, an act he referred to as "making strategic use of the information" he had ethnographically gathered,[11] Spradley made a decision not just to describe or explain social behaviors but to criticize directly the social patterns that he felt were morally wrong. He chose to act as an advocate because he did not believe that urban nomads were in a position, relative to the dominant institutions in society, to advocate effectively on their own behalf. Moreover, he did not see treatment providers or others who had regular contact with urban nomads assuming this role. Instead, he witnessed criminal justice and drug treatment professionals continually pointing fingers of blame at tramps for being the cause of their own problems.

Although many of the professional people who deal with tramps do not realize it, they have adopted a common strategy used by people in positions of power. This strategy is to blame the victims for all the problems they face. Instead of seeing jail as a place of oppression, they blame tramps for drinking too much. Instead of seeing arrest and incarceration as gross inequities based on the different lifestyle of tramps, they blame tramps for not being willing to seek treatment for alcoholism.[12]

Spradley's "value explicit" applied approach (i.e., choosing to act on the basis of specific values that are openly acknowledged) contrasts sharply with the "value-free" orientation supported by many theoretical anthropologists. However, it can and has been argued that the decision not to act in light of possessing knowledge about oppression also reflects a particular value orientation, while ultimately lending support to a continuation of that oppression. In short, the latter approach differs from a value-explicit orientation not in being value-free but in its reflection of hidden or implicit values. Either way, anthropologists can be accused of being guilty of the act of "side-taking." That being the case, it becomes critically important to acquire the best information possible by conducting rigorous, focused, and capable research, all characteristics of *You Owe Yourself a Drunk*.

The last challenge presented by Spradley's monograph is addressed to students. Beyond the field of anthropology as an academic discipline, beyond the domain of policymakers and the decision-making processes that shape our society and way of life, and beyond the domain of planned social intervention, this book constitutes an open invitation to students to examine the kinds of persons they want to be in a world of often vicious intolerance, great social suffering, rampant social inequality, and growing structural violence. It is hard to finish reading *You Owe Yourself a Drunk* without a feeling of encounter with James Spradley, the man behind the book, especially the profound sense of respect and compassion that characterized his interactions with people so demeaned elsewhere in society. Sadly, James Spradley died in September 1982, but this book stands as a lasting tribute to his efforts to go against the grain and to stand up to criticism in the cause of social justice. Students are similarly challenged to question their own storehouse of prejudicial stereotypes, pejorative assumptions, and culturally ingrained attitudes of intolerance. Ultimately, this is precisely what education is all about: disabusing students of perpetually fixed ideas, challenging official "truths," and breaking the chains of constrained thought.

In sum, while it is many years since *You Owe Yourself a Drunk* was first published, this book has stood up well to the test of what Shakespeare, in his *Twelfth Night*, colorfully referred to as the "whirligig of time." While many other ethnographies written before and after it have largely lost their relevance because of our evermore rapidly changing world, the continually evolving nature of our research methods, and the rapidly shifting theoretical perspectives that guide anthropological research and application, this book remains of enormous contemporary pertinence and value. Substance use and abuse, homelessness, social inequality, the expanding role of prisons as mechanisms of social control, the part played by the police in enforcing cultural values, and our societal and individual capacities for not only tolerating but celebrating social diversity are, if anything, of even greater importance today than at the time Spradley directly or indirectly addressed these issues in the pages of this book. At the outset of this introduction, the claim was made that *You Owe Yourself a Drunk* is a classic of anthropological literature. In truth, it holds the rare distinction of being a triple classic: it is, simultaneously, a classic in the ethnographic study of substance abuse and homelessness, a classic in applied anthropology, and a classic in the anthropology of North America. Were all of this not sufficient reason to make this an honored book, the unrestrained humanity and deep compassion of the author that permeates his portrayal of people long scorned and abused by our society would do so quite adequately.

NOTES

1. James Spradley, "Beating the Drunk Charge," in James Spradley and David McCurdy (eds.), *Conformity and Conflict*, Boston: Little Brown and Company, p. 358, 1971.
2. *You Owe Yourself a Drunk*, p. 252.
3. *You Owe Yourself a Drunk*, p. 259.
4. James Spradley and David McCurdy, "Culture and the Contemporary World," in James Spradley and David McCurdy (eds.), *Conformity and Conflict*, Boston: Little Brown and Company, p. 4, 1971.
5. James Spradley and David McCurdy, *Anthropology: The Cultural Perspective*, New York: John Wiley & Sons, 1975.
6. E-mail letter from Barbara Spradley to Merrill Singer, September 10, 1999.
7. Spradley and McCurdy, 1975, p. 626.
8. Spradley and McCurdy, 1971, p. 1.
9. James Spradley, "Foundations of Cultural Knowledge," in James Spradley (ed.), *Culture and Cognition: Rules, Maps and Plans*, pp. 33-38. San Francisco: Chandler Publishing Co., 1972.
10. Indeed, the first book Spradley wrote was entitled *Guests Never Leave Hungry: The Autobiography of James Seward, A Kwakiutl Indian*, New Haven: Yale University Press, 1969.
11. Spradley and McCurdy, 1975, p. 641.
12. Spradley and McCurdy, 1975, p. 634.

CHAPTER ONE

*A World
of Strangers*

The American city is convulsed in pain. It is in the streets and alleys, fills the air, crowds into our living rooms. People suffer from hunger, death, loneliness, and inequality. Urban institutions are being shaken to their foundations. Crime in the streets grows to menacing proportions despite police efforts to control it. Universities are closed by strikes and violence even as they are being reformed. Students and teachers alike drop out of the big city schools because of frustration and fear. The ghetto is wrenched by violence and burning while large sums of money are poured into it. Welfare programs are attacked by those who appear to be their beneficiaries. One need only look around him for signs of the urban crisis which arose during the 1960's, a crisis which will influence our lives for the rest of this century.

The American city is being rent asunder. Our sense of community is being shattered. As Moynihan has observed, "The mil-

1

lionaire who owns a plant and pours soot into the air does so because he doesn't know who you are and doesn't feel he has to act as if it matters to him. He doesn't have a sense of community. He's no different from the half-crazy kid snatching purses in the ghetto."[1] The cry heard from every corner of our land to "tell it like it is" eloquently expresses the death of what cultural unity we once felt. Students, with little sense of a meaningful future, attack the hypocrisy and injustice of our institutions. Some refuse to participate in society, they drop out of school, close down universities, resist the draft. Minorities point out that discrimination has become part of the fabric of our life, that institutional racism permeates our society. They clamor for a more equitable share of our wealth, for opportunities that are truly equal, and some even demand a separate society based on different cultural values. Suburbanites and other members of the middle class proclaim allegiance to traditional values and cry for more law and order to restore the tranquility of yesterday. At the root of these variant points of view about urban America and our shattered sense of community is the death of a great American myth. It is a cherished belief which has glossed over the cultural differences in our society — *the myth of the melting pot.*

Every schoolchild learns that America is made up of dissimilar social groups, people with widely varying cultural heritages. The waves of immigrants landing on our shores during the last 300 years have come from nearly every country in the world and they continue to come. They have come as slaves, land owners, seekers of economic, political, and religious freedom. Children are taught that those who came with different cultural backgrounds congealed into a homogeneous group with a common life style and culture pattern, and now they all share equally in the American way of life. Of course, the melting pot process has been slower for some groups: Italian-Americans may take a generation or two to become "truly American"; Indians take a little longer. But sooner or later a new way of life is adopted by all, a way of life that is *best for everyone.* American culture and its institutions are *for everyone,* created so that all could share equally in the responsibilities and benefits. America is seen as a patchwork quilt, composed

2

of many different pieces of cloth, each woven together with such skill that the seams are no longer visible. New pieces are added from time to time and small tears may need to be mended, but the essential unity is always there. Our national efforts, especially the wars of this century, reinforced this sense of unity and national purpose and lent a sense of reality to the myth of the melting pot.

With the emergence of the urban crisis of the 1960's many people have become pessimistic about the viability of our urban society. We seem to be "coming apart at the seams." Instead of a cultural unity and the resultant sense of community, we are like islands, each separated by wide stretches of turbulent sea. Puerto Ricans, the poor, suburbanites, police, Blacks, Indians, Mexican-Americans, students, moderates, extremists — all seem to practice and believe in different life styles, adhere to different values. The tightly woven pieces of cloth which appeared to make up a single fabric have been torn apart, revealing that the seams have always been there, perhaps more real than anyone was willing to admit.

With the awareness of the wrenching, segmenting, and polarizing process has come a variety of responses — most of which are aimed at restoring or creating cultural unity. Numbers of people have been overwhelmed with fear and confusion. They purchase guns for self-protection, elect leaders who pledge law and order. Their goal is to *preserve our institutions*, to restore a bygone sense of community and commitment to our basic values. Others, represented by some students and the disenfranchised, view the urban crisis with delight. The cohesion of our society must crumble so that a new society can emerge, one which is constructed on different values. Some openly proclaim the need to *destroy our institutions* as a first step to creating a new kind of unity. Schools, government, the police, the courts, the welfare system — all were created by those who hold the strings of power. They serve the middle class, but no others. Since our institutions perpetrate injustice they must be torn down. Although those who advocate destruction do not have a very clear idea about the nature of the new institutions they will construct, two things are apparent: they will not include the views of those who control society now and

3

the new order will demand allegiance to a common core of values — a new melting pot. Some responsible leaders in our society have responded to the crisis by seeking to *create new institutions*. They have recognized the weaknesses in our system; they have realized that all segments of our society do not participate in our institutions. New programs are needed to overcome these problems, to draw all Americans into sharing the blessings of equality, abundance, education, and justice. The civil rights act, the poverty program, the teacher corps, public defenders — these and other efforts have arisen in the last decade. Private enterprise and community groups have entered this field, creating new organizations which are aimed at alleviating some aspect of our urban crisis. All these responses are important. Some institutions, such as segregated schools, must be destroyed, others require preservation, and new ones need to be created. But all too often, these responses rest on the unstated assumption that institutions serve a homogeneous population, whose members share in a single culture pattern. It is believed that all Americans agree on the goals, the values, the life style to which we should aspire.

Is there not a deeper and more important lesson for us in the destruction of the melting pot myth? Perhaps what has been taking place is a healthy awareness of *cultural* differences which have always been present. A unity based on the suppression of differences and the belief in homogeneity is not realistic. Our society is *pluralistic* and we have hardly begun to discover the depths of this pluralism. Communication, transportation, and migration to the cities have all unmasked the extent to which we are a *multicultural* society. We agree with John Gardner that the great need of our times is to *renew our institutions* (1965). But they can only be renewed effectively, renewed so they serve *all* members of our nation, if we have a full appreciation for the pluralistic, multicultural nature of American society. Americans do not simply belong to different generations, classes, racial or ethnic groups. They have also acquired distinct values, goals, and life styles — they come from different subcultures.[2] America is faced, not simply with an urban crisis, but with a grand experiment in human community: can we create a society which recognizes the dignity of diverse

4

culture patterns? Can we renew our institutions so they are truly human with the full realization that there are a variety of ways to be human?

The first step in answering these questions is a more thorough understanding of American subcultures. The present study is intended to describe one urban subculture and its encounter with law enforcement agencies. It is intended as a study which mines a narrow but central vein in the life experiences of these men more deeply than has ever been done in order to show how these institutions affect the lives of these men. It emphasizes the cultural dimension of a very complex human situation and shows how repeated arrest and incarceration changes identities, facilitates the assimilation of the patterns of this culture, and motivates these men to take up the life style of urban nomads.[3] This description stresses social and cultural determinants of behavior, the ways in which law enforcement institutions function to create and sustain this culture. The value placed upon self-reliance in America has led to an overemphasis upon the prescription, "It's up to the individual!" Religion, education, psychotherapy, and other forms of rehabilitation seek to get the individual to change his behavior, cope with his problems, and adapt to the dominant culture. The structures of our society, our institutions, are all too often seen as *givens*, to which one must adjust. Such a view often leads to the persistence of forces which create human problems but lie outside the individual. It may seem bizarre to the reader to suggest, as the title of this book does, that incarceration in jail, intended as a *punishment* for public drunkenness, is a *cause* of public drunkenness. After all, that provides an alibi for those who get drunk, another excuse for their unwillingness to exert self-control over their behavior. Since everyone knows and believes in American cultural values, these men who do not follow them must be sick or stupid! But if the argument advanced in this book holds some truth it should command the attention of every citizen concerned about creating a better society through the renewal of our institutions. Effective renewal requires an exhaustive knowledge of our subcultures, a knowledge that can be gained by the kind of study presented here. This book is not written for urban nomads to

5

show them how to adapt to the social and cultural constraints placed upon them by our institutions; rather, it is intended for those of us who are not affected by these forces but who have the power to change them.

Anthropologists have a unique contribution to make to such urban studies. Their research has been carried out in small, often remote, natural laboratories and has resulted in a unique appreciation for cultural differences. It has also led to the formulation of methods which are especially suited to the discovery of the way in which *insiders* view their experience. As anthropologists turn their attention to urban subcultures they are bringing with them a guiding principle, gained by studying hundreds of so-called "primitive" societies: *discover the native point of view*. The men of this book are not geographically distant from other city dwellers. They inhabit the streets and alleys of most American cities; they sleep under our bridges, behind our buildings, and in our parks; they travel by foot and freight car from one place to another. They fill the courts, are statistics on police records, and spend much of their lives in our jails. The distance between most Americans and urban nomads cannot be measured in miles; they are separated from us by *cultural distance*. Their style of life is not only strange but also abhorrent to most Americans. They are socially alienated and culturally separated from us but still they are in our very midst! This book is an attempt to build a bridge of understanding by providing a description of their way of life from the insider's point of view.

Other points of view are possible and a complete study of the situations described in this book would consider all perspectives. The police, courts, medical personnel, social scientists, and the average citizen have all heard of these men and know something of their life style. But, what is known by these other people is usually based on the viewpoints of *outsiders*. No claim is made here that there are not other ways to define and evaluate the experiences of these men. The courts are presented with a massive problem in providing equal justice under the laws; the police have a difficult task in enforcing the laws which affect these men; even the average citizen encounters members of this group and is

6

repulsed because of the way they violate American values of clean-liness, steady employment, material possessions, and a commit-ment to home and family. All these perspectives are important in a multicultural society, but none of them "tell it like it is" in the widest sense of that phrase. Furthermore, the viewpoints held by those who are not urban nomads are easily accessible in the press and many scholarly publications.[4]

What, then, do we mean by the "insider's point of view"? How are we to conceptualize the life style of these men in a way which approaches their own definition of reality? In this book, we shall use the word *culture* to refer to the knowledge these men have acquired and use to organize their behavior. Their culture is the set of rules they employ, the characteristic ways in which they categorize, code, and define their own experience. "Culture" does not refer to statistical descriptions of overt behavior, but rather "the forms of things that people have in mind, their models for perceiving, relating, and otherwise interpreting them" (Goode-nough 1957:167). If we are successful in discovering the culture of urban nomads, the description should provide an outsider with information and rules to enable him to operate in a manner ac-ceptable to these men, to see the world as they see it, to adapt to that world as they do.[5]

Ethnography, the description of a culture, is carried out through many different methods by anthropologists doing field work, but the foundation for *all* ethnography lies in the complex relationship between the researcher and his informants. In this study, research was begun by months of *listening* to men talk about their ex-periences with law enforcement agencies in order to *discover* which questions could be appropriately asked of informants and, further, to ascertain the wording of these questions. The initial data were gathered through participant observation in a criminal court, an alcoholism treatment center, and on Skid Road. Subsequently, a lengthy questionnaire was administered to a sample of 100 men who had been in jail for public drunkenness[6] and, finally, many hours of formal ethnographic interviewing were carried out with a smaller number of informants. The discovery and testing proce-dures used in these interviews are discussed with the presentation of data in later chapters, especially in Chapter Two.[7] It was not an easy task to overcome the fear and distrust which informants felt toward me as a researcher; some suspected I was a police officer or a member of the Federal Bureau of Investigation. The research methods which required listening and consideration of the informant as the authority went a long way toward alleviating this distrust as it enhanced the development of congenial, trusting relationships.

The research was carried out from July, 1967 to August, 1968, and unless otherwise noted, all references to the court, jail, and police refer to Seattle, Washington. One of the major scenes in the lives of urban nomads is Skid Road, a name which originated in Seattle. It was first used to describe the street down which logs were skidded to the sawmill, a street lined with flop houses, taverns, gambling halls, and other places common to the lives of the men in this book. The name often became Skid Row as it was adopted throughout the country, but in Seattle it remains Skid Road. The experiences described here are not unique to Seattle. Informants reported similar ones in Portland, San Francisco, Birmingham, Minneapolis, Chicago, and a host of other towns and cities. It is not the intent of this study to single out Seattle as unique or to expose it to charges of injustice or discrimination. Civic officials in Seattle are making valiant efforts to correct the injustices reported here and provide more humane institutions, which will serve all segments of that city. During 1968 the Seattle City Council passed a resolution of their intent to repeal those ordinances which make public drunkenness a crime and to establish a detoxification center for alcoholics which will replace the revolving door of the jail. It is hoped that this study will stimulate the citizens of other American cities to make similar efforts to renew our institutions and include the urban nomad in our multicultural society.

CHAPTER TWO

Destination
Unknown

More arrests occur in the United States for public drunkenness than for any other crime; during 1965, of six million arrests, nearly two million were for this charge. The annual rate in Seattle, Washington, during the last few years has been nearly twelve thousand arrests, and in 1967 this accounted for more than half of all arrests during the year. The President's Commission on Law Enforcement and Administration of Justice has commented that this system of criminal justice "burdens police, clogs lower criminal courts and crowds penal institutions throughout the United States" (1967:233), an observation borne out in Seattle, where 70 per cent of police man-hours are spent on this type of offense and 80 per cent of the jail population throughout the year are the chronic alcoholic offenders. Any person arrested for public drunkenness in this city may post a bail of $20 and be released in a few hours, and most of those who post bail do not appear in court, preferring to forfeit their bail. Some chronic offenders spend hundreds of dollars each year in this manner. Those without sufficient funds to post bail must appear in Seattle Criminal Court, where it was reported that, during 1967, nearly 65 per cent of the cases were those charged with public drunkenness, or an average of about seventy persons per day. Ninety-seven per cent of those appearing in court are found to be guilty and sentenced to serve time in the city jail for their crime.

The effect of this system upon the individual, and especially on those who cannot post bail, has been seen as therapeutic by many members of our society. The President's Commission on Law Enforcement reported that:

The criminal justice system appears ineffective to deter drunkenness or to meet the problems of the chronic alcoholic offender. What the system usually does accomplish is to remove the drunk from public view, detoxify him, and provide him with food, shelter, emergency medical service, and a brief period of forced sobriety (1967:235).

During 1967, the Supreme Court of the State of Washington upheld laws against public drunkenness in the case of *Seattle v. Hill*. *The Seattle Post-Intelligencer* reported on December 22, 1967, the following:

Wayne J. Hill, 63, of Seattle, is in jail this morning on his 115th conviction of drunkenness in public. He undoubtedly will be back in jail again in a few hours after he is freed after serving his current sentence. There is no other haven for him. The State Supreme Court ruled yesterday the Seattle ordinance governing drunkenness in public applies to chronic and proven alcoholics such as Hill as well as the casual Saturday night drunk. This means the city need not attempt to furnish any other facilities or treatment for chronic alcoholics (1967:5).

On June 17, 1968, the Supreme Court of the United States ruled, in the case of *Powell v. Texas*, to uphold the laws which make public drunkenness an offense in every state of the union. One of the majority opinions stated the following reasons for this decision:

Jailing of chronic alcoholics is definitely defended as therapeutic, and the claims of therapeutic value are not insubstantial. As appellees note, the alcoholics are removed from the streets, where in their intoxicated state they may be in physical danger, and are given food, clothing, and shelter until they "sober up" and thus at least regain their ability to keep from being run over by automobiles in the street.

Apart from the value of jail as a form of treatment, jail serves other traditional functions of criminal law. For one thing, it gets the alcoholics off the street, where they may cause harm in a number of ways to a number of people, and isolation of the dangerous has always been considered an important function of the criminal law. In addition, punishment of chronic alcoholics can serve several deterrent functions — it can give potential alcoholics an additional incentive to control their drinking, and it may, even in the case of the chronic alcoholic strengthen his incentive to control the frequency and location of his drinking experiences (*Powell v. Texas*, 1968:2–3).

The dissenting justices in both of these cases argued that incarcerating those who are drunk in public has negative consequences which outweigh the therapeutic values of this practice.

Though the debate continues in our society over this issue, it is time to listen to those who are most deeply involved in the revolving door. Those in this minority group have not been heard and they have an important story to tell. Consider the case of Mr. John Hallman, a long-time resident of Seattle: he was first arrested for public drunkenness in 1947 and two years later declared by the courts to be a "common drunkard"; during the 21-year period, from 1947 to 1968, he was convicted more than one hundred times for this crime; he received many suspended sentences and posted $165 in bails which he forfeited; and there were 74 charges of public drunkenness on which he was sentenced to jail during this period. He was given a total of 5,340 days for these convictions, or *more than fourteen years*. If he had posted $20 bail it would have cost him $1,480. In this man's experience, then, a year of his life was worth only about $100! During 1966 he received two six-month sentences which he could have avoided for only $40. Although these facts are shocking to most Americans, they actually mean very little to those of us who do not undergo this process. What did it mean to Mr. John Hallman to do such a life sentence on the installment plan? What does it mean to the thousands of other men who lie at this moment in our city jails across America? These questions must be answered if we are to "tell it like it is" for this minority subculture. We begin by allowing one man to tell of his experiences with law enforcement agencies during one year of his life.

Mr. William R. Tanner is a 49-year-old Caucasian who has never married. His life style exemplifies some, but not all, of the characteristics of these men. The following personal document was compiled from letters, phone calls, conversations, and a diary written by Mr. Tanner. He arrived in Seattle during 1967 and stayed for less than a year, was arrested nine times for public drunkenness, and served nearly two hundred days on the drunk charges. During the past five years, he has held more than fifty jobs and reported that for 1966 his income was between $500 and $1,000. The author has lost contact with Mr. Tanner, who may well be languishing in a jail somewhere. Although the details of his experiences are unique, the themes which run through his story are common to thousands of men, the urban nomads of American society.

August 14, 1967

Dear Jim,

In all sincerity (as far as I'm able to be so) I'll be happy to write my own thoughts and you can sift thru the garbage and use whatever you wish. My only desire is that it would perhaps help some other in this bedlam. My background is peculiar: I was born in Minnesota, December 15, 1918. Father was a miner, mother a housewife. My brother Wayne, eight years my senior, was class valedictorian, a West Point nominee, a salesman and compulsive gambler. Died in 1951 — second heart attack. My "namesake Tanner," or my father, died of T.B. somewhere when I was born. Mother remarried my step-father. We were pretty tight; he said I was his true son. Several older people have as much as said so. I had a grand childhood. I now have a nephew and a sister-in-law who is remarried. I took my frustrations and self-anger out on her at my step-dad's funeral so thus far she has understandably refused to forgive. Thru a priest I found out that she does not wish to hear from me. Perhaps in fear that I may contaminate my nephew. I still expect to make amends if time will permit. I was tested by a psychologist a year ago in Minneapolis, the Minnesota Multiphasic

Personality Inventory. He said I didn't belong in jail at all, my I.Q. was 131. He said I indicated that I liked people and said he wished I'd go back to college and get a degree in anything and get into social work.

Well, I was pinched last Friday and they threw me in the drunk tank where I stayed until court time this morning. These Seattle police put you in the foam rubber drunk tank for maybe two-and-a-half to three hours. After that, on the weekends when there is no court, they put you in the cement tank. No beds or blankets. Sixty to seventy men in one of those tanks that was meant to hold maybe thirty-five. Some of those tramps were sick and going into DT's and the bulls just ignored them — sometimes as long as thirty minutes. I don't know if they are lazy or just too mean to help a sick man. The general consensus amongst the jail population is that this is the hungriest jail in the country — even the southern jails give of quantity if not quality. All seems to revolve around the pleasure-pain process. But why penalize the homeless, tortured, the ill? I reiterate, and Jim you're aware that in truth, none of us were slapped for being exuberant, jocuse, morose, bellicose, or comatose, but because of lack of a lousy $20 bail. My own stand is that booze has been with us as long as the "oldest profession." Since humanism is being back-seated (not without a struggle), money is what's respected!

I was surprised when they booked me, relieved me of my property, but no property slip or receipt was forthcoming. One of the few jails I've ever been in where that happened. I had no bread so it didn't matter but others lost all they had. Jim, here's a random thought — I'm not a cop hater, strangely enough I get along swell with guys like Anderson and most, it's just that arrogance and Mickey Mouse vindictiveness irritates the hell out of me — especially when a dozen or more tell me they've been robbed by the same. In my carreer I've been robbed exactly six times — twice by guys I toasted and aided, the others by the police in Oakland, Los Angeles, San Francisco, and Minneapolis. A drunk is always a pidgeon to all who trade on his weakness.

The good judge gave me a kickout — two days suspended — since this was my first appearance in his court. I'm now going to seek work and try once again to get a period of sobriety. Inwardly I suspect my talents are meager but I also fear that I haven't really made an effort because of fear of failure. It's 2:00 P.M. — I just sold a pint of plasma for five skins. I thank you much for your friendship and interest. I hope I do not cause you any embarrassment.

49er Bill

August 15, 1967
Tank #709 — Seattle City Jail

I entered a plea of guilty to the good judge — no other way to do it — and I'm on the steel for another 10 days. There's no chance of beating a drunk charge. My friend Joe was picked up for panhandling — he'd asked a man for a cigarette and when he was being booked, the officer in charge said to him, "Well, you haven't been picked up in this jail before so we'll just put down you were drunk, and then you'll get a kickout." He didn't want that but there wasn't anything he could do. He couldn't prove it, and he'd had a couple drinks so that's what they did. In this jail you might stay in the drunk tank from Friday until Monday and if so you look and feel like a bum whether you are or not. No razor or towel or soap. Before they locked me in #709 we all went to the delousing tank. They took off all our clothes and threw them into a barrel with everybody else's clothes. Some of those old tramps are the dirtiest people you've ever seen. Feces in their clothes and what not, and your clothes go in with theirs and into a machine to be sterilized. And they come back and smell, buttons are torn off, and those who had a pressed pair of pants — they were no longer pressed. One of the men here told me he has gone out of this jail in worse shape than when he came in.

Not much chance of getting out early this time unless there's an apple kickout. They tell me you used to be able to get some good time for giving blood. An oldtimer here told me about that. "I was in one time for 20 days and there was a sign in the tank that the bulls put up in there. Anybody who wanted to give blood could sign his name. And all the guys said if you give a pint you

14

get five days good time and two packs of cigarettes. And so I went up to the jail hospital. They didn't select all the guys — only those who were in good health and they took a pint of blood and I got out five days early." They say this blood went into the police department's blood supply. They stopped that now. I think they've got that blood bank quota filled up.

August 29, 1967
Tank #709 — Seattle City Jail

I was busted last Saturday and got 20 days this time. Walked out on Friday and back in on Saturday. Some towns in California pay $1 a day and smokes for work done by inmate. Most state pens pay a little and give a man "gate money." This bit of turning a man loose at 10:00 A.M. or later, stone-broke and hungry, with parting shots like "See you tomorrow!" First you must hustle pad, food, minus carfare — too late to seek work. . . . rough. It's always easy to spear drink or promote a jug of apple wine. In emaciated condition it's very easy to get loaded and then back to the "ballroom" and equal justice. Only it's not equal unless you got $20.

A lad of 71 was released Monday and is back today. Out for a day-and-a-half. Slept most of the time he was here, slightly deaf and senile. The judge should have his head examined. The man's harmless! So he got drunk . . . I suspect he probably got robbed too. Doesn't weigh 90 pounds. They let us walk ten minutes in the corridor tonight and I looked in on him — he was conked out on the ballroom floor with a hangover.

August 30, 1967
Tank #709 — Seattle City Jail

The 71-year-old lad was transferred here after being out a day-and-a-half. He got 30 days. He had two checks got robbed and tossed in jail. Poor guy is senile. He says it's not the first time he's been robbed. He gave a trusty a buck towards a pack of cigs. No result or return. I wonder.

In '61 made apples and jails in Wenatchee, Brewster, Okanogan, Omak. Wenatchee apples were done. About seventy or eighty of

15

us got ten days. Police chief gave spiel: "Well boys (ages twenty to seventy), the harvest is over. I haven't the funds to feed you. Tell the jailor which way you're headed, Seattle or Spokane." We did and about 2:00 P.M. they loaded thirty or so on gondola freight car. The squad car waited there until the train left. Most apple knockers were broke from wines, fines, etc. Mission accommodations — destination unknown. Have made wheat, hay, potatoes, pears, apples, grape, prune, walnut harvests. Sawmills, plywood, fell and bucked redwoods, pulp, railroaded, warehoused, longshored, drove truck tractors, horses, etc. But last year reached lowest rung of ladder. The only way I can go is up — bottom reached. Must use all means and invent others to begin a constructive life. All this must have been for some purpose. "For everything under heaven, time and season. . . ."

September 22, 1967
Alcoholism Treatment Center — Seattle

Stayed out a couple days. Ballroom was worse than ever. Judge asked me if I had a drinking problem. I told him I did and he asked if I wanted help with it. When I replied in the positive he told me they had a new treatment center for those who wanted help, but he said, "It's only for those who want help and will cooperate with the program. If you don't want to you can go back to the city jail." Well, I had 30 days hanging so I volunteered. It meant 180 days but they say you get out early — sometimes in twenty or thirty.

October 4, 1967
Alcoholism Treatment Center

We heard this morning that 25 guys in jail got kickouts to go pick apples. Some of the men here wish they'd stayed in the bucket — would have been out on that apple kickout. You had to volunteer to get out here but like one guy said, "I haven't had a sentence in three years and would have gotten a two-day suspended sentence. Did I volunteer? Well, I did and I didn't; I pleaded guilty and then the judge started to question me and he held my case over and he put a $500 bond on me and I couldn't bail out!"

The program here isn't started yet — this place just opened up a couple weeks ago with the first patients. The program isn't doing any of us any good. Of course they feed us well and they're building us up, but 30 days is enough to do that. It's not necessary for them to keep us in as long as they're going to keep us out here. It will take a lot of money to get this program off the ground. It may never get off the ground.

October 9, 1967
Alcoholism Treatment Center — Seattle

We had a meeting this afternoon and a lot of patients were angry about there not being much of a program out here. Alcoholics Anonymous meetings, lectures, vitamins, and work — most of the time we work! Routine and monotonous though it's a lot better than the jail. I had planned to bring up some questions — even typed them out on paper, but didn't even ask them. When do we get out of here? When does the training program and treatment program begin and what does it consist of? Who is going to decide about our release? Several patients asked why we had to be in here for six months and they said we could get out earlier if we had a job and a place to stay. So I guess I'll have to wait it out. I work every day cleaning up one of the dormitories. I have to mop and wax the floors, clean the commodes and sinks and mirrors. It doesn't take all day — but it is supposed to be work therapy. If I have to do this very long I'll become a zombie. This treatment program isn't much of a help — they ought to have speakers coming out here or something. One guy who didn't cooperate has already been sent back to the city jail to serve his time. It takes a lot of patience to be a patient here.

November 3, 1967
Holding Tank — Seattle City Jail

Jim, I'm back again. Released from the treatment center on October 30. It was done in a casual manner. Given a letter to the president of Local #6 for a job. They dropped me off at a half-way house for alcoholics at 5:00 P.M. The assistant manager said they weren't interested in the fact that I'd been at the treatment center,

I had to get on their program. I couldn't work for two weeks, had to attend Alcoholics Anonymous meetings seven nights a week, be in by 11:00 p.m. and do work at the half-way house. I felt as if I'd been transferred from one institution to another. When he stated, "The door swings both ways," I swung out — blew cool — ready for a drunk. When I presented letter to Local #6, he said, "Oh yes, the alcoholism treatment center, quite a place. I'll put you on the list." Sounded like, "Don't call us, we'll call you!" When I said I could wax, burr, strip, he said, "Well, maybe I can get you on right now," and made a call and did. I never showed. Had a beer. While in the rest room had a bag with two pair of slacks stolen, so off to the races. I don't know why I got drunk. I didn't intend to drink. It was really a combination of things. A long bus wait, plus the desire to drink. The pure fact is, I did hard time even at the treatment center. Hadn't made a dime, no smokes, and a sense of anxiety because I was broke. But, facilities like that are an improvement over jail in that they will restore the body at least with food and rest. The compulsion to drink — I would think the proper approach would be to try and find out what is lacking, what the person needs to help fill his needs. Myself, I had a small taste of sobriety in the five and a half months I wasn't drinking. Haven't been happy drinking since. Maybe that is all anyone needs — plus the ability to remember past miseries caused by booze.

When I went into court this morning the prosecutor said,

"You have been charged with drunk in public. How do you plead?"

I: "First of all, I'd like to ask the court for two sheets of paper and a pen or pencil, and then I'd like the court to contact Dr. James Spradley."

Judge: "How do you plead?"

I: "Will the court give me two sheets of paper and a pen, I want to contact Dr. Spradley. I can't talk but I have had two years of journalism and can write."

Judge: "How do you plead?"

I: "Not guilty. I'd like some paper and a pencil."

Judge: "Is this in preparation for your defense?"

I: "Yes."

Judge: "See that Mr. Tanner gets paper and pencil, and see that Dr. Spradley is contacted. Case continued until Monday."

I: "Thank you. I'm really not as hostile as I look."

When I got some paper I made out this Writ of Habeas Corpus and sent it up to the judge:

WRIT OF HABEAS CORPUS   'INSTANTER'

City of Seattle County of King Sovereign State of Washington	William R. Tanner
above herein designated 'Respondants'	The 'Petitioner'

To: Any law enforcement officer, jailor, deputy, warden or to any court officer/agent within Respondants' jurisdiction.

Such person is directed to deliver forthwith this written instrument to the nearest accessible magistrate, as provided for by both Federal/State constitutions and statutes.

Petitioner is a citizen of the U.S.A., resident of Washington subject to all laws and statutes enacted by governing bodies of aforesaid. Petitioner claims/seeks protection of all his personal rights as guaranteed by both Federal/State constitutions and statutes.

Petitioner claims only a layman's knowledge of law and in the event legal counsel is indicated is amenable to swearing to the "Pauper's Oath" as provided for by both Federal/State constitutions and statutes — in the belief that lack of fiscal resource should be no bar to equal protection of personal rights and dignity.

Petitioner feels that his rights may have been/are being abridged, infringed, or violated in the following instances, occasions, and particulars: —

To wit: —

A. 1. Petitioner is an alcoholic.
   2. Such being now defined by Federal court decisions as one suffering from an illness.
   3. Such allergy, sickness, or compulsion not punishable by extended jailing or immuration.

B. 1. The Fourth Federal District Court of Appeals has ruled that an alcoholic can not be convicted of the crime of public drunkenness.
   2. The Fifth Federal Circuit Court of Appeals sitting in Richmond, Virginia, has ruled likewise.

C. 1. Judge John Murtagh of the New York, N.Y. bench states:
      (a) "New York City will not arrest a drunk unless a disturbance is involved. . . ."
      (b) "An alcoholic is one of the most abused and misunderstood beings I know. . . ."

(c) "While it may give a policeman a sense of accomplishment to do so — it is a waste of time, money, and manpower — A policeman's services are more urgently needed elsewhere."

2. Judge George Hopper of Fresno, California, in concurrence says,
   (a) "I refuse to sentence an alcoholic because such a being does not possess the ability to become voluntarily intoxicated as a normal healthy person by reason of his affliction."
   (b) "No 'intent' can be established hence no crime."
   (c) "Imprisoning an alcoholic constitutes cruel and unusual punishment distinctly forbidden by both Federal/State constitutions and statutes."

D. 1. The object in jailing a criminal (most enlightened citizenry agree) is to act as a deterent to acts of similar nature upon the prisoner's release.
   2. This, jailing an alcoholic has admittedly failed to accomplish as witnessed by the repeater, or revolving door drunk.
   3. Jailing an alcoholic has no positive value whatsover.
   4. Petitioner feels that an alcoholic should be civily detained for only a minimal time, given proper and adequate medical care as one suffering from and exhibiting symptoms of any other illness or disease.

Petitioner firmly believes that:

1. Sentence is unwarranted for nature of offense or illness.
2. No crime committed — (No 'intent' established).
3. Sentence constitutes cruel/unusual punishment.

Petitioner respectfully prays that this application for Writ of Habeas Corpus be honored — in order that he be heard, that his rights be protected, and that justice best be served.

Now they tell me that the Municipal Court can't rule on this writ and so tomorrow morning I go up to Superior Court.

November 6, 1967
Somewhere in Seattle

Jim, my friend bailed me out at one o'clock this morning. I was asleep. I had about given up. Thanks for calling my friend for me. I couldn't make any phone calls from jail except in special cases. I feel like a Don Quixote fighting windmills with a broken lance. That jail is really bad. I was taken up to Superior court on the morning of November 3. The prosecuting attorney read off the bit

20

about having received my Writ of Habeas Corpus and then it went like this:

Judge: "Are you represented?"
I: "No."
Judge: "Do you wish to be sworn in at this time?"
I: "Yes."
Judge: "Do you solemnly swear to tell the truth. . . ."
I: "Yes. Is Dr. Spradley here?"
Judge: "How many arrests have you had for drunk?"
I: "Four."
Judge: "How old are you?"
I: "Forty-nine."
Judge: "Did you receive treatment at the alcoholism treatment center? How long were you there?"
I: "Yes. I was there for thirty days."
Judge: "Did you get any assistance?"

What could I say? The judge then denied my writ and set my trial in Municipal Court for November 6. He said my writ was premature and could only be submitted after I had been tried and found guilty. The judge said I could bail out before the trial or maybe I could get out on an RPR (Release on Prisoner's own Recognizance). I thought about going back to court today for the trial instead of forfeiting my bail, but I'd probably been found guilty and had to sit around that jail waiting for the writ to go through again. It's too much like fighting windmills and that jail is terrible. Nothing to read — starvation. When I came back from Superior Court the desk sergeant said to me, "Tanner, you broke your pick with me. Don't expect any more favors from us. Where did you find out about this alcoholism bit?" I told him it was from the newspapers and he said, "You mean you read the newspapers?" They know me by name now. I feel I ought to get out of town. Maybe I'll go to Minneapolis.

I feel like I let the treatment center down and yet that's a poor place — a political football. Most of the money is going to the salaries of the men who work there. It's nothing but a glorified jail . . . though still a lot better than the Seattle jail! It's still an institution that is trying to control people. Every so-called "pa-

21

tient" (or "inmate" — you can twist the English language around any way you want) — I'll bet you don't find one happy patient there who is really satisfied. They don't need psychiatric help — what they need is $500 in their pocket.

November 11, 1967
Tank #710 — Seattle City Jail

Wie Gehts? The salutation clues you as to my whereabouts — Am again expiating my sins and foibles.

Pardon the verbal intrusion — thru this tortuous trail of splintered syntax I merely wish to illuminate the more than somewhat sad fact that I have again tripped, stumbled, or lurched into the toils and accompanying travails this cushy Spa seems to abound with.

Now that I've preened my ego by above superabundant verbiage — I confess that I must be a hedonistic masochistic mental midget or just a nut. I do not expect to make the treatment center again —

I lack the ability, stamina and wherewithal to contest the charge. Just play the part of a passive dependent and hope for the best which undoubtedly will not be too good.

I had an interesting time on the way to the Public Safety Building. I was arrested on November 8 on Alaska Way, about 11:00 P.M. I approached the pianist (piano bar) and said: "Please play Lille Marlene."

He: "Will do."

I: "Waiting. . . ."

Barmaid: "Whad-ja-want?"

I: "One moment."

Barmaid: "You'd better leave."

I: "Soon."

Cops: "This the guy?"

The jailer said "No phone call and no writing paper." Who is the culprit? Equal justice? A MYTH! Believe it. City jail menu furnished on request!

The counselor from the alcoholic treatment center came into the tank just before court and I told him: "If you will take me back to the treatment center I'll plead guilty." He said: "That's against our policy. Obviously you have made no effort. We got you a job and a place to stay but you didn't even make any effort and there's no object whatsoever in taking you back at this time. Effort has to be shown that you really want to get over your problem and then we would be glad to help you. I heard about that writ of habeas corpus you tried. You are more interested in the legal problems than you are in your own recovery. You want out but you aren't interested in your problem." I pled not guilty then changed it to guilty under duress to be sure — the good counselor is understandably bewildered, bedazzled, bemused and betrayed by my dilatory and dismaying performance or lack of same.

If you detect a latent social hostility in this rambling rhetoric you may be right — but again I am more pained and tormented than anyone I know. To know the answers and not be able to perform acceptably socially irks me more than a little.

R. W. Emerson says, "Lose something and perforce you must gain something." So far I fail to recognize anything much on the plus side of the ledger except perhaps some insight into the good and bad about us.

Das ist alles! Vaya con Dios. . . .

November 18, 1967
#710 City Jail — Seattle, Washington

Greetings! I trust you are still pursuing your studies of the inebriates with tenacity and dedication.

Now to get to the toils and travails of Tanner — I pleaded guilty Thursday (November 16) — Was sentenced to 35 days — I handed the judge a Writ of Habeas Corpus directed to the Superior Court. Gave notice of intent to appeal and appeal bond set at $50. I don't have 50 cents. The bailiff told me my time does not start until after my appeal. Now, he must be wrong, or else I may languish here for a year waiting trial. The theory of "Equal Protection" is a myth. Possibly it is idiotic of me but I do feel more strongly than I can state that it is futile to jail a drunk — cruel and purposeless. I probably do not possess the ability, stamina, or wherewithal to successfully contest the sentence and I realize I do not possess even the minimal virtues but I am curious to see the outcome.

Will you contact the Civil Liberties Union and see if their attorney will see me?

Perhaps you could send me some writing materials.

Well this is the one and only letter I am allowed this week — I should contact some friends in Minneapolis.

Well, thank you and regards.

P.S. I gained 14 pounds at the treatment center. I'm now in the process of getting rid of surplus and back to my former slim self. Adios.

December 12, 1967
Tank #709 — Seattle City Jail

Greetings! I'm sending you this note via inmate friend being transferred from jail to the treatment center. Only way to communicate with the outside. Am gradually beginning to distinguish between appearance and reality. Equal justice is a myth. Power begets cruelty. Normally one does 30 days on a 35-day sentence. I've already served 34 and the end is not yet in view. The jailors refuse to answer any questions — just pass the buck — the old army game. Would you contact the University Bail Bond program for me? I'm in Tank #709. Or perhaps you could query the good judge as to my status?

I withdrew my appeal to Superior Court (it had to be passed on before the Writ of Habeas Corpus would be considered) because I was doing all this dead time. That was on November 29. I heard nothing until December 5 when the Superior Court notified me that my appeal had been set for trial on January 9, 1968! Then the next day I got this letter from the Municipal Court judge: (Dated December 6, 1967)

Dear Mr. Tanner:

Your letter of November 29, 1967 has been received and referred to the probation department for review, investigation and report. The probation officer will undoubtedly be talking with you within the not too distant future and when I have all of the information about your case I will then review your request and make a decision at that time.

24

Since the court always gives five days good time on a 35-day sentence, I decided to throw in another writ. I gave the jailor a copy of the following:

'Instanter'

WRIT OF HABEAS CORPUS

William R. Tanner
'Petitioner'

City of Seattle
County of King
    'Respondants'

To: Any law-enforcement officer, deputy, jailor, warden or to any court officer/agent of Respondants' jurisdiction.

Such person is directed to deliver forthwith this application for Writ of Habeas Corpus to the Judge of Seattle Municipal Court as provided for by Federal/State constitutions and statutes.

Petitioner feels that his rights have been/are being violated in the following instances and particulars:—

To Wit: —
Sentenced on 11/16/67 to thirty-five days on a charge of Public Drunk — credited for time served as of 11/8/67.

1. Petitioner feels that he is being discriminated against, harassed, and otherwise manipulated purely because of his having chosen to exercise his constitutional prerogatives.
2. Sentence has been served.
3. Cruel unusual punishment.

Petitioner respectfully prays that he be heard, that this application for Writ of Habeas Corpus be honored and that his detention be terminated in order that his rights be restored/protected in order that justice best be served.

The jailor said they needed six copies since it would go to the Supreme Court which is a multiple judge court. Now, I'm no attorney (curbstone perhaps), but you do not as far as I know jump from city court to Supreme Court. So I made six copies in my illegible scrawl so he came back and said they needed one more. Still waiting. My 35 days are up tomorrow.

December 14, 1967
Tank #709 — Seattle City Jail

Jim, do me a favor and call the ACLU for me. I was sentenced to 35 days on 11/16/67 on public drunk. Given credit for time

served from 11/8/67. My time has been served the hard way —
purely because I tried to exercise my rights. I'm sending this note
with another inmate who is being transferred to the treatment
center from the jail. Please explain to the ACLU attorney that I
have no means of communication other than this. This is absolutely the rottenest set-up I've ever seen. Thanks a lot, Your
Friend. . . .

December 19, 1967
Somewhere in Seattle

Again — your bewildered, dismayed, bemused, delerious, bedazzled, defunct scribe salutes you with some gossamer-like, misty
caperings. Yesterday they took me to court and the judge said,
"Well, since your time is served, your case has been remanded
from Superior Court to me." I said, "Your Honor, I served 40
days!" Judge said, "You will be released today." As I walked away
a fat cop says, "Get back in there!" I told him the judge said I
was released. "Oh no," he says, "It is the jailor who has to release
you." I thought they were going to give me 35 more days. Like the
sergeant said, "You broke your pick with us — don't expect any
favors." I'm afraid I'm becoming paranoid. When I got out the
letter you wrote me on December 8 with writing material and
stamps was in my property!

I'm gradually trying to introduce myself to society and regain
my civilian bearings. If you can trail me along this devious track,
you've a much better acumen than I. After 30 days in jail you owe
yourself a drunk.

December 20, 1967
"Hotel Flea-Bag-On-The-Sound"

10:00 A.M.

I will not even attempt to justify my "smart bastard" self-
projection of yesterday. I think I have the drunk out of my system.
It does seem, at least to me, that I do seem to be able to communicate (with some false bravado) when loaded, which same I
seem to lack when sober. I finally got to bed last night — first time

26

since release. Such fun being amongst people again, even though I'm still leaning on alcohol to lubricate my communicational office.

My only intention in this writ and appeal bit was purely to see what a person without a dime could do. I wish almost that I'd stayed in until January 9. But, let's face it — appearance and reality. The latter I've always dodged.

Now for 40 nites in tank #709 — City Sneezer, Seattle:

The tank is 18′ x 18′ — claustrophobic. Sixteen steel-double-decker bunks, one blanket, mattress cover, towel, one wash basin, one shower. The inmates are those such as I who for the large part (not always) are broke financially but not altogether morally. Jailors still carry enormous keys and they do have to rattle 'em. I still hear their discordanties. A jail-drunk phobia. The officer here is one with expressionless eyes, power, arrogance, and a sort of twisting the knife geniality. He appoints trusties. In jail a trusty gets three trays of anemic food unlike those doing it the hard way in the ten tanks with sixteen men in each. We get mush, one-half bowl of soup, and the evening meal (after waiting until 4:30 P.M.) always turns out to be a large disappointment in that it's garbage and the portions are near starvation. I bet I lost twenty pounds. Supper is the only meal with any variety from day to day. It has such things as meatless stew, chicken giblets, goat stew, beans, and meat loaf. Somebody is making a killing on the food, but who? A kitchen trusty told me a dozen turkeys went out the back door Thanksgiving day, and steaks, etc., walk out every night. Now Jim, it's almost impossible to bust anyone on this, but I defy the jail management to submit to a poll of the inmates in Tanks #701–711 on the seventh floor. Reading material is scarce — pencils and writing paper contraband (why?). Where there's smoke there's fire.

At various times in the 40 days I met the following: a newspaper man (15 years on circulation), a proper Bostonian, operating engineer, several seamen, and one man who professed to be an ex-A.P. correspondent. Some are defiant, some almost defeated, others surrendered, resigned or accept relief or a pension or even a sinecure with the Salvation Army — a job, flop and food. Myself, I refuse a vegetable existence, realize I need a goal — many or most being unattainable because I lack the wherewithal, ability or stamina or because of pure laziness. Maybe this self scourging does some good. For the most part the inmates accommodate and harness the irritations — sleep, talking, snoring. There was and is one young colored boy who I know came close to mayhem when one unthinking gent always and unconsciously used the word "nigger." I commend him for his restraint. I tortured myself with that line: "OK you of the gifted 5 per cent if you're so smart what in hell are you here for?"

The jailor, bland and bluff, buddy-buddy (until you cross him by writ-writing or failing to conform) was saying (not to me) check in hand: "Look! Out of $800 after all they take out I'm lucky if I clear $500. A man can't live on that of course. I have another job — got to." He sports a "rock" on his finger that I understand his spouse inherited. So I thought, "You poor bastard" (No! I'm the *smart* bastard). Every day or so I'd say to him, "May I make a phone call?"

"Look! Tanner, I've told you that I take care of the other side (five tanks on each side of the corridor). See the nite jailor." (They change shifts at 7:00, 3:00, and 11:00). So-oo-o I'd hit the nite jailor (and a lot of others — we took turns). He'd say, "No! I'm busy. See the man in the morning." In the morning "May I have some writing paper?" He: "Look, Tanner, Saturday is letter writing day — if you got a stamp."

I rest and recapitulate.

P.S. Pray don't join the throng and call me a smart SOB. I'm trying to cool it — not again!

January 2, 1968
Tank #709 — Seattle City Jail

Seasonal salutations (salubrious)!! This delerious denizen is demobilized for a toto of thirty sunsets — which same could conceivably give the cerebellum's circuits respite and recuperative space in the time continuum to regenerate and refurbish the dehydrated and debilated brain cells.

Now! The good magistrate commands my admiration for the

28

consummate ease, dispatch, skill, and judgment he exercised Tuesday A.M. Never, but never (it beggars verbal description) have these astigmatic orbs witnessed a more electric or superb judicial travesty. Judge Parker was a tyro. Even my own vile, loathsome self sufficed to wring a moisture from his compassionate honors. I felt like doing a Finnish Fling when he said, "I'm going to help you Mr. Tanner — 30 days." I tried to conceal my joy and queried, "May I use the phone and have some writing paper?" "Why certainly, the officers will take care of minor requests such as yours." I replied, "I beg to differ. . . ." "That will be all, Tanner. Next case."

January 3, 1968
Tank #709 — Seattle City Jail

6:30 A.M.

Had a monstrous, lumberjack breakfast — mush with powdered milk and a suspicion of sugar, two slices of bread with a dab of oleomargerine, ersatz coffee.

10:00 A.M.

Only gourmet spoken here. Had a delectable, flour-based, slightly chilled soup, bland for ulcerated stomachs, and a string bean, a carrot sliver, and two slices bread with oleo. Now replete and recumbent. Nothing is read — could strain the optics. I try and recall the inscription on the statue of liberty — "Give me your poor, oppressed, homeless, etc." I asked the officer if perhaps I could use the phone. I feel badly about it now. He said, "Tanner, you know I'm busy. See the night man." Now the night man is so damn busy — more than a Siamese on a smoking skillet — I find myself in a dilemma. I may wound the sensitive night jailor's feelings if I interrupt him in his dedicated duties (whatever they may be).

A normal society theoretically would be one which could fulfill its needs without undue injury to any of its parts. However, cannibalism seems to be the bent — in a civilized manner, of course. Drunks are defenseless, exploitable and expendable. An affluent or one successful in any profession (music, literary, artistic) — such drunks are merely jocularily dismissed as mildly eccentric or pursuing the muse. Some say an alky is a non-taxpayer. Federal tax on whiskey is approximately $11 per gallon. Then add state, county, city, plus twenty odd taxes on grains. I submit that our fraternity contributes considerably in blood, labor, sweat, fines, bails, bonds, provide sinecures for cops, judges, attorneys, bondsmen, pawnbrokers, work and maintain jails, sanitoriums, rehabs, confuse doctors, headshrinkers, win battles, lose wars. But, our grasshopper existence vs. bee-like norm of the materialistic out-do-the Jones is frowned on by those who (here I agree, the immense majority of people are fools) a là Shaupenhauer agree with the sages of past civilizations — but do the opposite.

But I digress into curbstone philosophizing. We now flash back or cut to the ballroom.

One soul states: "I had twenty-three bucks when booked. Now they tell me I've only got $3.30. I guess I'm a fucked duck — I've got twenty days hanging." Another says, "Don't feel bad, the cops need it worse than you do." Number three chimed in saying, "Three banks robbed in a couple weeks, where in hell were the cops then? Hell! man, they were busy chasing drunks." Just then two of Seattle's stalwarts tossed in a new arrival. The ballroom contained about thirty snoring, gagging, morose, passive and bone-sore gents. The cops said, "He's small — won't take much room." True! He weighed about 80 lbs soaked in wine. He was bellicose. Said, "I'm gonna sleep — keep quiet or I'll kill ya — All of you." A hefty gent built like a box-car said, "OK killer." He went into a willie pep dance — almost fell down. "Quiet! One more word and I'll kill ya. I mean it," "OK dago . . . ," etc. Next A.M. killer was subdued, ill — weakly cadged a Bull Durham cigarette. The possessors of $20 paid their dues at the jailor's convenience and left. Others, when permitted to phone, pleaded for twenty skins offering all sorts of inducements, such as, "I'll give you thirty the minute I crack a check," or "Honey, ma, buddy, get on the stick," etc.

January 4, 1968
Tank #709 — Seattle City Jail

I am scribling this by the refraction of lights from outside. It's about 11 P.M. The fifteen others in this 18′ x 18′ tank are reclined or simulating slumber — lights out.

Breakfast: ½ bowl mush, powdered milk, suspicion of sugar; lunch: flour based tepid soup, two bread, oleo; supper: terrific — baby beef, dressing, mashed "Irish Apples," 15 peas, two bread, oleo, anemic tea.

I now await my bowl of mush.

January 5, 1968
Tank #709 — Seattle City Jail

Had bowl of "birdseed" cracked wheat mush, powdered milk, two slices of bread/oleo, ersatz coffee.

10:00 A.M.

Flour based bland soup, tepid and putrid, 2 slices bread/oleo.

Been having my left ankle treated — infected contusion. One doll of a Florence Nightingale nurse. Has five kids, but top-shelf. Other two — negative personalities. That night jailor Wednesday again proved a point: good and bad are compensative, equalize balance. I know too that a cop's lot is not the happiest but if they do not like the work and people they must deal with, why not quit? Everyone knows cops have been busted in Denver, Chicago, Idaho Falls, Reno. Power breeds contempt toward the weak. Contempt/arrogance breeds dislike/hatred/disrespect and back to contempt. Suffering/pain breed compassion. Some measure of self-esteem is essential but excess is no good. Here I sometimes think that I detest myself but yet harbor a notion that I'm peer to any and all mentally should I choose to chase the buck.

I started imbibing at 17 — prom night — high school graduation. I danced with my history teacher. A lovely lass — tried to cop a feel. Next A.M. she held me after class saying, "William, what was that I smelled on you last nite, hair tonic?"

January 5, 1968
Tank #709 — Seattle City Jail

In fall of '41 I left Minnesota. Worked a dam job, drove truck in Montana, played stomach Steinway in a number of joints — free booze, easy broads — and majored again in the four B's: Booze, Broads, Bartenders, Boxing. Arrived in Oakland, October '41.

Made fair coin, won a couple amateur shots — worked for a doctor and sash firm. A gent who started same day is now superintendent.

It pains me to watch the illiterate, homeless derelicts shafted by an exploitive, monied, parasitical society. It seems that pity begets interest which leads to coercion. If a person chooses to disown society, leave the time clock and be nomadic, dipso, to blunt the pain of past errors and misfortunes by seeking oblivion or solace — that should be his prerogative. "The poor will always be with us," the MAN said, and I suspicion that drunks likewise. Others will continue to gain wealth, power, prestige by exploiting this. . . . Had money not been invented I wonder what would be.

Finally got a newspaper, January 4, if this Hearst Rag can be called one. I still would have won my bet: Indiana + 15 pts. Minnesota should have been there, they really clobbered Indiana.

Gourmetically: Evening repast: a fish mucilage on toast, mashed spuds, few carrots and salad green, thin H_2O with sweetish dampener, anemic tea. I should weigh out a trim 140 lbs.

A major crisis has developed! The weekly, two bags of Bull Durham, has not been issued. Tobacco withdrawal symptoms — irritability. I blew my cool at the medico. Asked for a sleeper and he offered A.P.C. Threw them back with, "Thanks much Dr." Temper, immaturity — you diagnose.

The army told me that despite academic ability I was alcoholic and unsalvageable as far as they were concerned. I often wonder why it took them two years to conclude thusly. Someday I may scribble my version of Pvt. Hargrove Tanner. But back to the ballroom.

6:00 A.M.

Mush, powdered milk, coffee, two pieces bread. At 6:30 a razor, soap (no mirror), 32 four-day beards, bone-sore-beat gents, bums, has beens, and some novices did a quick Braille defoliating. The blade was well blunted.

8:45

Three cops, one bailiff called the court docket sequence. I was number eight. Arrived Friday at 6:00 P.M. Then the rights spiel — I know it verbatum. "You are charged with Public Drunkenness.

32

No appeal if you plead guilty (a lie), 6 months and $500 fine max. If you plead not guilty the court will set a date in the not-too-distant future." I elected to plead guilty. I guess my forensic ability is zero. The judge said, "Thirty days." I could write a letter tomorrow but have no stamp or franking privileges. I still have one of your envelopes in my property — I've asked for it but with negative results. Well all for the nonce. I'm out of paper so I shall try and purloin some sort.

January 6, 1967
Tank #709 — Seattle City Jail

P.M. Supper: liver, mashed potatoes, squash, water tea, two slices bread. Hungry!

Wrote the judge — need no stamp. Expect no reply. Asked credit for overtime on last sentence. Medical department OK. Ankle healing fine. Bull Durham ration still nil — Reason?? I understand they have Bull Durham — possibly part of treatment. I should be released Tuesday morning, January 23. I wasn't asked if I wished trusty status. As the man said, "I've broken my pick."

Flashback to booze: Patent medicines (100 proof), home brew thrived during my kid-hood. Ma's remedy, if my nose dripped, a nice hot toddy or a sugar cube dipped in the sauce. Besides milking a cow, churning butter, she picked up pin money from visiting loggers with the brew. Gad it was dynamite and damn good. I liked the stuff before it turned — rich in malt sweet coca-cola — no competition.

Playing dances around '36–'39. We always were a bit high. I blacked out first when about twenty. Drove my car home, garaged it, no recollection. Generally only mildly high in order to bolster confidence and as social lubricant. Arrested a couple of times hometown but municipal judge merely reprimanded miners and loggers. All drank, fought in a friendly test of brawn. My dad was top dog, 6'1", 240 lbs. Pick up front end of ditched car unaided. Gad, if I were only one quarter the man. He drank but never missed a shift — never could understand me. I can't either. Once in dismay and shame he said, "I've never seen anyone like you,

you're always drunk." Still we loved each other much and worked together in '59 cutting pulp. We'd been on a protracted homecoming drunk reunion together. Both wound up in hometown jail. The sergeant sat behind me in school. Didn't recognize me. Said, "How'd you get so damn bald?" His cranial area resembled a cue ball. Said, "Shake your old man up and get out and get some coffee."

Dad died 11/16/64. I was in Minneapolis with fractured ankle, in cast. Psychic experience. I seldom called, but Monday nite, 11/16/64, I felt distracted and called dad. Learned he died at 11 A.M. and none knew my whereabouts. Glad I was able to say goodby. I, as always I guess, depended on sis-in-law and nephew who lived 110 miles away to make and take care of funeral arrangements. My responsibility, but I've never been a responsible person. Dad's mining friends did all. I was drinking vodka, lachrymose, crying jag. When my sis-in-law and new husband showed fifteen minutes before service, I asked, "What took you so long?" She, "We stopped and had the car washed." I said, "That's nice. Where's nephew?" "He had to take a music lesson." I said, "I hope the SOB turns out to be a Liberace." I'm really a nice kid of 49.

January 8, 1968
Tank #709 — Seattle City Jail

A.M. Salivation begins. Cups rattling, mush, bread, battery acid.

I borrowed an accordion and made every bar, played my ass off. Pops favorite Finn tunes — Vagabond Waltz, Remembrance Waltz, not good but loud. Never legally adopted, although Dad told me I was his blood — others seemed to suspect same. Died intestate. I had no legal status. Pop always expressed mild agnostic sentiments. I suspect he really was stronger in faith than many — lived straight and walked proud. Left no debits. Had a nice send off — excepting for my immaturity. Said, "Don't cry when I die — drink a toast to Tom!"

Judges (city) are notoriously capricious, careless, and at times, could care less when sentencing a drunk. I've faced blind, stoned, crippled, kindly, nasty, comedial, arrogant, senile, gentle, helpful,

34

the whole human range. In a small Oregon town, our gandy gang was paid off at 7 A.M. By nightfall about forty of us in jail. Local judge appeared at 7 P.M. I had $78 plus two weeks back pay. Fined $75 — others for whatever they had, or promise to pay next pay, released. I refused. Next A.M. police chief said, "You want to do your time right quick?" I replied, "How's this?" He, "Sweep streets." I said, "Sorry, sore back." He, "You're smart bastard. Wanna go to the county jail?" I said, "You're the chief." That noon, deputy drove me to county jail. Next A.M. chief called, asked if I'd pay $20. I, "OK, let's get out of this trap."

Towns and cities have no standard operating procedures but are distinct personalities as people. Duluth/Superior — Duluth has work farm — drunk bail $35. Haying time better have $35 or stay sober. Superior, across the bridge, bail $10, have to be performing some to be arrested. Cat houses, etc. Once judge looked at defendent — this was May — said, "I'm getting kinda tired of looking at you. This makes eighteen times this year." Wino said, "Going to apples." "OK, good luck," said judge. Oakland and San Francisco are the same situation. Oakland has Santa Rita Rehab (pop. approx. 1,300). Good chow, recreation, movies, gym, boxing . . . but got to keep place going. One kickout — then judge gets hostile. Drunk bail is $25. San Francisco is like Superior, Wisconsin. It possibly has more falling down drunks than any city. In 50's and 60's. Generally hold drunk three or four hours. Sgt. says, "OK all you bastards who can stand, get the hell out of here." Could be 3 or 4 A.M. Of course you seldom had very much money (cops need it for indigent police fund). Generally, though, they left a buck or two. Once on 81st and Howard Street (skid-row) a well-dressed gent, New Year's day, hand bums/dings a buck. Sometimes takes them in joint and joins bum (me for one) in a drink, then gives a buck. Him standing on corner watching bums when a cop came across street, saluted him, and said: "Lt., I've got enough trouble on this beat without you," but a sunburn or liquor burned complexion gave him away and he grinned and sauntered off, possibly to spear a drink.

My first appearance before a judge in Milwaukee — judge asks, "Where you from?" Like damn fool I answer, "Minneapolis."

Judge almost has a stroke. Addresses audience: "If you think they've torn down Milwaukee skid row — they really got rid of it in Minneapolis. That's why these bums are here. Ten days." Me, "I'm working." He, "No difference." Me, "You mean I've got to be arrested twenty or thirty times before my credit's good?" He, "True." Next time I took floater, 90 days suspended.

January 9, 1968
Tank #709 — Seattle City Jail

Approximately 3:00 P.M.

Got two recruits. Beat — hungry — missed their soup. Will get fed at 4:30. No rattle of metalware so this purposeless pup and prideless prodigal has not begun to drool. Someday may have a stroke if steak materializes. Now it seems I read a squib in the local rag of a group pressure chamber — was it 24 hours of continuous confrontation of different personalities? Now drunks must possess a homogenized or stoic acceptance or mayhem would ensue. The age differences are from early 20's to early 70's. There is tension and temper blowups but generally they're confined to verbal exchanges in fractured English. Have a gent light a cigarette and then flush butt down shitter when you are dying for smoke. Cruel and unusual punishment and then some! It's nice to call friend and ask for couple skins — promise will do and don't — almost makes one antisocial — but perhaps weak and witless gain strength, though not always wisdom, by deprivation and perhaps even enjoy the fact because not one in actuality is real proud of his status and has been conditioned to believe that he is parasitical, purposely squanders his life, money, talents, is unloved by friends, relations, society and God, the wheez God protects fools and drunks notwithstanding. Some guardian angel must have hovered over me many a time. Once in Minot, North Dakota I made the harvest — feeling no pain. Met man named Olsen — he's stiff. Said, "Whitey, want to take ride in my new car?" — Chevrolet hard top. Me, "Why not?" Going to Burlingame. We had two bottles — North Dakota has open container law. We're wide. Got glove compartment filled with miniature 2-oz whisky bottles, pitch empties outside. Stop at roadhouse, drink a bit til dusk. Take off — but fast

36

— hit soft shoulder — steep bank — car goes flippety-floppety. I flew out one door — him out the other. Car lands on wheels — radio still going loud and clear. Cattle truck stops. "Anybody hurt?" I holler.

6:00 P.M.

Slop supper — gravy goo, faint suspicion of meat, mashed potatoes, 2 mini-biscuits — crash diet. The butler must be buying swimming pool. Stomach has diminished to size of golf ball. Never die of overeating. They used to call me "heavy," now the salutation is "slim" or "skinny."

A brief course in the fifth "B" or Bumology which I originally meant to minor in, but possibly should have doctorate in. There are railroad (coast-to-coast on piece of toast — McArthur's contribution), rubber tire, mission stiffs, Salvation Army stiffs, working, non-working, bindle, stream-lined, Northerners are labeled snowbirds down South, Southerners are rebels up North. Riding freights has become hazardous — at least solo because of duos and trios of muggers and like. Of necessity, must have the difference on your person or travel three or four together. Hitch-hiking more difficult right along because of idiocies committed by psychos and freeways. Still possible by long-line trucks if you savvy lingo and on the quietus — insurance frowns on it as do carriers. But teamsters retain some measure of independence. Many drink considerably but seldom if ever on the road. Once known he's had it. A diesel duo will pull 110 loaded cars and cruise in over-drive at 70 MPH. Some manifests will change crews on the fly and make a quick look-over. Great Northern's Jim Hill is rumored to have said in his legacy, "The bums built my road so let 'em ride." Railroaders are also a different breed of cat, proud, competent, aware that banks, stockholders clamor for more profits. Railroads are making more $ than ever — true passenger trains are losers but even they could be made to pay but the gravy is in freight. Most rails will tell you what track and time your train is called for. In Superior, Wisconsin, going to Minneapolis, freight left at night so railroader said, "Go in that shack over there. Stove is warm and I'll wake you when it's time." I said, "Care for a drink?" He said, "Hell," looking at my Thunderbird, "I don't drink that crap — I've got better stuff." I sort of miss the steam days. Engineer and firemen are practically white-collar workers. Steam-heads as they're now called died hard — because of lower center of gravity a Diesel will take curves at greater speed, but on a straightaway I believe steamer still holds edge. I once saw engineer and fireman go three or four miles down single track R.R. and leave train. Must had interesting discussion. Used to take a casual approach — if drinking on the job they could be black-balled on road — would say, "Hell there's lots of railroads but only one me." Times are changing and so is the breed.

Footnote — if this inextricable garbage lacks conciseness, consecutiveness or continuity, a weather-vane-like many tangented timid and dampish mental apparati have short-circuited and circumsized by Ethyl, Iso Propyl and other liquid viables. . . . At least I'm happily stringing words together in desultory dead seriousness.

11:00 P.M. (One dim night light)

This seventh floor section has eleven tanks (#701 to 711). Ten are approximately 18′ x 18′. They have one wash bowl, one shower, eight double decker steel bunks, and sixteen men each. Then, there is one trusty tank with possibly 50 or 60 men. Trusties get three trays of food a day, a trifle better than us. We get aforementioned, unmentionable, unsavory provender as befits bumptious, abominable winos, dinos, dingbats. Steel partitions separate tanks. This tank is relatively somnorous day and night. The tank next door has a different metabolism, vocal effect peaks after lights out — so a gentle harassment . . . they bug us nites, we retaliate A.M. I catnap — . . . we exercise the puny tri- and biceps. In your letter you erred when you said, "I admire your courage." I would in retrospect name it stupidity or plain idiocy. I really needed that Reality Therapy book you were kind enough to fetch. Appearance and reality. I'm going to try and bury romantic misnotions I've thus far carried. Comes possibly from reading too much trashy fiction in younger days.

I still find it hard to believe that cops are subject to same human

38

weaknesses and foibles — such is their public image — tarnished some, 'tis true, of recent years. I know too that not all are tarred with the same brush. I've some friends in same — knew some great ones as a kid. Got lost in town of 5,000 once and about four years old — usual treat — ice cream bit. I believe, treat others as you would like to be treated yourself. Now I'm a Bible thumper — I don't succeed though. Tend to react quick to any hurt or what I possibly imagine to be, as in the case of nephew and sis-in-law. My ma was same, would blow her stack — but five minutes later not even a ripple showed, and harmony prevailed. I err often and quick but repent at leisure — and too late.

January 10, 1968
Tank #709 — Seattle City Jail

10:00 A.M.

Await bread and tepid flour thickened soup. Had mush, powdered milk, bread, and battery acid for breakfast. Went on sick call — Nice Florence Nightingale nurse. Passed banter — ankle OK — but she suggested I come anytime to break monotony. Portly, pill pusher passed me vitamins, APC, asprin. I asked for pill for acute melancholy and nicotine withdrawal. The portly purveyor of pills daily dispenses asprin, APC's, and pheno-b's, librium to the vibrating clients. I wonder why he hasn't retired. Understand he's had three cardiacs. But I suppose he'd be in a vacuum if he did so — nice gent — perhaps needs the bread. May have beatnik or alky offspring who requires sanitorial seclusion. Heaven forbid.

Most cops merely counting months and years 'til retirement. Impersonal — inmate just a nonentity. Jail personnel generally the most stupid — have sinecures — perhaps I'm prejudiced. All this crap for a harmless drunk. I've got to blow town. They call me by last name. Do not intend to leave broke. But hesitant about gambling on my sobriety. I'm a diff person when drinking and am arrest prone. Worked nites in San Francisco, longshoreman. Don't require much sleep, five or six hours plenty. Like to wander nite spots — restless — enjoy nite air. Once in Racine, Wisconsin I sat on rocks of Lake Michigan. Foggy, couldn't see ten feet out. A

39

prowl car drove up — me half-crocked. Cops, "What ya doin?" Two jugs nearby, me, "Watching boats go by." About 3:30 A.M. They laughed. Took off.

January 11, 1968
Tank #709 — Seattle City Jail

At lunch had bird-seed and flour water. Now it's approximately 2 P.M. Hungry!

That Alcoholics Anonymous has been as successful as it has amazes and puzzles me. How drunks, in far more advanced stages, have been able to kick booze and I haven't. Made my best try in Minneapolis, 1961. For five months and fifteen days I was a fair non-haired boy. Was nite man at Alano Club — 11–7 A.M. Lots of work but enjoyed it. Then took day job too. In a hurry to make bread. Finally began experimenting with one or two shots Vodka. One day took bus to St. Paul. In bus station met old drinking acquaintance. Offered me slug of wine. Same day blacked out. Blew about sixty bucks. Group meetings two weeks later I was to get my six months pin. I told them to forget it that I'd been on one. Never got tracked again. Wound up blowing both jobs. Just took off to Superior and Duluth. Came back in three weeks, picked up my checks. Higgins, at wheel at the Grain Exchange asked me where I'd been and why I hadn't let him know — said he'd hired another man — said his wife (she was a character) liked my work. I told him I was alky. He said, I think my wife is one too. Made a lot of friends at AA — lot of phonies too. Many really not alkys at all — con artists and congenital liars — others jockeying for status in club — or kicked booze and on pills, Dexedrine, I guess, or barbituates. The club bent over backwards to help me. In my opinion the pro's are moving in — it's obvious that plenty of bread — State, Federal and County, is going to be spent supposedly to aid alky. But salaries for social workers (I use the term loosely) brain pickers, counselors (good and indifferent) and the many channels (hands) the funds pass thru . . . I'm afraid only a small percentage will actually go to the aid of the alky. Then too, the alky personality is multi-faceted. I've tried self-analysis (in fact this scribble now is another attempt) to see if I can't find the answer. Why? I've been blessed with good health, good parents, education, childhood, friends. I possess no rabid fears (height, some, but I've forced myself to climb when roofing), etc. I think I've got to begin to use the intellect I'm supposed to possess — try Napoleon Hill's approach. Set a modest goal, shelter, food and flunky job and cool it for two years — just stay sober and see what happens.

This is a test of concentration. Sixteen persons about me in this cage, ex-mutton conductor, ex-pug, four Indians, three colored, two Finns (myself, included), one retired army (20 years). Ages from 22–70. Four B's and Bumology — the munificent past and dismal present — I wish I had a tape recorder. Saw the nice nurse — killed an hour. Portly pill pusher gave usual asprin, APC, vitamins and a couple of others. Now am starved. Could eat south end of a north bound skunk. To twist the blade at intervals I recite the menu at the treatment center just to break or brighten the day. Or the Milwaukee menu — seconds. Just now they're discussing horsemeat, pork, chicken, I now await the "big" meal — goat stew, chicken wings — small portions you may be assured. I'm armed against disappointment.

8:00 P.M.

Supper was even less than expected: mashed potatoes, dab of rice and bone (possibly ox-tail-meatless) suspicion of spinach, bread, tea.

Bumology II: Salvation Army. I worked as truck helper at Men's Social Center — 8:00–4:30 — Breakfast, Lunch (two sandwiches, coffee, apple), Supper. Single room. Must be in by 11 P.M. Hired Monday — blood test, X ray, two changes of clothes, got canteen ticket for $2 (tobacco — ice cream) on Friday. Got paid $1 day — 32 trucks. Saturday I met friend — got high — sober Sunday A.M. They said I had to reapply Monday. Didn't have permission to stay out all night. That was enough. Salvation Army stiffs are clanish. They spot a non-stiff and feel superior. Some are young and husky but prefer sinecure of bed and room plus conviviality. Salvation Army exploiting drunks for labor, but do some good such as clothes, 50¢ or 65¢ meal ticket. They are listed in Dunn and Bradstreet as American Salvage Company. Assets (and how) in real estate alone, plus trucks, Appearance — reality?

Really ridiculous when I can work Van Lines for $3 plus an hour

— but it's OK to recuperate after long drunk. Besides I had broken ninth rib in Wenatchee in early July. Man came at me with full fifth of wine. I fell off loading dock, landed on back — bottle broke. Guardian Angel again present. Mission stiffs: Once at Bethel Mission, Duluth, I was coming off one — Guy sits down next, asks, "How's this place?" Said he just left Minneapolis. Knew this racket. Noticed he had Bible under arm. Everytime Reverend opened larnyx he intoned "Amen," next night he was behind desk, smoking hard rolls, white shirt — definitely executive type. I can't do that route. Missions are tax-exempt — solicit through mail and through different denominations. Appearance — reality?

Bar owner said he was behind Mission operator once in bank — Said, "I'd like to trade places with her." In Los Angeles Sister Sylvia's Mission is open at 6:00 A.M. On the air 6:15 to 6:30. She says, "When red light goes on sing nice boys" (20 to 80). Light goes on and we sing Old Rugged Cross, etc. Then a straight 10 minutes solicitation on behalf of poor, honest, hungry, homeless, harmless, unhappy bum — need coffee, warm food, clothes, etc. After red light is off she settles down. Says you don't have to take "nose dive" my place. Does a vocal and suggestive dance — we get rancid coffee, peanut butter sandwich. Heard she'd been in what's known as the circuit. Lady friend asked her how come she got in this racket. Says Sylvia, "Beats hustling!" Appearance — reality?

In Union Gospel Mission an honest bum gets three nites plus bowl of soup. Must attend service, then must pay 65¢ nite. Approximately 70–80 "boys" in the dorm. No 65¢, no flop. Three or four floors — tax exempt! Appearance — reality?

In a convivial (easy on the "con") mood I met alky Catholic Friar in train station, Minneapolis. Asked, "How come so many good friars go alky?" Reverend says, "Well, you listen to all these problems, and we do have the wind." I was reared on the Lutheran catechism and confirmed in Finnish. Learned to read and write native tongue — but seems that I lean towards Catholicism (disregard past history of same). Catholic Friars generally sympathetic and understanding. Once hung-over — put bite on Friar Freeley, Minneapolis. "Need a dollar, Father." Friar, "You hungry?" Me, "No." "What do you need a dollar for?" "Don't feel good. Buy jug of wine." Friar, "Well, at least you're honest." (Like hell.) "Here you are. Come see me sometime when you're in better shape." I did. One priest who seemed to possess the peace that passeth. . . . He's in Rome now for further studies. Have meant to but neglected to write. Soon I hope.

Minneapolis has reformed or there's a new court system. Judges rotate — suburban and urban. There are fourteen different judges in municipal court. They are all different — run the gamut of chromatic scale. But go largely by screening past record. I recalled some of habeas corpus writ from what I learned in Milwaukee. Got thirty days from Judge Stone for drunk. Was pinched coming out of a music store by rookie cop whose sensitivities seemed . . . Feeling mellow, jocose, he was leaning on building. I say, "Hi. How's business?" He, "Looks pretty good." I make move to heel and toe. He, "Hold it. You're not going nowhere." Me, "I beg your pardon." So when I got to work-house Thursday I composed the first alky writ to Stone — practiced up on ping pong. Monday morning they take me back to court. Just Stone, me, county attorney and recorder. Stone (Chief Municipal Judge, collaborator on Minnesota Statute and Crime Law Reform) may be sympathetic to drunks. Says, "All U.S. court judges agree you're right. Now, if I release you, what do you intend doing?" Me, "Go work." Stone, "OK, Mr. Tanner, promise me one thing." Me, "What?" "Try and stay off Seventh and Henn." (Where I was apprehended.) Me, "Will do." "You may go." A space later I came afoul Judge Winton (millionaire judge). I'd met him before. Got pinched 9:30 A.M. — rode 'round paddy wagon till 3 P.M. At 7 P.M. call Winton at residence. "What's your trouble now, Mr. T.?" I say, "Would appreciate an R.P.R. Nice and sober now — protect job, etc." Judge, "You won't go out and get drunk again?" "Never happen." So out in time to make liquor store, get sauce. Go to Copper Squirrel strip joint. Two strippers have Texan buying $10 ponies of $2 champagne. I join the table, in my well-oiled manner. Soon have double double scotch. Again (1:00 P.M. close-up) I hit street. Second floor, next door hotel where area boys are put up while waiting induction and physical, having a party. Holler down — "Whitey, where's a cat house? Where's bootlegger?" Just then a cop on bike pulls up. I

43

start to lope. I ask the usual friendly, "How's business?" Start to move. He, "Hold on," so back to jail. I try to say I just got R.P.R. No sale. Desk sergeant, "Jeez Cris, this guy just RPR'd." Who's on bench next day? Winton. My charge now was drunk — drunk and him handing out 10–20–30 days. He came to my case looking like cat ate canary. Say, "Well I did you a favor last nite. What happened?" Me, "Well I run into a couple of friends. How about a stayed sentence?" Judge laughed so hard he almost fell out of his chair. Audience laughed. I feel like crying. Judge, "I'm gonna give you a stay — 90 days stay on first drunk and 90 days stay on second drunk. That's 180 days." And he tells the prosecutor, "If this character is back in front of any judge, I want him referred to me." The same week I was in court on Saturday but hit a different judge. Got seven days, six with good time. So I made like bugs bunny and rabbited to St. Paul. But I was back in Minneapolis and got pinched. Ten days for escape plus 180 days Winton revoked. I appealed and wrote State Public Defender Judge Chapman. Did sixty days.

Good night. Await my oats.

January 12, 1968
Tank #709 — Seattle City Jail

Best supper of the week — fish, gluey spuds, tomato and onion salad. Hungry.

Bull Durham ration still withheld but lucky ones with money . . . about four guys got Pall Malls — can spear one or two — for all purposes have quit.

Ten days left — Have lost weight. Judge never answered my request for credit for overtime served on last sentence. More appearance — reality.

Skid-row bars and taverns most lucrative beats for cops. Alkys always pidgeons, blacked out, careless with money, can't very well accuse when cannot recollect. Subject to being drugged, mugged, slugged, or jugged. Gets to be a way of life. Regardless of financial status. I seem to gravitate there — there are kindred souls there and that's where the action is. Really cheaper to drink in better establishments. I've become careless of dress and self. Neglected teeth, toilet, etc. Actually ill at ease in dress clothes, prefer casual sportswear in dusky hues or "thousand miller." Must remedy that when in Rome. . . . Morals or lack of same showing. Believe that approximately $500 would erase most problems, teeth, clothes, general appearance. Surely I can become stable enough to work two months at any flunky job if necessary. This is worse than ridiculous. Sobriety's got to be first. The past, I find while I've missed and abused it, is not as dismal as I've thought. The good far outweighs the bad. So it's about time to accent the positive — get out of dreamland — face reality — 49-years old, need overhaul and personality. I've been stepped on but only because of passive acceptance — a vegetable existence. Have health, strength, some ability, not the most moronic. Pick up your bed and walk . . . I can't change police procedure, courts, people, but I can change myself. I can't do much about the past, but I do not have to drink. I'll find a habit easier to live with. Surely staying on an even keel. Food, shelter, clothes, work — try AA again. False pride out. Nothing to be particularly vain about. Antagonism is a negative emotion. Establish regular eating and sleeping pattern — work — play — master of own ship — get off ship of fools — Now — Why drink to lose use of elemental faculties — gain courage nothing to fear. Am peer of most — have worked menial jobs — No sweat — appearance — reality. Am only average Joe, give writing a try in spare time — music — settle for less — aim lower — settle for hash — happy medium is better than dreams of never-never-land — school maybe.

Thesis: Alky can gain sobriety.

Why: It's a frustrating, unhappy, abnormal, self-punishing, uncontrolled, lonely, desire-defeating, progressively worsening, habit pattern and expensive in terms of money and friends — really makes you low man on totem pole. Jails, bails, judges, cops — A defenseless moneyless pidgeon, exploited and exploitable — ridiculed, censured, pitied, despised, abused, misunderstood, pauperized, untrusted, unloved, unwanted.

How: Break pattern, substitute, improve, strengthen desire, AA, medical — Fill basic needs first — Modest goal for first year. Avoid impatience, spot judgements, cool. Not in position to be critical, can't boast, don't knock substitutes: coffee, candy, gum, soda, milkshakes, occasional movie, short trips, YMCA, walks, swim, gym, library, music, visit and make acquaintances. Write freelance, avoid boredom, bars, bottles, boozers, renew correspondence, write home and friends. After basic needs, begin to overhaul clothes, teeth, general appearance. Reason and experience indicate it should be easier, happier, and more profitable to stay sober. Appearance — reality? Time is motion, man's invention. Remember past insofar as to prevent repetition. Pleasant memories, but if tempted to drink dredge up and profit by past. An educated man is one who can assess the consequences of his actions and perform accordingly. Any action to prevent drinking cycle. On release from jails I have always gone on one self-defeating drunk. This time I will break pattern. Basic needs then — job — make AA connection. No time like present — no close friends. Work should be relatively easy.

January 13, 1968
Tank #709 — Seattle City Jail

Mush — soup — Supper of small meatless stew.

Why drink? AA speaker once said, "If I decide to start drinking again — get couple cases 'canned heat' — That's what I always wound up on — that way stay drunk longer — Why pay six-bits a shot? I don't drink for flavor but for effect." Got a point. Likewise here — Know Skid Road bars — clip joints, poor booze, company, surroundings, strictly exploiters of defenseless, toss you out, call law in minute if broke. I am trying damdest to impress on my dim wit that there's no percentage — ratiocination. Maybe, just maybe, I'll defeat this self-destructive pattern and drive. Crib freely from any source if I feel it will help me.

Once in Portland I came off steel gang and got drunk. I'd rented a room and left $100 under newspaper top dresser drawer — to make sure I don't wind up broke. Next day couldn't find hotel, never did. That money came hard way. Shock treatment: saddest moment — pretty shakey in Los Angeles at Christmas season and called brother in Minnesota. Was gonna ask, "What is your wish for Christmas?" His wife answered. Me high, "Like talk to Wayne." She, "Can't." Me, "Why not?" She starts to cry. "Talk to your father." Tom comes to phone. Me, "Where's Wayne?" Ole Man says, "Dead and buried — six months ago." I'm floating around Montana and Wyoming. I owe booze a lot. This should be titled, "How to torture yourself."

Two or three of us under a railroad bridge in Redding, California. Rubber-legged gent comes up — Got $200-fiddle (suit) on —Comes up and says, "Hell, this is where I belong. Those damn waitresses can't keep their orders straight." Head chef in the best hotel in town — makes $800 a month. Sauce flows freely and we end up in the bucket. I owed judge ten days. We both face the judge and I get ten. The chef, a tall red head says, "Your honor I'd like ten days too. Then Whitey and I can get out together." Judge blows a gasket and says, "I'm not running a boarding house! Ten days suspended! You come back, I'll give you ninety." Few months later I stop at a greasy spoon in Sacramento to have coffee. I look up and the cook is the tall red head in a dirty, greasy apron. "Hi red." "Whitey!" Me, "What the hell you doing in this dive?" He, "I won't be here long. Looks like you need a drink. Hell, a drink won't do you any good, you need a jug (Taps the till.) Here's a buck, get well. See ya."

Idaho Falls, I'd just come out of jail. In a bar and cafe where hiring is done this guy hollers from the back. "Whitey wat-in-ell you doing here?" Was a guy I met in Eureka, California, with a broken ankle (hit by auto) in a cast. I gave him a fin. Now he says, "You broke?" "Yeah." Got out a coat, pulls out a roll, and hands me a sawbuck. Let's go liquor store. A few months later I see him in Portland, broke, no flop. I'm holding this time so all OK. Brotherhood of the road. Law of compensation. Balance the good and bad. Bumming is habit forming — Old wheez rolling stone — no "green" — I've decided this is my last go-round again. No percentage laws getting stricter. One really loses ability to relate to people. It's free, irresponsible, seldom dull but it's no good. Friends are casual and all alkys subject to temptation. Old saying

— First one up will have all the money. Seldom been robbed by drinking companions. Has happened three or four times which isn't a bad average.

January 14, 1968
Tank #709 — Seattle City Jail

Breakfast: Had bowl of raisins and applesauce. First fruit seen in 17 days. Coffee, Bread.

Why drink? My stability declining all along. Was occasional, then weekend, now extended drunks. Don't sleep or eat for days on end — but when left alone most always stop, recoup and go to work. Now I make jail practically every drunk. Try and stay fairly clean so possibly I look like I'm good for $20 bail! First blackout I've experienced for years was last two times prior to this one. No recollection of arrest. This time I wasn't drunk. Was high and happy. Remember all. Just wrong place — wrong time. Believe I'm not being "spanked" for being drunk but for not having $20 license fee for drinking. Cannot convince me that being drunk is a crime. Being broke is. I speculate as to what use drunk bails are put to. One $20 would mush and soup the whole jail population for weeks — suppers too, such as I've seen. How a $20 bail can grow into 30 days, 60 days, 6 months and $500. Appearance — reality? Exploiters — exploitable. Vicious life-consuming, drive-destroying circle. Liquor industry and bar owners equally culpable. Common sense approach would be to make own potables — have control of quality and cheaper. Modern beer pales in comparison to home brew, wines and liquor likewise. Understand one private producer has operated unmolested making quality liquor for select clientele in Washington. Shows ill repute of drunks when bondsmen are reluctant unless they have gold-plated credit and bank — even then $20 service charge is a trifle exorbitant — only more so. Be a nice racket to bail drunks only, but probably bondsmen got closed shop union. Misdemeanor inmates have no collectiveness. Subtle form of coercion used by jailors to have inmates practically run the jail — feed, clean-up, wash cars, cycles, do cooking, run errands, hospital, orderlies, gun range, sub-stations. Paid help supervise. Every city

48

has its regulars. Have more and better food, freedom to hustle more restricted prisoners. Some have been in so often they are almost part of the force. Should have honorary badges. Will do a favor for price or to a pal who may return same. Otherwise, you're solely out of luck. I've known some who have done equivalent of life sentence (17 years in Minnesota) for drunk. Two brothers, Pat and Les, in California. Les, a top sign painter, could in free-hand make many a pro blush. Painted all signs in City Hall. Both brothers were personable and talented but unpredictable. Together they donated much of life to the city of Oakland. I did some also — was in Bay area 16 years.

Friend, a design electronic engineer who was in Los Alamos and Oak Ridge projects, I.Q. 167 — overboard on religion but a very good man and friend. He took me to Willmar State Hospital in 1963 for their 60-day treatment — on voluntary commitment — can leave in 3-day notice. I stayed 30 days. Felt cured — good program, food, recreation, library — worked about three hours daily in the kitchen. Good program. Daily lectures by pro-speakers. Then group meetings. Various I.Q. and personality tests — great counselors. Should have stayed the full sixty days. But it was Indian summer and I jumped the gun. Was in bad shape when I entered — bleeding internally, but recovered rapidly. Fat and confident. Worked in Minneapolis but same routine — blew my cool — excuse to have a couple. No better — always able to con myself. Not this time. Like the man said, "Can't remember past so repeat performance." People and events move on — but time appears to have halted for me. Yesterdays seem as vivid to me as today — yet I do not seem to profit by past errors — a paradox. Case of arrested development. Again! Champagne appetite, less than beer income. Must lower my sights or raise my income. Convinced I cannot drink. How to overcome compulsion and break the pattern — substitute another habit — establish regular eating and sleep pattern — Get work, avoid snap judgements, anger, Etc.

Supper, insofar, below par — even here. Small portions of beans and spaghetti, limp greens.

Impressions of the alcoholism treatment center in Seattle: I presume personnel disenchanted by now with clientele — But really they have a soft touch. Most alkys are fairly congenial and not demanding. I was well treated — gained 16 pounds which I've now returned with interest. AA I know fully having had over-exposure. Why did I not crave a drink now or when confined? A paradox — yet am overwhelmed by desire when I'm released. I was bored to death at the treatment center. Am not much of an eater — felt that again I was being suckered — 29 days. No one coun-selled or hardly asked me a thing. I suspect city and county are getting ready to put the bite on Federal Government for grants to help sick sick drunk. Really a pork barrel — salaries and paper work and other lucrative bifs will be worked. Eventually drunk labor will be exploited and it will be a glorified jail, or as in Cali-fornia, an honor camp. Yet get 400 men to work four hours a day = 1600 hours of labor. I sound and am pessimistic because I don't understand myself. What in hell's the matter with me? I've been helped by experts — get dressed up, working, make friends. Liked and been liked by employers and all but seem to dodge "success" and the norm as if I didn't deserve it. If I have any guilty complex it's buried in subconscious. Educated in richest school district in the country. I've had advantages many haven't. Don't feel any bet-ter than any other — but sure as hell feel I'm equal — money not withstanding. About $500 would probably cure my problems. Try and stay straight long enough to earn it. Well, I'm straining eye-balls again. Others sleep. Await mush.

January 15, 1968
Tank #709 — Seattle City Jail

Mush, soup, ball (mostly filler — faint aroma of sausage), mashed potatoes and turnips.

Appearance — reality. Understand they have a lovely printed menu below for public consumption, only trouble is menus not digestible or edible.

St. Louis, I understand, will hold drunk 20 hours — maximum — sounds sensible. Jailing drunks to my notion is like bailing ocean with sieve — drunks multiplying faster than jails. Have been in so many jails — really appreciate privacy rather than being in any.

Am going try my way this time. See if I can't use own initiative. Sail my ship alone — see if can't take star fix and find direction. Perhaps I'm overly distrusting, or simply empathetic. No more half-way houses, missions, or Salvation Army. Possibly poor thinking but I've been "had" so many times that I question people and motivations. I have met sincere people but believe me, not often. I can count them, if not on one hand, at least on two. To be able to give freely of yourself is a quality I never cease to marvel at — especially those who receive no compensation or perhaps not even recognition. Milwaukee — I thought was ahead in that prior to a man's release a welfare worker interviewed and made an appointment with him, then set him up for a minimum of four weeks. What to do with the alky? Make him wear scarlet letter on forehead? Give him smart pills? Jails waste men, time, man-power. Jails, AA, clergy, I've tried all — but remain optimistic none the less. I'm going to attempt rational approach or combination of all. Have a lot of catching up to do — start living for one — start thinking — a lot of life has slipped by. By some happy chance might get back and face reality instead of drifting in alky dreamland. Pete just came back — got 30 days. Nice Joe. I wonder what he thinks about. Am curious. Well, according to my scientific minded friend, I've only got seven days left. It should go relatively fast if time speed-up theory holds. I hope so. Supper.

January 16, 1968
Tank #709 — Seattle City Jail

Breakfast: Mush, powdered milk, coffee. Lunch: Soup. Supper was miserable: Bread, meat loaf, mashed potatoes, carrots — insufficient and poor. Hungry!

Once in Chico, California, I got pinched A.M. Asked the jailor "How's judge?" He, "Never turned man loose yet." To judge I give the pitch, "I work at Hammond Lumber in Eureka. I'm on vacation." This was May. He, "When's pay day?" Me, "First of June." He, "Fine is $40 or 8 days. Can you remit the first of the month?" Me, "Surely." Judge, "OK. You may go, don't want you to lose a good job." Somehow I wound up in Eureka in September. At 7:00 A.M. I was going in joint. Prowl car pulls over. Cop says, "Hi Tanner. When's last time you were in Chico?" Me, "Where in hell is Chico?" Cop, "Sorry, hop in." They sent two men through four counties by auto, approximately 1200 miles both ways. Returned me, bought me steak, ice cream, cigarettes. Judge asks, "How come you don't send 40 bucks?" Me, "Was told OK as long as I stay out of Chico." Judge, "Oh, you must have talked to a curbstone attorney. You have 40 skins?" Me, "No." He, "Sorry — you've got to do eight days." I did four. Brought in an elderly electrician, emptied a pistol in neighbor, says, "Neighbor won't kick my dog no more." Then he complained, "This steel sure hard on my arthritis."

In Minneapolis the drunk bail is $25 but you cannot merely forfeit. You still must appear in a court or a bench warrant is issued. Then you're liable to contempt of court and lose your bail and still may get jail sentence.

I made a trip to San Francisco in 1961. I avoided Los Angeles like the plague. Heard that drunks were being given two waivers (kick-outs) then the third time around they were tried and sentenced on all three, or $3 \times 90 = 270$ days for ambulant drunk. Believe me, you do not have to be drunk to be taken. When the paddy wagons load up they just grab anyone handy. Once in a California drunk tank, over the audio-system speaker Judge Ashton said, "Well, we have 250 drunks this morning. That's average. You'll be appearing before me soon. Have your plea ready. If you feel that you need help indicate same and I will give you 180 days in one of our rehabilitation center's honor farms." Appearance — reality? What a racket. That kind of help I do not need! They hold court 7 days a week. I was robbed right at the booking desk of forty some dollars. Asked for property slip and the sergeant signified by putting on a pair of black leather gloves, saying, "You don't have any property do you?" I wound up in a cold shower, suit coat split in back. Great judge did turn me loose. Had to walk a few miles to town. I s'pose by now you're aware that not many of the affluent patronize the alcoholic treatment center or this crowbar hostelry.

Returning or flash-back to my own sad and peculiar problem. If I'd finished my education, married, hadn't gone to California, probably if I'd made the army a career I could have been an officer — and a dozen other possibilities. At any rate I've lost a lot of time — have many regrets — missed opportunities, but in many respects have been more fortunate than many. I know my condition hasn't happened overnight and that I most likely can't correct it overnight. But am a young-old man in a hurry — and I know too that I can't afford to be so.

January 17, 1968
Tank #709 — Seattle City Jail

Breakfast: Birdseed mush. Lunch: one-half bowl of soup. Supper: Dab of spuds, few chips of beets, meatless stew — more of a gravy — worst yet. Wonder how they get away with it. Stinks.

Bull Durham ration returned Tuesday so nicotine withdrawal symptoms are diminishing. It's bad enough being hungry *without* being out of smokes. Society must be callous and indifferent to let conditions as this exist — perhaps unaware. Inmates are all aware — money for food is appropriated. Lack collectivism to do anything — the easy way is to do your time and hope you're not back. Who would one appeal to, City Hall? The old adage: "You can't fight city hall," holds. I doubt if I weigh 150 — drink a lot of H_2O. Noticed a couple groups on "Guided Tours." Strange they never come around at chow time. Jim Klobuchar, Minneapolis Star Tribune had himself "arrested," spent part of a nite in the drunk tank — gave a superficial account — cops knew who he was, so really he only saw what they wished him to see. I stopped at the Tribune one night and left him my version. Perhaps I'll follow up on some ideas — Sobriety comes first though.

I seem incapable of a sustained effort in any direction. I wonder why. Raised in a rural and mining community, where everyone knew one and all. There were the usual village drunks, primadonnas, and odd-balls — all nationalities. Most were bi- or multilingual. I've got to try and get acquainted with myself. Money I'll never need much of but as a friend of mine put it, "It's no disgrace to be poor but it is inconvenient at times." Amen, brother. Had a dominating mother — died far too young (50) of a sudden, massive brain hemorrhage — Nice way to go — but rough on survivors — Self analysis is impossible. Self inventory same. Matter of perspective — bound to be prejudiced, for or against? Am not vindictive. Aware good is not always rewarded nor evil punished. Guess the whole race has self-destructive notions. Have no conscious suicidal bent. Been accused of being a wise bastard a few times. Am cynical and doubtful of professional do-gooders — many are busy feathering their own nests while professing to aid or rehabilitate others. I readily see why a drunk fails to inspire anyone to great pity or any emotion except disgust seeing it's self inflicted — but a society which condones sale of intoxicants certainly has no valid reason for imposing criminal sanctions on those who are allergic or are compulsive drinkers when that same society takes a hefty tax bite out of every dollar spent — licensing fees, etc. Then turn around and jail and starve the drunk who doesn't understand the why-fors himself and is already in bad nutritional shape.

Pensioners, itinerant workers, paupers, the unmonied are the ones who are rounded up by a well-paid, well-fed, police force. Every city jail has its inmate crew of "trusties." Those hardy gents who have become so inured or benumbed by repeated arrests that jail has become a way of life — the cops know them by nicknames. Instead of changing scenery and towns they elect to stay. I've elected to leave Minneapolis — no doubt to their advantage — if not mine. At least Minneapolis does provide comestibles in sufficient quantity and even of some quality. Seattle could well pick up a few pointers.

Now I'm to be released January 23. Jails haven't sobered me. AA has helped. Now I shall try a rational, selfish, self-propelling urge of my own. See if I can't stick by a decision to avoid emotion that would cause me to even think of a drink. Try to keep up a sustained effort. It's either/or, appearance/reality. Any method, any habit is preferable to what booze has done to me and cost me in years, unfilled desires, pain, friends and relatives.

January 18, 1968
Tank #709 — Seattle City Jail

Birdseed — Soup — Turkey wing, potatoes, spinach.
Food obviously is the dominant thought here — everyone con-

54

tinually hungry. Have three weeks in today. Have seen fruit once — Last Sunday for breakfast a thin apple/raison sauce. My neck cords are quite prominent. I guess have dropped 20–25 pounds. One library book a week. One letter a week if you have stamp. Sorry this is somewhat illegible. The only paper available here are these scraps torn from the front of old books the inmates have borrowed from library. Can't mail — everything censored. Hope to be able to smuggle out and give to you. Wrote Judge twice, no reply. Nice equality. Man's inhumanity to man — 16 men in 16 x 16 tank. Ten tanks this section; 160 men plus 50–60 trusties.

A stray thought: I would think that if camps or dry-out stations patterned after the old CCC forestry camps were established on a voluntary basis where men could perform constructive work and get room, board, essentials, plus a stipend, say $5 a day, I would think that would be performing a better service to community and alcoholic. He would be paying his way, still could attend AA, listen to outside speakers (there are real good ones). When discharged he wouldn't be a charity case and it would then be up to the individual which is where the balls winds up anyhow. I don't know if it would work either.

Now a bit of appearance — reality therapy. Eye-ball the sign in the courtroom: "Equal Justice for All under the Law." It seems that is largely negated by the lack of twenty bucks. How can twenty bucks plummet up and up until a man can do six months if he doesn't have it? And sometimes have a $500 bail on top of that?

Today I feel listless (more so than usual). The perimeter I'm surveying isn't particularly stimulating nor conducive to inductive or deductive mental gymnastics — so I'd better lay this bit of graphite aside and lay the 7½ inch head down and contemplate my navel.

January 19, 1968
Tank #709 — Seattle City Jail

Mush — Soup — Beans, spaghetti, limp salad — small portions! Three more days. Hard to plan. So many variables. Make the blood bank for plasma donation, possibly $5. Dishwash job if possible. Promote clothes, flop and food. Possibly go to San Francisco — Return to Minneapolis in the spring. Essential to gain period of sobriety. Try AA club. Maybe do self some good, friends and sociality. Check Pioneer Industries. Not particular what I do. Start small and play by ear. Either/or, appearance/reality. Time to awaken: I'm 49, reasonable health, intelligent, also stupidity, lazy. Try rational self-improvement program. Disassociate from drinkers and attendant aberrations. No need to continue thusly. No haste, slow and easy — nothing to be anxious about — eliminate difficulties by simply not taking drink — it's poison to self — think selfish and for self. I can say I haven't had a drink this year. Keep it that way. There isn't one good reason for taking a drink — Eat a candy bar, cup coffee, chew gum, soda, milk shake, anything. Need to gain weight — start going to movies, write, walk, visit, shop. . . .

January 21, 1968
Tank #709 — Seattle City Jail

My last day — Kickout tomorrow A.M.

Hard to imagine doing six months in this 16 x 16 cubicle and on this diet but it's being done and just for drunk — cruel and unusual and then some. It seems a long time ago that I was apprehended as an ambulant drunk and derailed and detained in the drunk tank or "ballroom" at this 16 x 16 steel and bar cubicle is jocularly described by the local citizenry. I made my entree feeling jocose and mellow at about 6:00 P.M. Smokes, matches, billfold, belt, pens, pencils all extracted at the booking desk. Fellow traveler had stashed a fin in his sock, gave it to a jail trusty to get smokes. Received a bag of Bull Durham, no change. I surmise a drunk is a pidgeon to all. Luckily he made bail of twenty skins or he would be here with me now. Being indigent I remained.

I think I'd better get back to Minneapolis or anywhere. The alcoholic treatment center kills you with kindness and boredom. This place is a pressure chamber and then some. Audio system plays some taped melancholic crap either so low you can't hear the news or so loud you can't hear each other or think — a sort of brain washing — torture. Understand ballroom is loaded. The circle continues, where she stops no one knows. . . .

March 29, 1968
Edgecliff Sanitarium
Spokane, Washington

Bibaceas (sp?) Bill is now a T.B. suspect. Have been on a marathon drunk. I was pinched in Seattle on March 10 and the good judge gave me sixty days suspended. Next time in his court I would have gotten that sixty plus additional so I blew town. I left Seattle March 11 on the 2:30 Mainstreeter and was ejected by a nasty conductor in Ellensberg, was arrested three minutes after debarking.

Next morning a trusty (named Warren) tells me they only have court twice weekly — Monday and Thursday afternoon at 4 P.M. Bail is $15. Have $11 check, pint of vodka and gear. Ellensburg cops detest alkys. (I wonder why?) I blew my cool. Tried usual tactics to avoid going berserk. Write a writ, threaten to sue Northern Pacific Railroad, conductor, and police for false arrest . . . , etc. Had my second meeting with wet-brain via alcohol. In the next cell is a damp brain (George). Had a beautiful baritone voice, but limited repertoire, sang Eddie Arnold's Tennessee Waltz with improvised new lyrics. Two good meals at 8 A.M. and 4 P.M. First morning got five hot cakes, coffee, etc. George was happy and sang 'til approximately 8:30 A.M. (I gave him three of my cakes). George then called to trusty Warren (other wet brain) "Wat time is it, Warren?" Warren, "I'll go see." Half hour later Warren returned. George, "Wat time was it?" Warren, "I forgot to look." George: "I'm hungry, go get me a couple spuds. Those punk cops are busy playing grab-ass — they're all queer. I know, I used to run a joint in Frisco. . . ." Warren came back with a few raw potatoes (Irish apples) and I could hear George masticating same. Then the "Tennessee Waltz" (butchered lyrics) from 9 A.M. 'til 4 P.M. George would ask, "Wat time is it, Warren?" "Have they gone for food yet?" Warren, "You want 'nother pill, George?" "Might as well bring me two." (I wonder what in hell he was taking — appetite stimulants or what). By Wednesday A.M. I'd smoked the two packs of Luckies I had. A young cop about 19 years old — nice lad — gave me two bags of Durham. My wrist wound reopened somehow — slight suppuration. I sent a note to chief (Larsen), "How come you Swedes are picking on poor Finlanders, me?" Show him my minor but nasty-looking wound. Took me to the "pill roller" — dressed wound and gave me sulfa ointment. I asked for sedative pills and got about thirty samples of some new tranquilizers. So I wrote and rewrote a couple of epic poems and did isometrics til court time on Thursday, March 14 at 4:00 P.M. Saw judge — told him it was the first time I got stoned in one town and arrested in another. Found Smirnoff Vodka potent potion. I was arrested at 1:30 A.M. so I must have ridden the 9:45 Limited from Seattle instead of Mainstreeter — Judge OK. Ten dollar fine suspended. "Thank you, Your Honor." I cashed check at depot and caught the 5:30 Limited. Got friendly with couple of colored gents in dining car. Beg pint of bourbon. At Pasco two colored gents give me long-green ($) to run for two pints of scotch and two pints of Walker Delux. Get same and another pint of Vodka. Arrive in Spokane 11:44 P.M., debark and get a room. Make rounds, worked a couple days. Get arrested on Sunday morning, March 24.

Now Jim, meet gentle Judge Lowry. Forty drunks — traffic cases first, drunks finaly at 10:00 A.M., 20 at a clip. Judge, "Rise when I call your name, plead guilty or not guilty and sit down." We all do — plead guilty — sit down. Every drunk who'd not been arrested for seven days received one day suspended. Judge looks at me, "Your face is familiar. When were you here last?" I said, "November, 1961." He, "Has it been that long? One day suspended. I must say this is the finest looking group of drunks I've seen for a longtime. Now gentlemen I have a policy. You *must* have some sort of policy. Mine is that you must not appear before me twice in one week. Monday — Don't be here 'til next Monday. Tuesday — not 'til next Tuesday. Clear?"

Damn if I don't get busted 2 A.M. Tuesday! See gentle Judge Lowry and hand him a written pitch: "Have train ticket and medical appointment." (Yes, Jim, I guess I strained or sprained my vocal apparatus again — have to quit smoking and drink more or visa versa.) Judge says, "Against my better judgement I'm going to make an exception. Perhaps I should have my head examined. One day suspended and good luck. But if you're back within a week you may get 30 days." Me, "Thank you, Your Honor. You may throw the keys away if I am." Judge, "No, I won't do that." On that note we parted.

However, I'd had an X ray that A.M. When I went to claim my property, damn if they didn't have a T.B. suspect health hold. Wednesday afternoon a deputy brought me here. I have a touch of flu or pleurisy — plus a three-week drunk, plus that crash diet supplied by the avaricious butler of the Seattle city clink — I weighed 172 when I left the treatment center, now I weighed 147 clothed.

Monday nite two jack rollers tried to take me in my hotel corridor. I was busy (and drunk) with the one in front when the other tripped me from behind, kicked me in the ribs. The hotel clerk came to the rescue and ran them off. I, fool that I am, went back to a joint where the action is — had slight nick over left eyebrow.

They're killing me with kindness here a la the Seattle treatment center, only more so. X ray showed rib fracture, can't be very bad though it hurts to cough. I guess this is a better place to dry out than any jail but I'm in a locked ward.

P.S. I did intend going straight to Minneapolis but I second thoughted. I can go to work here or anywhere "IF" (another behemoth of a word) I can lay off the sauce. I had a grand-daddy of a drunk and now feel no tension. I believe I must and can whip this thing. I would feel more than a little defeated if I returned to Minneapolis the same sloppy drunken slob I was when I left there last June. I've contacted the AA here and talked with a Catholic Father (St. Patrick's day) even though I'm supposedly a Lutheran. Seems the good fathers understand us conning drunks better. I can get help here *if* I can somehow convince them of my sincerity and convince myself that the big clock is running. "Time is on the wing," it's a now or never proposition. I am always short on gratitude. The facility here is of the best. I'm a man in a hurry, a derelict, rudderless ship, have various goals in mind — but the fear of failure so strong that at least thus far I have really not extended

59

or expended myself to reach any of them. I seem to have both an inferiority and superiority complex — mayhaps I'm a schizoid split personality. What's your diagnosis and prognosis, Doctor?

I'm quite positive I do not have active T.B. A week or so here will build me up physically and heal my rib. This is "Paradise Regained" whereas the Seattle's Bastille would, in allegory, be "Paradise Lost."

I've become a paper "freak" as a result of my immurations in Seattle jail. Paper and pens are available here though stamps are not too loose and I hesitate or am reluctant to borrow from the more affluent patients.

Well that is all for the nonce. May you father a hundred children and all of them sons. Ancient Chinese verbal curve. Friend, Bill.

April 14, 1968
Edgecliff Hospital
Spokane, Washington

Dear Jim:

Lean over a bit and listen closely dear doc' — but first "Warmest Easter greetings." I've been suspect for some time of having loose morals and of being prone to peculiar pecadillos — now I am, amongst my other endearing qualities, also a T.B. suspect.

Damn X ray again showed old T.B. scar so here we go again. Tried to tell nice people that in the last ten-month period I'd been thru the X-ray, sputum, urine, and serological series twice (Minneapolis and Seattle) and found negative by the leading lights of the medical fraternity. NO SALE! "Now, now, Mr. Tanner, why are you angry? We don't care about Seattle or Minneapolis — it's for your own good — purely a precautionary measure." I, at times, wonder if traffic in T.B. bug hasn't slumped to such a point that they must beat the brush for clientele. So I ask, "Bill, watinell u bitching 'bout? You got a good pad, good chuck, hand and foot catering service, and nice nurses — killing me with kindness — But just think of Seattle clink — mush, soup, chicken necks!" Buddy, I'm traveling in a parabolic circle. Treatment center in Seattle fattened me to 172 — Seattle clink slimmed me to 145 — now in 2 weeks I'm back to 160. Truth is I'm intelligent enough to realize even if I do not have the bug they quite probably are adding time to my terrestial sojourn. I am going to try to fly straight when they complete their reading in not more than a week or two — I hope.

It's Saturday noon. Soon I'll hit the public trough again. I do hope I am found negative again. I have been crowding my luck — I've been able to rebound thus far. . . . I do understand that there is a limit to the mental and physical abuse one can subject himself to. Thank you for past favors and for bearing with me. Cheers! Friend, Bill.

April 30, 1968
Billings, Montana — City Jail

Evil Entrapments, entanglements continue to bedevil bewildered Bill. I've advanced as far as Billings, Montana, on my dilatory and bit sanguine journey. Was a trifle abruptly halted by my predilection to derelict demeanor — and attendant derailments. Need I elaborate? Still pursuing my involuntary post graduate studies of bucket — hosteleries. Lovely weather (I'm more than less under same). I'm fine fettle though and glad T.B. diagnosis was negative. I do not believe the "bug" could long survive in my alky cooling and fuel stream. Law of compensation. Weight zoomed to 165 but am now on a crash diet again.

My mail, if anyone has bothered to reply to the 20 odd letters I wrote hither and yon, is probably snafued. I guess I'm an elusive target for any praiseworthy replies I may have received at Spokane.

Once back in "The City of Lakes" I will check on the squirrel population and watch them stash their goodies — Then if times are tough next winter I can always steal or beg a crumb or two. That's it. If you answer at once I'll be here, perhaps a week or so. Address: City Jail, Billings, Montana.

May 20, 1968
Division of Corrections
Minneapolis, Minnesota

Greetings! Heavy, heavy hangs the time. I must have an urge to seek self punishment — But like a homing pidgeon I returned here

— knowing damn well I'd wind up here. Slightly mellow, I walked or ran a red light — Damn if I do not get accosted by the most dedicated cops (I use the term loosely).

I hope you're not getting the impression that I'm getting a father complex writing you (bugging you). I've already got a "mother" complex as far as institutions are concerned. Everything was going good. Had a job, pad, clothes, etc.

Perhaps I'd better volunteer for a cure or start a flood of writs to bug the judge or judges. I guess I'm involved with about three. I had ninety days hanging from the millionaire Judge Winton (He had offered me a 45-day sentence or 90 days suspended. One week later I hit Judge Christiansen and got 10 days — on a Saturday A.M. I knew the 90 would follow so I flew or stumbled into Seattle. That was last June.) Now I found Judge Johnson — Man! We have the judges! All sizes, shapes, and dispositions, about 14 or more — they alternate. The good judge Johnson, a bald, beefy, 300-pounder, asked me what my trouble was. I couldn't answer — I was so disgusted. Here went my clothes, pad, and job. I didn't even make a pitch. I think I got 10 days, 90 days, 90 days, and $25 fine or five days on all charges — past and present. The bailiff said they ran concurrently. The judge referred me to AA in 30 days — so time will tell. I'm in "dead-lock" a 6 x 8 cubicle with restricted diet and movement — only two meals. I should scream double jeopardy — got 90 days for escape, plus this durance vile.

Enough of that: I picked up enough material last year to write a hundred books. How's your work coming or have the lushes driven you to the sauce yourself? I remain the optimist. Something will happen — things will improve. I could spring from here — I do have an out but I hesitate to use it. You may surmise what it is — I was fattened at Edgecliff; now I go thru the slimming process again.

July 7, 1968
Glen Lake Sanitarium
Minnetonka, Minnesota

Hello! How's your corpus cavernosum? As a dedicated savant pursuing my study of spirits fermenti and alcoholism feckfully

62

and recklessly for many a year I guess I neglected to take elementary precautions. I've been here a little better than seven weeks. Takes eight weeks to get a sputum culture return. I will then know if some discriminating T.B. bugs have been studying my anatomy. Meanwhile, I'm furiously comesting the comestibles — giving the corpuscles time to regroup and start corpusculating or whatever they do in perilous times.

I see the Supreme Court ruled 5 to 4 that alcoholics may be jailed — Too bad. A writer in Time magazine suggested that an alky who could stay sober for a few months would be doing his fellows a signal favor if he brought another case to court. I can very well understand minimal jailing — say five days — or so. If I do have T.B. it is of recent vintage and most likely due to the starvation and unhealthy Seattle jail. I wish I knew who to contact in regard to the same. I can visualize breakfast — damn near sugarless mush, two slices of bread, one cup of ersatz coffee — that flour-based soup for lunch and the pitiful supper. Man it was pathetic. Ah well, perhaps the law of compensation will take over somewhere along the line.

August 28, 1968
Glen Lake Sanitarium
Minnetonka, Minnesota

I was surprised and very happy to receive your letter and report on Seattle City Jail. To be honest I had about decided that I'd offended you somehow — Tact or lack of same seems to be one of my failings. I thank you very much for remembering this skid-rogue. I wish I could have helped you more. I'm going to try very hard to overcome what I feel is an emotional and mental instability. I can, when rational, understand that liquor has thrown me for a loss almost every time — that it has cost me in friends, jobs, money and the whole bit.

I've been here almost three months. I'm rather glad that I've only been on one drunk — I'm not locked up either. The temptation to take off is strong — a bus at the door — beautiful weather — I'm having my dental needs taken care of and I am glad that all tests thus far (cultures and all) have been negative. I've written the judge a few verbal curves and perhaps the cockles of his stony heart may relent and he could dismiss my rabbit time. There are a few activities here — leathercraft, rug making, belts, etc. — let me know if you are in the market for a hand-tooled belt or billfold — I may send you one anyhow — if I knew your waist size. No accordion here but I give myself a piano lesson daily on the baby grand — such schmaltzy tunes as "Walking My Baby Back Home" and "It Really Makes No Difference Now."

Well, Jim, I do not imagine that you are very popular with the police department but you really let them off lightly. I know I lost a few bucks the last time I was booked. I'd been to the newspaper and had been given a complementary ball point pen. So I tell the good officer when my property was being returned that I should have a couple of pens. Hell, you never had any pens. Just then I glanced at his shirt. I was looking right at my pen — in his shirt pocket; Penny ante thievery such as that I do not dig.

Time hangs heavy at times — am getting wonderful care — weight back up to 175 — teeth, and glasses. I begin pursuing the babes. A set of ivories, I get them next Monday, and I will then turn on the wolfish grin and charm.

I would like very much to hope and think that your writings and research will help improve the lot of the drinking man in Seattle — I agree without any reservations that the jail there is one of, or the worst in the country — food-wise and in all the aspects covered. For that matter, the Minneapolis jail and court procedure is also strictly a kangaroo — but at least when sentenced one does have fair and sufficient comestibles and medical care.

Your friend, Bill

CHAPTER THREE

*A Bucket Full
of Tramps*

Mr. Tanner's behavior and experiences often appear bizarre and irrational: at times he is torn by inner conflict about the meaning and value of his life, and, like many men with similar life-styles, he determines to stay away from Skid Road but seems irresistibly drawn there. He experiences periods of sobriety as well as marathon drunks, vacillating between fighting for justice and passively submitting to those institutions which control him. He values his "grasshopper existence" yet feels constrained to return to the "bee-hive-like norm" which defines this life as undesirable. How shall we account for men such as this who seem to be running from one drink, town, and jail to another in rapid succession? Is it possible that this way of life is based on cultural rules? Do these men share some kind of cultural pattern? This minority group has been present in American society for a long time and many attempts have been made to comprehend and explain their behavior. A decision as to their social identity will not only enable us to identify *who* they are, but also help explain *why* they live as they do; most or all attempts to understand and identify these men have been based on at least four *models*.

These men are most often characterized by other Americans in terms of their *popular identity*. They are seen as people who fail abysmally, are dependent on society, lack self-control, drink too much, are unpredictable, and often end up in jail for their criminal behavior. In a word, they are *bums*. A recent issue of *Newsweek* magazine cogently expressed this approach.

At worst, they're treated like criminals scooped up by the bum wagon, hauled into court, sentenced to dry out in jail, then tossed back to the street to be swept up again in what amounts to a revolving door. At best, they're left to drift by themselves, here picking up a welfare chit for a flop, there cadging a few dimes for a bottle, eventually ending their lives in an unmarked grave in potter's field (1968:78).

A number of other widely used names reflect this popular identity: "derelict," "wino," and "transient." This is the viewpoint of the outsider who sees this way of life as irrational, immoral, and irresponsible, but it is important to understand this model since it has influenced professional and layman alike. As part of American culture it is learned early in life and taken for granted. Although most of the men studied were aware of this popular image and even used these terms, they defined them differently.

A second model assumes that the most significant way to characterize these men is by their *medical identity*. They are defined on the basis of a disease: alcoholism. It is an interesting identity because it has only recently been considered by the medical profession to be an illness or disease, and it is one of the few diseases which one *becomes*. In our culture we *have* heart attacks and are *victims* of cancer, but *become* neither of these diseases. The criteria used to identify an alcoholic are hardly better defined than those used to identify a bum, although different kinds of alcoholics are recognized by professionals.[1] The men described here had all heard the term "alcoholic" and had been in one or more alcoholism treatment centers, yet this identity was not too significant to many of them.

66

Studies which have been carried out from the medical point of view have, interestingly enough, come to conclusions which are very similar to the popular model. Such a man is seen as resembling "a burned-out, back-ward schizophrenic who has forgotten what his troubles were and why he retreated from life" (Solomon 1966:165). They are characterized as "unable to maintain themselves in society without the imposition of external controls" (Chafetz 1966:137) and "incapable of planning or perceiving the consequences of his initial actions" (Levinson 1957:210). Such statements imply that Skid Road alcoholics are almost without culturally organized behavior.

The third point of view stresses the *legal identity* of these men. They are seen as criminals, guilty of many minor crimes, but especially of public drunkenness. The police refer to these men as "drunks" and "vagrants" and view them in much the same way as the general public does. A recent study of the police quotes a high law official who stated:

We're pretty tough on vagrants here. We give them summary justice and send them to jail. There, the police rough 'em up a bit and then we send them out of town. These people could work if they wanted to. There's plenty of jobs here, what with all the construction going on. . . . The only reason these men don't work is that they don't want to work (Wilson 1968:147).

In Seattle the criminal court had a special file for keeping track of this population which officially identified them as *common drunkards*.

The *sociological identity* of these men has been constructed using a variety of criteria. Some social scientists have adopted the perspective of the medical or legal models while others have selected geographic boundaries and focused upon that section of American cities known as Skid Road. One of the most widely used criterion has been the lack of a home, giving rise to the concept of the *homeless man*. Age, race, sex, income, and drinking behavior have all been used by researchers for identifying this population. Most of these criteria have implicit values drawn from the popular image of the "bum." The focus upon drinking behavior and homelessness, for instance, reflects the dominant values in American

67

society of sobriety, self control, and the home. The popular image has influenced social science studies of these men in many ways.

When the sociologist arrives on skid row with pre-coded, pre-tested, survey questionnaire in hand, every one of his questions implicitly assumes the person is a failure and asks why. Even though this question remains unstated, both questioner and questioned perceives its fundamental reality (Wallace, S. 1965:159).

Studies which have attempted to discover the culture and identity of this population without defining in advance what is significant are rare, and even these do no more than superficially discuss what the men themselves consider extremely significant — their encounter with law enforcement officials.[2]

The popular, medical, legal, and sociological models used to identify these men and their style of life are not devoid of practical value and for certain purposes they are extremely useful. Providing definitions of social situations which make interaction predictable, they enable average citizens, physicians, police, judges, and researchers to account for what appears to be strange and irrational behavior. A man who has no family, travels from town to town, seldom works, and drinks a great deal is not easy to comprehend. By defining such people as *bums, Skid Road alcoholics, vagrants, common drunkards,* or *homeless men,* the average citizen or the professional person knows how to relate to them. He knows that they ought to be ignored, pitied, arrested, jailed, run out of town, or rehabilitated. Studies of this minority group based on these models may not describe this subculture at all. Instead, they may describe how members of the larger American society define this minority group, and as such, they are descriptions of the dominant American culture! Whatever their value, they do not go very far toward providing a description of the way in which members of this group define their own identity and culture, which is the aim of this book.

The ethnographic study of social identity has a long history in anthropology, particularly in the study of kinship systems.[3] In many non-Western societies these systems are the most important social identity networks and early anthropologists soon discovered that kinsmen were not classified or defined in the same way from one society to another. Native words used to refer to one's father or mother might include individuals who, from the outsider's point of view, were not one's father or mother. In some societies those who are mother's brothers have a social identity which is similar to the identity of fathers in American culture, and behavior patterns which first appeared strange and exotic became comprehensible only after the anthropologist had mapped the native definitions of such social identity systems. Once the underlying cultural rules for classifying and relating to kinsmen are discovered for a society, other patterns within the culture begin to emerge. It seems reasonable that the ethnographic study of social identity in urban subcultures will also be a productive enterprise. How do members of the group being considered here classify and define themselves and the social identity of those with whom they interact? The answer to this question could not be found by using questionnaires on social identity, nor was it appropriate to ask informants to explain their identities to the researcher. Initially the data were gathered by *listening* and *observing,* not to discover answers but to find which questions to ask. The core of the ethnographic method is this search for questions in the field situation. Black and Metzger have made this very point:

It could be said of ethnography that until you know the question that someone in the culture is responding to you can't know many things about the response. Yet the ethnographer is greeted, in the field, with an array of *responses.* He needs to know what questions people are answering in their every act. He needs to know which questions are being taken for granted because they are what "everybody knows" without thinking (1965:144).

Participant observation and recording casual conversations among these men made it possible to formulate many hypotheses and hunches which were later the basis for more formal ethnographic interviews. Specific question frames were then developed along with a variety of sorting tasks for testing the adequacy of these hypotheses. The result presented here is an ethnographic description which approaches the way insiders of this culture define their own identity, environment, and life style. Although listening, engaging in participant observation, formulating hypotheses, and testing these hypotheses with specific eliciting techniques were all used throughout the research, some tended to precede others. In this chapter the formal questioning and sorting tasks will be discussed in some detail but it should be understood they were used in gathering and analyzing the data presented in later chapters also.

The men were first identified *hypothetically* as Skid Road alcoholics, an identity based on the medical model. They had all been arrested for public drunkenness and subsequently committed to an alcoholism treatment center. Among the large number of verbatim statements by these men that were recorded, many appeared to relate to social identity and these included such references as the following:

> We are really *inmates* out here.
> They sure treat us *patients* well.
> Some more *tramps* arrived today from the city jail.
> These men are all a bunch of *bums*.
> This is no way to treat a *citizen* of this country.
> He's an *ex-convict*.
> We are all really *prisoners*.

In order to reduce the influence of their translation competence, data were gathered when the men were talking among themselves rather than to the researcher or the staff at the treatment center. Although they were often referred to as alcoholics by the staff and had acknowledged this identity at the time of admission, they seldom used the term among themselves. Individual interviews proved less effective on this point because many men identified the author as a member of the alcoholism treatment staff and would not speak in the dialect of their own subculture, but group interviews, which developed into discussions among informants rather than direct responses to the researcher, were most effective.

In order to further check the saliency of different identity terms, two questions were asked a group of fifty men. First, they were asked to place in rank order those terms which they felt best described the men at the treatment center. They were presented with the words *inmate, patient, tramp, bum, citizen, convict,* and *prisoner* and instructed to include additional words which would better describe the population. Although only two men (4 per cent) responded with *alcoholic*, many new terms such as "mission stiff," "hustler," and "dingbat" were elicited. No one referred to the men as Skid Road alcoholics. This same group was asked to indicate the major illnesses, diseases, or sicknesses they had had during the last two years. Only four men (8 per cent) responded with "alcoholic" or "alcoholism" in spite of the fact they were constantly reminded that this was their medical condition! Some of the men reported such illnesses as hangovers (6 per cent), alcoholic seizures (4 per cent), wineache (2 per cent), and drunk (2 per cent), but these were seen as consequences of drinking, not as diseases which led to compulsive drinking. Thus, concepts such as "alcoholic" and "Skid Road alcoholic" were discarded and those terms identified by informants as culturally appropriate were selected for further research.

The terms used by these men reflect their life style and where they are anchored in social space. *Citizen* was most often used with reference to their rights under the law and indicated their membership in American society, but the term most frequently used as an identity reference in *all* the scenes of their world was *tramp*. There are five major scenes in this subculture: buckets (jails), farms (treatment centers), jungles (encampments), skids (Skid Roads), and freights (railroad cars). Informants would make such comments as, "All the men on Skid Road are tramps of one sort or another," and "All those guys they throw in the drunk tank in the city jail are tramps." This term referred to their identity as men who have learned a particular style of life — the culture of the tramp. *Patient*, on the other hand, referred to their identity when in some treatment center, work farm, or sanitarium. Such terms as *inmate, prisoner,* and *convict* specify their identity in relation to law enforcement agencies, especially when incarcerated in jail. Though all these identities are important, we shall focus upon only two: tramp and inmate. Their selection is partly determined by research interest in law and order for minority groups, but it also reflects informants' feelings about the relative importance of their different identities.

If a person is identified as a tramp, what does this mean? When a police officer refers to the man he has arrested as a tramp, does it have the same implication as it does when a tramp uses such a term? How are we to discover what it means to be a tramp? The first step was to elicit descriptive statements from informants, statements much like dictionary definitions. One man reported:

A tramp is a fiddlefoot. One-hundred and fifty years ago he would be an explorer or adventurer. These are men who don't want a steady job, no desire to compete in the rat-race. Society looks on him as a man who can't keep up when he is one who doesn't want to keep up.

Another suggested:

A tramp is a good person who works and supports himself but who doesn't have any roots.

Some men reported that a tramp was the same as a hobo. Others felt that tramps and bums were different; still others used these terms synonymously but such statements do not go very far toward understanding what it means to be a tramp. Ethnographers have developed two other approaches for analyzing the meaning of terms and these lead to *taxonomic definitions* and *componential definitions*.

One of the most important functions of language is to classify unique objects into categories so they may be treated as equivalent. The American English term uncle classifies into a single category different individuals who are related to some person in different ways. Different kinds of relations are thus *included* in a single concept. At the same time, terms such as uncle, father, mother, and grandson are all included in the more general term relative or kinsman. There is some evidence to suggest that this relationship of inclusion is a universal feature of language related to basic cognitive processes since in every language, terms which refer to more specific objects and events are included in more generic labels or cover terms.[4] Such relationships are usually described as "taxonomic" and are illustrated in Table 3.1.

It was not readily apparent just *how* the term "tramp" was related to other categories for distinguishing social identity and it might well have turned out that tramps were simply one kind of alcoholic or alcoholics were to be classified as tramps. Such was not

TABLE 3.1 PARTIAL TAXONOMY OF AMERICAN
KINSHIP TERMS

Relative					
Blood relative			In-law		
Mother	Father	Brother	Mother-in-law	Father-in-law	Brother-in-law

the case. In order to discover whether this was a general cover term for a variety of social identities or a specific term for a single identity, informants were asked, "Are there different kinds of tramps?" An affirmative answer to this question was followed by asking: "What kinds of tramps are there?" This resulted in the terms shown in Table 3.2, each of which refers to a different type of person identified in this culture as a tramp. The terms are arranged in a folk taxonomy.[5]

Other terms used by informants are not included in Table 3.2, but most are synonyms and reflect variations in dialect among the men. These appear to be related to the area where a man was socialized into this subculture and the length of time he had been a tramp. Those who were from the southern United States often used "tramp" and "hobo" interchangeably but preferred the latter; others used "bum," or even "drunk," in a manner which was synonymous with "tramp." These were tested by asking, "What kinds of bums or drunks are there?" The answer to such a question led to lists similar to the ones shown above. Mr. Tanner had been socialized in the midwest and more often used the term bum. He writes:

A brief course in the fifth "B" or Bumology. . . . There are railroad. . . , rubber tire, mission stiffs, Salvation Army stiffs, working, non-working, bindle, stream-lined. . . .

Mr. Tanner speaks of "stream-lined stiff," whereas most informants spoke of a "box car tramp" or hobo who was characterized by traveling streamlined. By this they meant such a person rode freight trains without carrying any personal belongings. A careful analysis of all synonyms and various regional dialects is important,

TABLE 3.2 TAXONOMIC DEFINITION OF
TRAMP DOMAIN

Tramp												
Working stiff					Mission stiff							
Construction tramp	Sea tramp	Tramp miner	Harvest tramp	Fruit tramp	Nose diver	Professional nose diver	Bindle stiff	Airedale	Rubber tramp	Home guard tramp	Box car tramp	Ding

but it is beyond the purpose and scope of this work, and the terms presented and analyzed here were selected because of their wide usage by long-time tramps who had spent considerable time in the Pacific Northwest.

The language of a society, as we have noted, classifies different objects together as similar. "Tramp" is a cover term which functions in this way, grouping many identities into one category. Language also identifies significant contracts among similar objects. The acquisition and communication of *meaning* is achieved not

74

only by identifying things for what they *are*, but also by implicitly recognizing what they *are not*.[6] Except for words with identical meaning, every term in a language contrasts with every other term. A "bindle stiff" contrasts with a "mission stiff" as well as with an "elephant." But, to the ethnographer and those interested in the study of meaning, the difference between "bindle stiff" and "mission stiff" is far more significant than the difference between "bindle stiff" and "elephant." The former terms are said to be in *restricted contrast* while the latter are in *total contrast*.[7] The identities of "tramp," "bull," and "professor" are all different, but "tramp" and "bull" share many similar features of meaning which are not shared by "professor" and are thus in restricted contrast. The discovery that there are fifteen kinds of tramps is a recognition of similarities among a set of labels. It also points to the fact that they are in restricted contrast, and that the differences among them will be significant according to their respective meanings, and, more generally, it tells us what it means to be a tramp.

Many descriptive statements that were gathered suggested differences among kinds of tramps. Informants reported the following:

I was with a ding one time and he made $30 begging while we walked back to town from West Seattle.

Joe over there is a mission stiff — he hangs around the missions all the time. A mission stiff just goes from one mission to another.

You can't trust a rubber tramp. He will drive off in the middle of the night with anything not nailed down.

If I see a group of fifteen men, I can tell which ones are tramps. I can tell in forty words if a guy is a mission stiff.

Such statements add to our understanding of differences among tramp identities, as does the taxonomic relationship shown in Table 3.3; but, since a very large number of attributes *could* distinguish among the different kinds of tramps, we must establish which ones informants consider *significant*. This was done by asking informants to perform a variety of tasks aimed at eliciting criterial attributes; a triadic sorting task developed by George Kelly (1955) was found to be most useful.[8] An informant was presented with terms for three kinds of tramps and asked to indicate which two were *similar* and which one was *different* from the other two. One response to such a question often was: "How do you mean, similar or different?" Informants were told to select any criteria they felt important for grouping two kinds of tramps together and distinguishing them from a third. Only after the terms had been sorted into two groups would the informant be queried as to the basis for his action. For example, when an informant was presented with the terms "bindle stiff," "airedale," and "box car tramp," a typical response was, "The first two are similar because they both carry a pack with them where they have a bedroll and other belongings, but a box car tramp travels streamlined." The systematic application of this approach with many combinations of tramp terms led to the discovery of the dimensions of contrasts which informants used to recognize differences among tramps.

This approach to finding significant differences in meaning among a set of terms is referred to as "componential analysis."[9] A componential definition of the eight core terms in this domain is provided in Table 3.3.

TABLE 3.3 COMPONENTIAL DEFINITION OF
TRAMP DOMAIN

	Mobile[10]	*Mode of travel*	*Home base*	*Livelihood*
Working stiff	Yes	Freight Commercial	Job	Specialized— Works
Mission stiff	Yes	Commercial	Mission	Specialized— Missions
Bindle stiff	Yes	Freight	Pack	Generalized
Airedale	Yes	Walk	Pack	Generalized
Rubber tramp	Yes	Car	Car	Generalized
Home guard tramp	No	Ø	Town and Kinsmen	Generalized
Box car tramp	Yes	Freight	None	Generalized
Ding	Yes	Freight	None	Specialized— Begs

The first dimension is *mobility,* which was expressed in a variety of ways: "A rubber tramp travels from harvest to harvest," or "An airedale travels from town to town." The "home guard tramp" was always defined as one who stayed around town year in and year out. When a man arrived in a new town, it was the home guard tramp he looked for to find out about police practices or to seek other helpful information. From Seattle, a home guard tramp might go to eastern Washington during the apple harvest, but he would usually return to Seattle. He was defined as being psychologically tied to this locale, even though he was still a tramp.

The next dimension of meaning, *mode of travel,* was a relevant criterion for all but the home guard tramp. Tramps use many ways to get from one place to another; they may hitchhike along the highway or go to a truck stop and seek assistance, or they may apply for a job in another town with the railroad in order to receive free transportation to that town. Some men would work for a time and then fly to another city, and others who had money for commercial transportation would prefer to ride in a box car. One man reported:

I've traveled by freight and sent $600 on ahead. I don't like to ride the bus, even though I had the money. On the freight I could rest, sleep, walk around, get off when I wanted and cook up.

Although most tramps are willing to use any means of transportation under specific conditions, they tend to develop customary modes of travel which became part of their identity. These include freight trains, commercial transportation, walking, and traveling in one's own car.

The next criterion which informants used to distinguish among the tramp identities was their *home base.* This does not refer to where their home was or what it was, as defined by American culture, for tramps have learned to make a home in a variety of places. Rather, it has to do with where they are *anchored* socially and psychologically. Some men are linked to a particular kind of job, although not in any permanent sense. The sea tramp is different from other merchant seamen primarily because he never stays on the same ship, even when he has such an opportunity. Though they do loathe a steady job, they are not men who dislike work. The home base for a rubber tramp is his car; for a mission stiff it is the mission. The home guard tramp is psychologically anchored to one city or several towns in a single locale, usually where he has some relatives to fall back on in case of dire need. He learns to know the policemen on the beat and often has an almost permanent position as a trusty in the local jail. Two other kinds of criteria on this dimension stress a higher degree of independence: the bindle stiff and airedale carry all their belongings with them and their home base can be created wherever they are; the box car tramp and the ding are the most independent, defined by informants as nearly devoid of social anchorage. They are the most highly mobile, free to come and go as they like, with no need to maintain a car or look for a mission or a job.

The outsider always wonders how such men manage to survive. This is an equally important consideration for insiders and they distinguish among the different kinds of tramps by their ways of earning a *livelihood*. Many strategies are used by tramps to meet the basic requirements of living: they can beg, sell their possessions, work, go to welfare agencies, collect discarded items such as bottles and sell them, steal, sell their own blood, as well as a variety of other activities. Most men, at one time or another, may have to use all these strategies, but some tramps become identified by their customary way of making a living. These men, in a sense, have become specialists in the tramp society, while the others are still generalists. The working stiff specializes in working, the mission stiff in making the mission, and the ding in begging. Each has developed skills which suit him to these occupations and many become experts, if judged by the standards of this culture.

The values of each of these four dimensions are sufficient to distinguish among the eight major kinds of tramps. Although these are the most important differences recognized by informants, they do not exhaust the discriminations which were reported. For example, working stiffs, mission stiffs, and rubber tramps might be women as well as men, whereas only men assume the other tramp identities. Most of the types would include men who received pensions with the general exception of box car tramps, dings, and bindle stiffs. Some informants would refer to all such men as "pensioners," an identity which crosscuts the domain of tramps. Another dimension of contrast was the degree of trustworthiness one could expect to find in each kind of tramp; mission stiffs, airedales, rubber tramps, and dings are considered by most men to be untrustworthy. Mission stiffs are disliked because of their ties with missions and their tendency to boss other tramps who come there for food or a place to sleep. Airedales and dings are few in number and reported to be social isolates and thus to be avoided. The rubber tramp is untrustworthy because he steals from other tramps and can easily escape in his car. Although informants described the attributes for each tramp identity as if they were static, they also recognized that this was not always the case. Some rubber tramps did turn out to be trustworthy and some home guard tramps were known to have traveled to distant places by freight. The information contained in the componential definition of tramps enables a man to predict with high probability, but not with certainty, the characteristics of other men. In addition, these terms refer to *identities*, not to persons. Interest, ability, and other personal traits may lead a man to discard his identity as a home guard tramp and become a box car tramp, a ding, or one of the other kinds of tramp. One informant reported, "If a home guard tramp were to change he would probably become a bindle stiff because he would feel he needed a lot of things to get along."

The ethnographic study of identity seeks to find out how people in alien societies organize their knowledge about themselves, but it does not prescribe which criteria should be significant, allowing these to arise from the empirical situation. The present study might have been done with questions derived from the popular, medical, legal, or sociological models of identity; instead, the questions asked were first discovered from informants. They define their primary identity with the word "tramp," and in order to understand the meaning of such an identity this word was defined both taxonomically and componentially. The underlying semantic principles for organizing their knowledge about their own identity are intimately related to their nomadic style of life. Mobility, how one travels, the degree to which one is anchored to some kind of home base, and the strategies for survival — these are the features of identity which are significant. The man who is independent, travels constantly, and uses a wide variety of survival techniques is both trustworthy and respected. Even the type of tramp who commands little respect is still evaluated by these same criteria. Many identity features which are of interest to the outsider go unnoticed by tramps. An almost infinite number of criteria could be used in any society for signifying differences among people. Every culture defines a limited number as significant — the rest go unnoticed. From an ethnographic point of view, then, these men are tramps. The underlying logic of this social identity reflects many other patterns in their culture.

Another important identity shared by all the men is *inmate*. When a man is released from jail, this identity is discarded or simply recognized as part of his past — he is an ex-convict. The relationship between the identities of "tramp" and "inmate" is tightly interwoven because the men who are picked up repeatedly for public drunkenness, and are too poor to bail out, are the *tramps*. One informant summed up the feeling of many men when he said, "*If a man hasn't made the bucket, he isn't a tramp.*" Mr. Tanner's diary, covering less than a year, has many references to his life as an inmate. Like most urban nomads, he had been in jail so many times he had lost count. A group of slightly more than 200 men were asked to estimate the number of times they had been in jail with the following results:

Less than 10	9%
10–25	24%
26–50	23%
51–100	25%
101–200	12%
Over 200	7%

Most responses were general, such as "over fifty," or "about a hundred times," and, if anything, the number was probably underestimated. In contrast to these figures, we may notice the number of times they reported receiving inpatient treatment for drinking prior to their commitment to the alcoholism treatment center in Seattle.

Never	59%
1	18%
2–5	18%
6 or more	5%

Though they had all been patients, such an identity was much less significant as measured by the length of time in such a role. In fact, for some men, much of their adult lives had been lived as inmates in local jails. An understanding of what it means to be an inmate in one city jail (Seattle), then, should help us understand their social identity.

Tramps refer to any local city or county jail as "the bucket." A wide variety of statements were recorded about life in jail, a number of which contained references to the social identities a tramp and others have there. It is difficult to grasp the full meaning of any aspect of life in the bucket without first identifying *who* is there. If a man says, "Some of them bulls are sadists — they knock hell out of drunks and laugh about it," who is he talking about? Are all policemen the same kind of bulls and do all inmates have the same identity? What does it mean *to be a drunk?* Tramps often made such comments as, "The trusties usually run the jail as far as the lock-ups are concerned . . . if you are able to give them a candy bar or good cigarettes they will give you sandwiches and extra favors." An understanding of such behavior first requires a definition of those who are labeled "trusties" and "lockups." Interaction in jail, as in any social setting, takes place between people who are identified as occupying certain positions or having certain kinds of identities. After discovering the many kinds of people in jail, systematic interviewing was done with the question, "What kinds of people are there in the Seattle bucket?" This led to a long list of terms used by tramps to refer to these people and a folk taxonomy of the major ones is shown in Table 3.4.

When a tramp enters the jail, he is recognized by himself and others as having a particular identity — one which is part of the

TABLE 3.4 PEOPLE IN THE BUCKET

Inmate				Bull								Civilian		
Drunk	Lockup	Trusty	Kickout	Matron	Turnkey	Bailiff	Sergeant	Kingpin	Inspector	Booking desk bull	Court liaison officer	Cook	Doctor	Nurse

jail social system. Although a man is identified as a drunk it does not necessarily mean he is intoxicated or was at the time of his arrest. Whether he is drunk or not is irrelevant — when a tramp is brought into the jail, he *becomes* a drunk, in much the same way that a woman who is brought into a hospital and has a baby *becomes* a mother. The tramp is not only locked up in a cell, but he *becomes* a lockup or timer; he not only works as a trusty, but *becomes* a trusty; and he is not simply released from jail, but prior to his release he lays aside these other identities and *becomes* a kickout. He sees himself, and others see him, as merged with these roles. It is extremely difficult, if not impossible, for a man to remain detached from this social network — the meaning that such identities have becomes internalized as part of the self. The behavior of tramps, then, both inside and outside the bucket, must be understood by considering what it means to be an inmate.

There are socially accepted rules in American culture for assuming the roles and identities of "drunk," "trusty," "lockup," and "kickout." These rules are known to tramps and policemen alike, and are often violated by both. These men are arrested for their *public behavior*: drinking, urinating, sleeping, begging, and for their very presence in the Skid Road area. Once arrested, for whatever reason, they are placed in the drunk tank where they assume the identity of a drunk. A man can even become a drunk by going to jail and requesting to be admitted! After going to court and receiving a sentence, a man may immediately assume any of the other three identities. If his sentence is suspended, he becomes a kickout and within a short time he will be released. If he receives a long sentence, he has a good chance of becoming a trusty or, if he becomes a lockup, he may at a later time move to the position of trusty. The reverse is also true: as a trusty he may violate some rule or offend some officer and be "busted" back to being a lockup. After serving his time, he will become a kickout and be released. For many men, the identity of kickout is followed very soon by that of drunk, once again to repeat the pattern. Some tramps are able to escape from the Seattle city jail and assume a new identity which is outside the system — that of a "rabbit." The complex relationships among these social identities are shown in Chart 3.1. The arrows indicate the possible changes in identity which may

CHART 3.1 IDENTITY CHANGES IN THE BUCKET

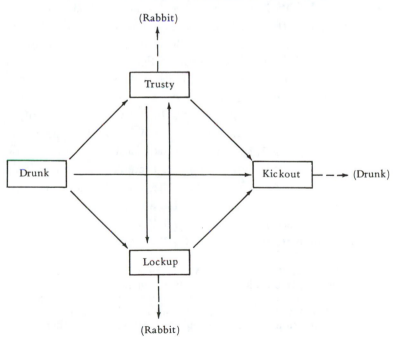

occur. A more complete analysis of these processes will be made in later chapters.

This discovery that a group of related identities was included in the cover term not only added to the impression that *inmate* was an important domain in this culture, but it also gave the investigator relevant questions to ask of informants. One set of questions was: "What kinds of drunks are there?" "What kinds of rabbits?" "What kinds of lockups?" and "What kinds of trusties?" Though most of these questions were not very productive, the last one produced significant results. It was discovered that there were about 60 categories of trusties! Those who become trusties in the Seattle city jail work at an enormous number of jobs: they staple targets, mow lawns, mop floors, change tires, wash cars, clean boats, clean toilets, make coffee, usher in the court, care for the sick, press clothes, make pastries, wait on bulls, carry messages, wash pots, run elevators, cut hair, and a variety of other tasks. In this jail, which has a capacity for approximately 500 inmates, nearly 150 trusties are required each day to work. It was estimated by one police official that 80 per cent of the inmates at any time are those charged with public drunkenness and these are the men chosen to become trusties because their crimes are not serious nor is there much difficulty if they escape. The police know that if a tramp rabbits from the jail he will either leave town or they can easily arrest him again in a short time.

How do tramps feel about this practice of working to maintain the jail and other city agencies, such as city hall and the police department firing range? Although they seek trusty positions because it makes their sentence more bearable, there is a widespread feeling that they are sometimes arrested because trusties are needed. Tramps have become an indispensable and cheap labor force for jails and other institutions throughout the country. One man reported the following experience in another part of the state:

Do you know what they did in Walla Walla? You couldn't hardly walk down the street. They were putting a new addition on the jail and ran an ad in the paper trying to get labor to help. They couldn't get them so they were picking up the tramps at that pea harvest. I got picked up three times . . . they had me working around there doing everything — roofing, painting, helping the plumber and electrician. They were getting that free labor.

Another, a tailor by trade, came to Seattle from a California city because he couldn't stay out of jail. There he would work as a trusty, mending officers' uniforms and making dresses for their wives, in return for cigarettes and spending money. Some men in Seattle had even been told they were being arrested to fill a quota or to work as trusties. One man stated, "I was picked up and the cop told me, 'We need some good trusties,' " and another reported, "One cop told the other cop, 'Let's pick up this Mex and we'll only have one more to go for our quota for the day.' " Another tramp who was working as a trusty in the jail kitchen overheard the cook ask an officer where a certain man was who had been a good cook. The officer indicated they knew his whereabouts and would pick him up in a few days. Most tramps were aware that in some jails the inmates are paid for doing trusty work. Other men in the Seattle jail are doing time to pay off a fine — at the rate of $9 per day whether they are working or not. At this rate, every tramp who is arrested for drunk could be release in three days if he were *fined* $20 instead of having a *bail* of $20! Bail money cannot be earned by doing time. When a man works month after month as a trusty for the sole reason that he did not have $20, he finds it hard to escape the conclusion that he is being used for cheap labor.

It is interesting that this perception of being "used" to work in the jail is not entirely one-sided. A court official reported that when there had been a change in policy resulting in shorter sentences for public drunkenness cases, an officer in the jail had objected. The tramps were only receiving thirty days in jail, or occasionally sixty, rather than up to six months as had been the practice, and the officer complained that he just had a man trained to do his work as a trusty when the court released him! Some law enforcement officials also felt that the number of arrests for public drunkenness each year was almost *too* consistent, as indeed Table 3.5 seems to indicate.[11]

During 1968 the International Association of Chiefs of Police investigated the Seattle Police Department and reported that some

TABLE 3.5   ARRESTS FOR PUBLIC DRUNKENNESS

Year	Population (Seattle)	Drunk arrests
1960	557,087	11,198
1961	557,087	11,047
1962	561,000	13,633
1963	563,000	14,851
1964	564,000	13,707
1965	567,000	11,645
1966	574,000	11,328
1967	580,000	11,367

trusties were doing custodial work outside the jail in privately owned facilities. These trusties, referred to by tramps as "rangers," maintain the grounds and a pavilion at the police department firing range, a facility also leased to other groups by the owners. The report also stated that the prisoners received no monetary compensation for their services and recommended that trusties not be assigned to this type of work.[12] During 1968, the county jail, located in Seattle, had several escapes which came to the attention of the public, and the jail superintendent was reported in the press to have explained these and other problems of security. The work in the jail had always been done by tramps who were sentenced on drunk charges; then, in 1967, a new alcoholism treatment center began operation and received these men from the jails. He stated:

Before then, we had all the vagrants and drunks on the top floor. They were the trusties, and did all the work. Many of them stayed for the winter and you couldn't have chased them off. But since the alcoholics have been going out to the Center, we've had to put felons on the top floor, and use them as trusties. And most of these guys are smart. They've got 24 hours a day to think up schemes to get out (*Seattle Post-Intelligencer*, 1969).

The way in which this official refers to these men reflects their changing identities in American culture. As trusties in jail they were *vagrants* and *drunks* — that is the appropriate place for such people — but, when they were transferred to the treatment center they were defined as *alcoholics*. Urban nomads not only make reliable workers in jail, but, because of their life style — mobility,

86

drinking behavior, and sleeping habits — the police have little difficulty locating them when the need arises. You cannot be a tramp if you *don't* make the bucket, but you cannot run a jail unless tramps *do* make the bucket.

The work of trusties is not only a convenience for the police department, it is eagerly sought by most tramps who must do time in this jail. As we shall see, the freedom, food, and opportunities to augment their meager resources are all much greater for trusties than lockups. The assignment to a trusty position is used by jail personnel as a reward for conformity and passivity on the part of an inmate. Mr. Tanner was not allowed to be a trusty, in part, because he fought the system with his writ of habeas corpus. Those who "buck the bulls" or have a record as "rabbits" are seldom given such a position. Many men have worked at dozens of trusty jobs and have had this identity over ten or fifteen years. This inmate identity, then, is of special relevance to tramps and will provide additional insight into the culture of urban nomads. A taxonomic definition of this domain is shown in Table 3.6. The figures after each of the major terms indicate the number of men needed each day to fill these positions.

The sixteen core terms for the major kinds of trusties share many similarities in meaning. An inmate knows that if he is in any of these positions it means work, more food, and more freedom; he also knows that there are important differences among kinds of trusties. What it means to be a ranger differs from what it means to be a runner. From the ethnographic standpoint, these terms are in restricted contrast. Although inmates, bulls, and civilians in the jail all distinguish one kind of trusty from another, it is very likely that the criteria used by each group are different. An understanding of how tramps define these terms was first gained by recording statements which implied contrasts. Informants gave a variety of definitions: "I'd rather lay it out than be a floor man — you work too hard," and, "When extra food comes up the floor man can trade it to the lockups for commissary." Additional contrasts were gathered using the triadic sorting task. A man was presented with terms such as "ranger," "kitchen man," and "floor man," and asked to indicate which two were most alike. Typical of the responses elicited in this way is the following: "Kitchen men

TABLE 3.6 TAXONOMIC DEFINITION OF TRUSTY DOMAIN

Trusty			
Ranger (16-18)	Pistol shack man	Bullet man
		Target stapler
	Rifle target man	
	Pistol target man	
	Lawn man	
Odlin's man (4)	Floor man	
	Paper presser	
Garage man (8-10)	Window tire man	
	Car washer	
Georgetown man (5)		
City Hall man (2)		
Harbor Patrol man (2)		
Wallingford man (2)		
Floor man (24-28)	Sixth floor man	Pusher
		Water wheeler
		Sweeper
		Mopper
		Bucket man
		Mop cleaner
	Seventh floor man	Head trusty
		Sweeper
		Dish man
		Mess hall man
		Mopper
		Bucket man
		Mop cleaner
		Toilet man

TABLE 3.6 TAXONOMIC DEFINITION OF TRUSTY DOMAIN (Concluded)

Trusty		
Clerk (2)		
Bull cook (2)		
Court usher (2)		
Hospital orderly (4)		
Blue Room man (11)		
Kitchen man (36)	Elevator man	
	Laundry man	
	Presser	
	Dishwasher	
	Pastry man	
	Pot washer	
	Clean-up man	
	Vegetable man	
	Coffee man	
	Tea man	
	Storeroom man	
	Butcher	
	Waiter	
	Cook's helper	
Runner (6)	Day runner	
	Night runner	
Barber (2)	Inmate barber	
	Bull's barber	

and floor men are alike because they are inside the bucket while rangers are outside." Many combinations of terms were used to find the criteria considered important by informants and five dimensions of contrast economically define these terms but do not exhaust the informants' knowledge of them.

The most important theme which appeared was related to differences in the *restricted mobility* for these different identities. All inmates are locked up in jail, and, from the outsider's point of view, all appear to have about the same strictures on their movement, but tramps who have spent many years in this jail have learned to make fine discriminations among the degrees of freedom which different positions allow. This theme involves three dimensions of contrast. The first identifies the way in which a man is related to the *bucket* itself, very generally, and has two values: a trusty may be *inside* or *outside* the bucket. This way of identifying trusties is so important that men often refer to those who are more restricted as inside trusties and those who have more freedom as outside trusties. Even the more restricted trusties who are inside the bucket have a great deal more freedom than those confined to lockup or the drunk tank. An inmate who is allowed to work outside the bucket has opportunity to steal, beg, escape, and smuggle contraband back into the jail to sell. He can meet friends or relatives who may bring him things he needs, such as cigarettes, a privilege not allowed those who are inside the jail. Though these are important advantages, the feeling that a trusty who is outside the bucket has an easier time results from the sense that he is not as isolated from the rest of society. Many men are struggling to maintain a respectable identity even though they are being labeled by others as tramps, Skid Road alcoholics, inmates, and convicts. Being a trusty who is outside the bucket much of the time offers some support, although admittedly meager, for maintaining those identities not held in disrepute by the rest of society.

A second dimension of contrast, applicable only to trusties who work outside the jail, identifies the four major degrees of *freedom* these identities have:

1. Harbor Patrol and Wallingford men live outside the jail in another part of town. They eat at restaurants, are free to go to stores and movies, and may have visitors throughout each week.

2. Rangers and Georgetown men leave the jail each morning and return in the late afternoon. They must eat a lunch prepared in the jail. They have some opportunity to go to stores to make purchases, but these will have to be smuggled back into the jail.

3. The Garage and City Hall men leave the jail in the morning, return at noon to eat lunch, and then go back out until late in the afternoon. Opportunities for begging or making purchases are more limited than for those with more freedom.

4. Odlin's men follow the same pattern as those above who must come back to the jail for lunch. In addition, they must work within the same building which houses the jail.

The degrees of freedom which informants recognized show a heightened awareness on their part of the extent to which they are anchored to the bucket and all that this institution means for their own identity. The symbols which so securely link a man to the identity system of the jail are the building itself, distance, food, access to outside resources, and the number of times each day a man must return to the place he feels is changing him into a different person. Although these men inwardly struggle to keep from internalizing the identities which are thrust upon them in the jail, they find it is necessary to submit passively to this system if they are to be rewarded with trusty positions which give them the most freedom. A man who seeks to be true to *himself* discovers that after repeated arrests and many months in jail, year in and year out, he is no longer himself. His true identities are fading and he is slowly becoming what life in the bucket says he is — a man without a destination who must move on or be swallowed up by this system.

The third dimension of contrast, applicable only to trusties who work inside the jail, identifies the different degrees of *confinement* for these identities:

1. The kitchen men leave the sixth and seventh floors of the Public Safety Building and travel by elevator to the kitchen on the first floor. On their return at the end of the work day they will often be examined for contraband.

2. The runners must stay within the bucket itself, but they have freedom to move throughout most of the two floors. They know what is taking place, who the new drunks are, and which men become kickouts each day.

3. All other trusties who work inside are restricted to a single floor, an area on one floor, or an even more confined place such as a barber shop.

The variety of opportunities which present themselves for men in these positions will be discussed later; most of them are related to hustling other inmates. The important factor for most men is that the less they are confined the more contact they can maintain with the outside world. This may be seen especially in the matter of making phone calls; trusties have much greater opportunity to telephone than lockups do, and it is one important reinforcement of their other identities not associated with the jail. Although the jail policy is to allow one phone call per week, in the sample, 45 per cent of the men who had done time as lockups reported they had been refused permission to make their call. A young college graduate who had been in the Seattle city jail many times on drunk charges summarized the emotional significance of this sense of isolation:

There are two places where a person is very emotionally distraught in the jail: one is on the sixth floor at the booking desk where his money and personal belongings are taken away from him; another is upstairs when he is placed in a cell and cut off from making phone calls. A man is particularly distraught about being shut off from the outside society and he has a major question in his mind, "How can I make contact outside?" This is a very major problem because phone calls can be almost impossible to make. You can try two or three times a day all week to get permission — each cell is given permission on one day of the week to make a phone call, and often it's after 5 o'clock and the person you wish to call — you only have his office number and it's only open during the day. You ask the day officer all day if you can make a phone call and he'll say, "You can, I'll tell the night man about it," and the night man will say, "I'll tell the next man." They just pass the buck on and on. . . .

In summary, the most important criteria for defining trusties and inmate identity generally involve the extent to which one is restricted in his mobility. These restrictions have great psychological significance for tramps by cutting them off from people, places, and activities which reinforce their more respectable identities while anchoring them more firmly to the social system in the jail — the world of tramps and inmates.

Two additional dimensions of contrast are also important for differentiating all the core terms. Each trusty must perform certain duties which are necessary for the maintenance of the jail and each kind of trusty is closely associated with certain objects which provide a *work focus*. The objects which form this dimension of contrasts are guns, buildings, wheeled vehicles, boats, food, and people. And finally, each kind of trusty is linked to others in the social identity system of the jail; some of these relationships are casual, others are intense and may be friendly or antagonistic. Of special significance are those relationships in which inmates are required to render *direct service* to other people, service which can sometimes be onerous. One man recalled, "A hospital orderly has to wait on people hand and foot. If a guy comes in with shit all over him he has to clean it off of him." In other situations trusty jobs may provide opportunities to earn money, such as the barber who cuts the officers' hair or the kitchen man who presses their clothing. Sometimes a man has an opportunity to choose the kind of trusty he would like to be, and he will do so on the basis of these five dimensions of contrast. He will seek to maximize his mobility, select a work focus to his liking, and choose people to serve who can provide the most opportunity for meeting his own needs (See Appendix B for a more complete componential definition of the core trusty terms).

The ethnographic study of these two systems of social identity reveals an important and pervasive theme — both domains are defined in reference to an underlying cultural value which may be called *environmental anchorage*. Tramps are identified in terms of their ties to geographical locations, specific modes of travel, some kind of home base, and some means of livelihood. Independence from social institutions is highly valued. The home guard tramp is looked upon as overly dependent: "They try like hell to be one of the boys but they can't, gets too rough and they go home." The mission stiff is held in greatest disrepute because his life style constantly reaffirms the definition most outsiders have of tramps — hopeless derelicts in desperate need of help from others. A box car tramp, on the other hand, is respected because of his independence from institutions and possessions. He is the least anchored to his social and physical environment — he will "jump on a box car without tobacco and water, he travels streamline, and if he sees anything loose he can turn into money he will steal it."

Informants used a variety of symbols to contrast their life style with the rest of society: tramps are grasshoppers rather than bees, plants without roots, explorers and adventurers, and men with itchy feet. As tramps, these men are *far less anchored* to their environment than most members of American society.

In contrast to his tramp identity, when a man becomes a trusty or other inmate he is very securely anchored to a local jail. Trusties are identified according to their restricted mobility, firm ties to specific work objects, and those they must serve. As trusties, these men are *far more anchored* to their environment than most members of American society. In the bucket, men are told when to sleep, when to get up, what to do, and how to do it. The scope of control exerted by others encompasses much of their behavior — they make few choices for themselves. The experience of being controlled, restricted in movement, and anchored to this institution is in extreme contrast to the unrestricted movement and limited environmental anchorage which the tramp experiences in other scenes of this subculture.

One result of these extremes in social experience is that the way of life in the bucket complements other aspects of a tramp's life. One who is on an extended drunk, travels from one spot job to another, and has unrestricted movement, may find the bucket a desirable place for a time. In the sample of those who were asked if they had ever gone to jail and turned themselves in without being picked up, 11 per cent indicated they had done so. One man stated, "I realized that I had reached the point where I needed help, especially from the standpoint of my health." While most men felt intense resentment toward those who jailed drunks and agreed there were better ways to handle this problem, they also admitted that such a practice saved the lives of many tramps. One young man summarized this therapeutic aspect of jail from the tramps' point of view:

Sometimes some of them got so darn tired of not being picked up. They feel, "I wish the devil I could put an end to this and get a few days rest." And this is when he begins to act erratically and in a few hours he will be picked up. He's sick and tired of drinking but he really doesn't know how to stop, because he knows if he goes someplace and lies down he will get weaker and weaker and no food, and he knows he won't be in any shape to get some food, and so he has to keep going until he's picked up.

Once a man has been in jail for a time, he may find a period of unrestricted mobility a desirable thing. Many men felt that "after 30 days in jail, you owe yourself a drunk."

These two identities are not altogether different — both of them are defined as deviant in American culture. These men become inmates and trusties because they lack $20 bail money at the time of their arrest. They are labeled as "common drunkards" by the court and committed to do their time in one or more of the inmate roles. They become tramps, on the other hand, as a result of many social and psychological processes, one of the most important of which is a result of this public labeling:

From the point of view of responsible society, the skid rower has become desocialized. From the point of view of skid row society he has become socialized and acculturated. It is in this phase that the individual may be publicly labeled a deviant through arrest, sentence, and incarceration. Incarceration throws him into intimate contact with fellow associates from skid row and intensifies his socialization into the subculture. The label of deviant serves as an important credential for the admission to the innermost circle of skid rowers and at the same time additionally isolates our recruit from his society. Private self-acceptance must inevitably follow public recognition and that most important element of all emerges — the individual now thinks of himself as a skid rower (Wallace, S. 1968:101–102).

The men studied were all at varying stages of self-acceptance of their tramp identity. Some had been tramps for thirty years or more and clearly enjoyed their way of life; others were fighting hard to keep from being drawn into this subculture, though with each new arrest their attempts grew more futile. They were aware that one criterion of trampness is to make the bucket. The following discussion among a group of tramps suggests the differing degrees to which they have accepted their identity:

Hal: If they want tramps, all they have to do is come out to this treatment center — there are lots of tramps all over the place here. There are new tramps coming out every day of the week.
Jim: That's not so. I'm not a tramp.
Hal: Oh yes you are! What do you think a tramp is?
Mac: A tramp is a good person who works and supports himself but who doesn't have any roots. There is a difference between a tramp and a bum, but everyone at this treatment center is either one or the other. A bum is just no good — he's different from a tramp.

Hal: That's right. I agree with you.

Jim: I disagree — I still don't consider myself to be a tramp. There are different classes of alcoholics. . . .

Hal: Oh, bull shit! A tramp is a tramp . . . if you are on Skid Road, you are on Skid Road!

Jim: Well, Hal . . . you are a professional tramp — you probably don't want to help yourself — you enjoy being on Skid Road.

Hal: That's true! Now, in your case, Jim, you may feel different about it. Here you are, 50 years old, and you hit the skid just three or four years ago. You have a tough time accepting it because you were about 47 years old when you hit the bottom. I've been a tramp since I was 19 years old and I've enjoyed every bit of it.

In studying this population, it would have been possible to begin with any of the identity models discussed earlier, but each would have led to asking a different set of questions. The popular model would lead to asking, "Why don't these men work? Why are they so lazy?" The medical model would have focused on their drinking behavior, asking "Why are they alcoholics?" The legal model would ask why they break the law so often, even though they are punished repeatedly. The sociological model would have investigated their age, race, income, and homeless state, and many other questions. The ethnographic approach has led to the discovery of those identities which are significant to those inside this subculture. It is now possible to ask other questions on the basis of these discoveries. The important questions are related to the *identities* and *values* in this subculture. What factors lead men to give up or lose their former respectable identities in American society? What are the forces which result in their acquiring their tramp and inmate identities? What forces are at work in the lives of these men and in their subculture which increase their mobility? Why do they appear to resist being anchored both socially and physically? The ethnographic approach will provide some of the answers to these questions. It will also lead to the discovery of *new* questions which tramps are asking as well as answering in the way in which they conceptualize their experience. While we have entered the insider's world, we must move on to comprehend more fully what a bucket full of tramps means to urban nomads.

CHAPTER FOUR

Pick Up Your Bed and Walk...

I sacked out in this penny arcade but I got pinched. This bull comes in and he says, "All right, take a walk." And that S.O.B. was right on my tail. I'd walked about a half a block, and I thought, "I ain't gonna be ploughing around in this rain, because I'd conked out in the Colombus Tavern but they kicked me out of there about 1:30 in the morning when they closed. I couldn't score enough for no flop money so I went into that penny arcade again. And the second time I come in there, I'd just sat down and dozed off again and the same two bulls came right back about a half hour later. They must have figured I'd come back. One said, "I told you to take a walk, come on you're goin to jail!" You know, they run you from one spot to another all night long. A tramp puts in twenty-four hours but a cop only puts in eight.

The emphasis on mobility which characterizes the culture of urban nomads has many sources and expressions. Some tramps travel to seek adventure; others are run out of town by the police or move on because their criminal record in a particular place limits their freedom. Some tramps travel in the continental circuit, around the entire United States; others ride the freight trains from town to town in a smaller circuit in the Northwest or Southwest. Mobility, as a life style, means more than moving from one job to another, one mission to another, or one town to another; it often means constant movement, without a destination, in order to survive in urban America. These men are urban nomads, because they live much of their lives in public places where our culture demands that people appear to be involved in some "legitimate" activity. Loitering is still a crime in many parts of the United States and one of the quickest ways to come to the attention of the police is to stand, sit, or lie in a public place with no apparent purpose. Urban nomads are poor — they live in the nooks and crannies of our civilization and, when discovered by other citizens or the police, they are "run out" and told to "keep moving on."

Within American cities are a variety of ethnic and social groups. Each has developed different strategies of adaptation which are coded in its own classification systems or cognitive maps. The problems and vicissitudes of urban nomads differ from those encountered by other categories of urban dwellers and, as one is socialized into this subculture, he learns varied strategies for satisfying biological needs, achieving his goals, and adjusting to his environment. In each of the major scenes in the world of the tramp there are traditional ways of solving such common problems as earning money, acquiring clothing, getting alcoholic beverages, avoiding police, traveling, and finding a place to sleep. A complete analysis of the culture of tramps would involve a study of each of these strategies and more. An ethnographic description of tramp sleeping places is singled out here because it provides insight into many facets of their culture as well as an understanding of their relations with the police and factors important for the survival of urban nomads.

It was not initially anticipated that this domain would be culturally revealing or significant because most Americans sleep in a few conventional places. Also, the popular image of the "bum" or "derelict" in American culture portrays these men as sleeping in

98

cheap hotels or passing out in a stupor from too much alcohol. In-formal conversations recorded among tramps revealed many refer-ences to "making a flop." Friends were identified as someone you would make a flop with and sleeping was often linked to other important activities such as traveling, drinking, and being arrested. It became clear that, as one informant expressed it, "The most important thing to a tramp is something to eat and a place to flop."

A number of domains or category systems within the general area of making a flop may be analyzed. These include the kinds of flops, ways to make a flop, ways to make a bed, kinds of beds, and the kinds of people who bother you when you flop. Some of the names given these domains refer to objects, others refer to modes of action. In this chapter, we will consider mostly the kinds of flops, or places to sleep used by tramps. *Flopping* is the most common word, but such synonyms as *sleeping, corking out,* and *crap-ping out* are also used. The radical difference between the impor-tance and meaning of sleeping places for tramps and for most other Americans will become clear, but it is interesting to compare the usage of the two terms *flop* and *sleep.* "Flopping" is used to identify an activity which other Americans refer to as "sleeping." When we consider the tramp's use of these two terms in their noun form, an interesting difference appears — they are not syn-onyms. *Flop* refers to a place in the physical environment where the activity takes place. *Sleep* refers to the bodily state of rest or the occasion of sleeping. It is not appropriate for Americans to say, "I'm looking for a sleep for the night," or "I paid for my sleep last night." Tramps, on the other hand, frequently make such refer-ences: "I got my flop for the night," and "He ran me out of my flop." Tramps stress the place where sleeping occurs, whereas other Americans do not. When informants were asked, "What kinds of flops are there?" they reported places which seem incredible to the outsider. Nearly one hundred categories of sleeping places were dis-covered, and these do not exhaust the knowledge of long-time tramps nor are they specific places to flop, but rather *classes* of sleeping places.[1] Table 4.1 provides a taxonomic definition of one

99

TABLE 4.1 TAXONOMIC DEFINITION OF FLOPS

- **Flop**
  - **Paid flop** — *Flea bag (flop house)*
    - Motel
    - Hotel
    - Apartment
    - Dormitory
    - Wire cage
    - **Flop house**
      - Globe
      - Grand Central
      - Puget Sound
      - Stevens
      - New England
      - Yesler
      - Travelers
      - Pacific
      - Clarkston
      - Howell
      - Nord
      - New Central
      - New Lucky
      - Milwaukee
  - **Empty building**
    - Motel
    - Hotel
    - House
    - Apartment
    - Abandoned
    - Under construction
    - Being torn down

TABLE 4.1 TAXONOMIC DEFINITION OF FLOPS (Continued)

Flop

Weed patch			
Pasture			
Cemetery			
Viaduct			
Bridge			
Riverbank			
Field			
Orchard			
Between buildings			
Park			
Sidewalk			
Jungle	Town	Own	
		Main	
	Railroad	Own	
		Main	
Railroad track			
Alley			
Dump			

TABLE 4.1   TAXONOMIC DEFINITION OF FLOPS (Continued)

Flop		
Railroad flop	Switchman's shanty	
	Conductor's quarters	
	Coal car	
	Box car	
	Flat car	
	Reefer	
	Piggyback	
	Station	
	Gondola	
	Passenger car	
	Sand House	
	Crummy	
Mission flop	Sally	
	Dawes	
	Pacific Garden	
	Holy Cross	
	The Mitt	
	Joe's	
	Wheeler's	
	Toby's	
	Bread of Life	
	City	

TABLE 4.1 TAXONOMIC DEFINITION OF FLOPS (Continued)

Flop			
"Places in paid flop"	Closet	Clothes
		Broom
	Bathtub	
	Hallway	
	Toilet floor	
	Lobby	
Window well		
Under building		
All night Laundromat		
All night bar		
Car flop	Own car	
	Car on street	
	Harvest bus	
	Transit bus	
	Junk yard	
	Used car lot	
	Truck	

TABLE 4.1 TAXONOMIC DEFINITION OF FLOPS (Concluded)

Flop
Loading dock
Haystack
Apple bin
Doorway
Trash box
Church
Penny arcade
Park bench
Stairwell
Tool house
Bucket
Harvest shack
Scale house
Brick yard
Bus depot
Night club
Bar room
Newspaper building
Furnace room
Hay barn
Cotton wagon
Paddy wagon
All night show
All night restaurant

term, *flop*. When a tramp says, "I had a flop last night," he could mean any of the nearly one hundred kinds of sleeping places shown in this taxonomy.

Some sleeping places are not included here because they are extremely rare or very little information could be gathered on them. One informant recalled:

My wife and I were hitchhiking to Chattanooga and we slept in an old filling station that was closed, in an old *mortar box*. We picked up some grass they had just cut along the highway and used it for a bed.

Further research may reveal that there is a category of flops called "boxes" which will include mortar box and trash box, but only the latter was included here because it is used much more frequently. Another informant reported that a friend of his flopped in a "junky cart." Tramps have a variety of ways of earning a livelihood, one of which is called "junking." In this case, two tramps had acquired a junky cart and were traveling the streets of Chicago picking up bottles, metal, and other objects of value to sell to the junk dealer. Their junky cart was large enough to sleep in, so one man would crawl in and cover himself with an overcoat to keep out of sight while the other pushed the cart along. It was not possible to discover the frequency of this practice nor could we locate any other information which would enable us to define the junky cart from the tramps' point of view. There is reason to believe that further research would illuminate such terms and would uncover other categories.

In the buildings of American cities are many places where these men find a bed, only a few of them included in the list of flops. Many such places, accessible to tramps, make good sleeping quarters because they are heated. These include: depots, business establishments, police stations, libraries, and hotels. Closets and bathrooms were those used most frequently, but in talking about them informants always referred to the "closet in an empty building," or "toilet in the depot." The specific place was always located in its larger context. One box car tramp reported, "I slept in a jail in Mississippi. We went into the jail toilet and slept all night." Another man said, "I've slept in a railroad station toilet and a bus depot toilet." The taxonomic status of these terms which referred to places in larger buildings was difficult to ascertain, and the final decision was based on informants' responses, intuitive insights, and some ordering of the categories during analysis to satisfy the aesthetic values of the researchers! *Toilet floor* and *hallway* might have been treated as cover terms for a great many location concepts such as "in jails," "in paid flops," etc. Since most informants reported that they usually found such places in flop houses or hotels, it was decided to consider "places in paid flops" as the cover term. The following is typical of the most frequent designations:

I have no trouble walking in a second floor, second-rate hotel — going upstairs and curling up and going to sleep in the men's room. If it's very late at night I know there's a very poor possibility of anyone wanting to take a bath, so I just sleep in the bathtub. I've done that many times.

This taxonomy of flops throws into bold relief a fundamental concept which anthropologists have known from studies in non-Western societies but which is all too often overlooked when studying urban subcultures: objects in the physical environment may be defined by their *form* or structure, but their meaning also arises from their *function*. In one sense those who live in cities share many facets of urban life, including climate, scenery, streets, parks, law enforcement agencies and other institutions. In another sense, members of the same city do not share these things since their function and meaning are different. Intangible aspects of human experience are socially created but, if bathtubs, cars, trash boxes, and cemeteries differ from one subculture to another — if, in fact, physical space and objects are socially constructed — we may be sure that men who live together in the same town may actually be cultural worlds apart.

The taxonomic definition of flops elucidates that objects are often defined by their function. It may appear to some readers that a paddy wagon and a cotton wagon are both kinds of wagons and therefore would be classified as two kinds of "wagon flops." Although tramps recognize they are both kinds of wagons, this is not culturally significant. In their scheme of things they are not primarily wagons but *flops*. An outsider might define both of these wagons as vehicles and classify them together with cars, trucks, busses, and freight cars. Tramps have learned a culture which classifies a toilet floor, night club, sand house, truck, car, and a bucket into the same category. Several terms in the taxonomy include the phrase *all night,* such as all night laundromat. When asked to sort these into similar categories, or when asked if they were to be considered as similar kinds of flops, informants refused to include them in any term more than the most generic: flop. The discovery of taxonomic relationships for similar terms in two or more urban subcultures is one way to test whether they are homonyms or not. When the criteria for contrasting kinds of flops are discussed (componential definition), the importance of distinguishing between form and function will become even more apparent.

What does this taxonomy say about the subculture of urban nomads? How culturally revealing is it to elicit the categories which these men use to order their environment in relationship to sleeping behavior? Again, although this category system is not exhaustive, it does contain nearly one hundred categories of sleeping places and has five levels of contrast which could have been extended to at least six by including more specific terms. Several tentative conclusions may be drawn from these facts. First, the importance of non-drinking behavior, such as sleeping, appears to have been underestimated by most researchers. One recent study of Skid Road in a Midwestern city emphasizes the importance of flops:

A place to sleep is, in some ways, more important to the men who live on skid row than food to eat or something to drink. This is so for two reasons. First, a man sleeping in the open is an easy victim for the weather, as well as for assailants be they jack rollers or police. Secondly, the law uniformly requires that "everyone must have a bedroom" if he is not to be charged with vagrancy . . . (Wallace, S. 1965:29).

This author then discusses the different places where these men sleep. He reports only eleven categories of flops: single room hotels, cubicle hotels, mission hotels, dormitories, transportation depots, busses, subways, movie houses, flop houses, box cars and hobo jungles. Whereas the initial participant observations led to the *impression* that "making a flop" was important and would be culturally revealing, we now have a basis for comparison with other domains, both intraculturally and interculturally. Although a simple count of the number of terms or the levels of a taxonomy is not conclusive evidence of importance, it cannot be easily dismissed. Preliminary work with other domains in this subculture has not revealed any other category system which organizes so much of the environment or in such a detailed fashion. There are many different kinds of *bars, bulls, time,* and *ways of making it,* but none of these domains appears to be as elaborate as that of flops.

How does this elaborate taxonomy of sleeping places compare with the same domain for others in our urban society? Frake has proposed the following hypothesis related to taxonomic differences between cultures:

> The greater the number of distinct social contexts in which information about a particular phenomenon must be communicated, the greater the number of different levels of contrast into which phenomenon is categorized. . . . If the botanical taxonomy of tribe A has more levels of contrast than that of tribe B, it means the members of tribe A communicate botanical information in a wider variety of sociocultural settings (Frake 1961:121, 122).

A casual comparison of urban nomads with most Americans reveals no other group with such a complex scheme for categorizing sleeping places. Tramps communicate information regarding places to sleep in a wider variety of sociocultural settings than do members of the larger American society. One is not surprised that sleeping behavior has been largely overlooked by those who have studied this group. The social scientist in his own culture has learned that there are relatively few places to sleep, that places to sleep do not enter into a wide variety of sociocultural settings, and probably holds the implicit assumption that places to sleep are not culturally relevant. Although the major basis for designating these men as urban nomads is their own definition of their social identity, this taxonomy strongly supports such a designation. And although a nomadic way of life does not necessarily require an extensive category system for places to sleep, we might expect to find it so for these men. We might well be surprised to discover a group which is sedentary and also has such an elaborate way of categorizing places to sleep.

A taxonomic definition tells us that tramps have many places to sleep but it does not tell us very much about what they consider significant about each place for sleeping purposes or about how they choose one place to sleep instead of another or which places are important in their encounter with police. A very large number of criteria could be used to define such objects as cemeteries, box cars, bridges, and bathtubs, but in order to understand what meaning these places hold for tramps, it is necessary to discuss the underlying semantic principles which tramps use to differentiate one kind of flop from another. Though all the terms in the taxonomy are flops, some are more alike and included in cover terms which are, in turn, kinds of flops. Thus there are different kinds of weed patches, missions, car flops, railroad flops, etc. The terms within each of these subcategories are at the same level of contrast and make up contrast sets which may be defined componentially. Some criteria used for distinguishing among kinds of flops are useful only for one small category of sleeping places within the taxonomy; others are applicable to all flops. The monetary resources necessary for one kind of flop constitute one dimension of contrast which provides important information for tramps about all possible sleeping places. Another criterion, whether one must take a nosedive or an earbanging, is relevant only to missions, the only category of flops which has such requirements. Fifteen dimensions of contrast are used here to define most of the flops in this domain (Table 4.2). The terms at the first level of contrast are componentially defined in Table 4.3. Eight dimensions of contrast are used to define this set; the numbers correspond with the values for each of these dimensions. The symbol "X" is used to indicate variation among the more specific terms of a subcategory and a question mark (?) indicates insufficient information for defining a term.

MONETARY RESOURCES

A complete analysis of the semantic principles which define all categories of sleeping places is beyond the scope of this discussion but componential definitions for several other contrast sets are

TABLE 4.2 DIMENSIONS OF CONTRAST FOR FLOP DOMAIN

1.0 Monetary resources
    1.1 Not required
    1.2 Required to pay for the flop
    1.3 Required to pay for something else

2.0 Atmospheric conditions (weather)
    2.1 Almost no protection
    2.2 Out of the rain/snow
    2.3 Out of the wind
    2.4 Out of the wind, possibly out of the cold
    2.5 Out of the wind and rain/snow
    2.6 Out of the wind and rain/snow, possibly out of the cold
    2.7 Out of the wind, rain/snow, and cold

3.0 Body position
    3.1 May lie down
    3.2 Must sit up
    3.3 Should sit up but may lie down

4.0 Intoxication
    4.1 Must be sober
    4.2 Must be drunk
    4.3 Any state of intoxication

5.0 Drinking restrictions
    5.1 Low risk drinking
    5.2 High risk drinking
    5.3 Purchase drinks

6.0 Civilian interference
    6.1 Waitress
    6.2 Night watchman
    6.3 Bartender
    6.4 Manager
    6.5 Owner
    6.6 Farmer
    6.7 Engineer
    6.8 Tramps
    6.9 Anybody
    6.10 Minister or priest
    6.11 Truck driver
    6.12 Probably no civilian

7.0 Police interference
    7.1 Police check and may also be called
    7.2 Police check
    7.3 Police must be called
    7.4 Police do not interfere

8.0 Security
    8.1 Public/concealed/protected
    8.2 Public/concealed/unprotected
    8.3 Public/unconcealed/protected
    8.4 Public/unconcealed/unprotected
    8.5 Non-public/concealed/protected
    8.6 Non-public/concealed/unprotected
    8.7 Non-public/unconcealed/unprotected

9.0 Urban location
    9.1 In town
    9.2 Out of town
    9.3 Either location

10.0 Permission
    10.1 Required
    10.2 Not required

11.0 Number of nights
    11.1 One night a month
    11.2 Three nights a month
    11.3 Every night of the year
    11.4 Ticket to hotel

12.0 Requirements: listening (earbanging), praying (nosediving)
    12.1 Neither action necessary or important
    12.2 Neither action necessary, listening important
    12.3 Neither action necessary, both important
    12.4 Listening necessary, praying important

13.0 Work opportunities
    13.1 Work at the mission
    13.2 Work out of the mission
    13.3 Work at and out of the mission

14.0 Meals
    14.1 Meal ticket
    14.2 Soup and sandwiches

15.0 Clothes
    15.1 Available
    15.2 Not available

TABLE 4.3 COMPONENTIAL DEFINITION OF FLOPS (HIGHEST LEVEL OF CONTRAST)

Dimensions of Contrast

Flops	1.0	2.0	3.0	4.0	5.0	6.0	7.0	8.0
Paid flop	1.2	2.7	3.1	4.3	X	X	7.4	X
Empty building	1.1	2.6	3.1	4.1	5.1	6.2, 8	7.1	8.6
Weed patch	1.1	X	3.1	X	5.1	X	X	X
Railroad flop	1.1	X	X	X	X	X	X	X
Mission flop	1.1	2.7	3.1	4.1	5.2	6.8	7.4	8.4?
Car flop	X	X	3.1	X	5.1	X	X	X
"Places in paid flop"	1.1	2.7	X	X	X	X	7.3	X
Window well	1.1	2.4	3.1	4.3	5.1	6.8	7.2	8.7
Under building	1.1	2.6	3.1	4.3	5.1	6.8	7.2	8.6
All night laundromat	1.1	2.7	3.3	4.3	5.2	6.5	7.2	8.4
All night bar	1.3	2.7	3.2	4.3	5.3	6.1, 3, 4	7.1	8.4
All night restaurant	1.3	2.7	3.2	4.3	5.2	6.1	7.1	8.4
All night show	1.3	2.7	3.3	4.3	5.1	6.8	7.4	8.2
Paddy wagon	1.1	2.5	3.1	4.2	5.2	6.12	7.2	8.8
Cotton wagon	1.1	2.5	3.1	4.3	5.1	6.12	7.4	8.6
Hay barn	1.1	2.6	3.1	4.3	5.1	6.6	7.4	8.6
Furnace room	1.1	2.7	3.1	4.3	5.1	6.2, 7	7.3	8.6
Newspaper building	1.1	2.7	3.1	4.3	5.2	6.4	7.3	8.6
Bar room	1.3	2.7	3.2	4.3	5.3	6.1, 3, 4	7.1	8.4
Night club	1.3	2.7	3.2	4.3	5.3	6.1, 3, 4	7.1	8.4
Bus depot	1.1	2.7	3.2	4.3	5.2	6.9	7.1	8.4
Brick yard	1.1	2.7	3.1	4.3	5.1	6.4	7.3	8.6
Scale house	1.1	2.6	3.1	4.3	5.1	6.8	7.3?	8.6
Harvest shack	1.1	2.7	3.1	4.3	5.1	6.8	7.4	8.1
Bucket	1.1	2.7	3.1	4.3	5.2	6.8	7.4	8.4
Tool house	1.1	2.5	3.1	4.3	5.1	6.12	7.3	8.6
Stairwell	1.1	2.4	3.1	4.2	5.1	6.5, 8	7.1	8.7
Park bench	1.1	2.1	3.1	4.3	5.2	6.8	7.2	8.7
Penny arcade	1.1	2.7	3.2	4.3	5.2	6.12	7.2	8.4
Church	1.1	2.6	3.1	4.3	5.2	6.2, 10	7.1	8.6
Trash box	1.1	2.5	3.1	4.3	5.1	6.12	7.2	8.6
Doorway	1.1	2.1	3.1	4.2	5.1	6.8, 9	7.1	8.7
Apple bin	1.1	2.5	3.1	4.3	5.1	6.12	7.4	8.6
Haystack	1.1	2.7?	3.1	4.3	5.1	6.12	7.4	8.6
Loading dock	1.1	2.1	3.1	4.2	5.1	6.2, 8, 11	7.1	8.7

provided in Appendix C. Some of these principles reveal important facets of the relationship between urban nomads and law enforcement officials. Consider the first dimension of contrast, monetary resources. Of the nearly one hundred categories of flops shown in Table 4.1, only fourteen require some expenditure of money. It cannot be assumed that a man who sleeps in a place that does not *require* money does not *have* money since he may be saving it for other purposes or be sleeping in such a place for other reasons. A tramp may have rented a room in a paid flop and still sleep in one which does not require money in order to stay out of jail. One man reported the following experience, which occurred during 1967:

Where I used to sleep, you know, right across from the county jail park? Up on Yesler, well that shrubbery was pretty thick. I had a place to sleep (rented) but I'd had a little too much (to drink) so I ain't gonna chance it. So I got me 10 or 12 newspapers back at the Frye Hotel. Every night I picked up these papers and I had a bed a foot thick. Had an overcoat, that was January, February and March. It'd rain, but I'd never get wet, and there was a lot of heat coming out of that tunnel and it hit you. Get braced there between the shrubbery and the wall so I wouldn't roll off, it was quite a drop you know. And John asked me where I was sleeping so I told him, "Right there is my room!" And he got to crapping out there too, even though he had an apartment, rather than risk walking all that way to it. Oh, I slept there a long time.

This man, a home guard tramp, spent nearly three months sleeping in this weed patch in order to avoid arrest. The short walk of several blocks to his rented room could have been navigated but not without the risk of going to jail on a drunk charge. The same man reported that he had sometimes been arrested within several hours after his release from jail and he felt he had become a "marked man." This is one of the problems faced by home guard tramps and it increases their mobility. He recalled:

I've got so bad that way I finally had to leave town. That's when my mother was living here, and that judge — I finally had even him convinced. Sometimes I would get out of jail, someone come and bail me out, I wouldn't get a half-a-block and that same son-of-a-bitch would come and say, "Let's go!"

This is not an isolated incident, as shown by the fact that in the

112

sample, 20 per cent reported they had been picked up for drunk the same day they were kicked out of jail when there hadn't been enough time to get drunk, and 30 per cent reported they had to leave Seattle because the cops had gotten to know them and consequently were picking them up more frequently.

If a man wants to sleep in a place which requires payment and he has no money, he can use one of many strategies, some of which bring him into contact with the police. He may steal something which he will later sell or "peddle" on the street. Some men purchase rather expensive jackets or other possessions after a period of work so they can sell them during lean times. The police are aware that these men shoplift and engage in other petty crimes and arrests are made when they are suspected. A few weeks before Mr. Tanner left Seattle he met a friend on the street and after a drinking spree they went together to his rented room. The next morning the friend was gone when Mr. Tanner awoke and he found that he was being arrested for larceny because some items in the room had been stolen. A tramp who possesses or tries to sell valuable articles often comes under the suspicion of the police.

On April 3, 1968, I was in a hock shop on First and Pike trying to pawn my radio when I came out and I met a cop. He said I stole the radio but he could not prove it so he took me in to the city jail and booked me as drunk.

It is general knowledge among tramps that peddling must be done with great care or one may end up in jail on a drunk charge, also losing the item he was going to sell. Another man recalled:

I was walking along the street carrying an overcoat when a squad car came by and stopped me. The officer said, "You stole the coat," and I said, "I bought it at a thrift shop." They took me in and the booking desk officer said, "Well what should we book him on?" and the other cop said, "Stealing a coat." So I said, "Fine, I'll have a good suit against the city because I can subpoena those two witnesses who know that I bought it." Then the officer said, "Put him down for drunk . . . he had a few drinks." I pleaded guilty because you can't beat it. The judge always takes the policeman's word for it — you can't win. When I got out my coat was gone.

The most widely used means for getting money for a place to sleep, or as a tramp would say, "scoring for some flop money," is to beg or "panhandle." A tramp who is not able to score for any flop money may have to walk the streets all night or "carry the banner." The man who attempted to sleep in the penny arcade was in the worst of all possible positions: either he had to keep walking and carry the banner all night or go to jail. Whereas men are able to beg and get enough for a paid flop, sometimes 50 cents is adequate, they also run the risk of being arrested for begging, a misdemeanor offense in Seattle as well as in many other American cities. Since this practice is a crime, it is possible to trap a tramp quite easily. Plain clothes policemen who work in the Skid Road district are referred to as "rag pickers," a term used to refer to all police in some towns. One tramp summarized what can happen when a man is begging in order to earn enough for a place to sleep or to purchase a jug of wine:

A rag picker would see you with change in your hand and ask if you are short. You tell him, "Yea, I'm short 20 cents," and when you ask him if he can spare it, he says, "Yes!" — gives you the 20 cents, shows you his badge, and gets you for bumming or stemming.

Although uniformed policemen will sometimes do a tramp a favor and give him some money, at other times they will "try to get you to accept their money, asking you, 'Are you a little short?' and as soon as he drops the money in your hand he gets you for panhandling." These experiences are common to many tramps, and an awareness that they can happen is probably universal. Their culture defines the danger inherent in all these situations and their choices of places to sleep are based on a sophisticated knowledge of police behavior. Those without money must take risks; they may even use their poverty as an excuse as this tramp did:

I wasn't drunk, no bottle, and was sleeping down in a stairwell. Officers came by and asked me, "Couldn't you get inside?" I said, "I had a ticket to the Union Gospel Mission but they're filled up. Can't get in and I just have 35 cents." That bull said, "You got a cold night ahead of you." Well, the next morning it was 24 degrees.

Urban nomads are almost all characterized by *periodic* poverty, which is reflected in their choice of place to sleep, and this lack of money is an important factor in their encounter with the police. A man without enough money for a paid flop has a greater chance of being arrested and then spending months in jail for lack of the $20 bail.

The exigencies of the weather are one set of conditions to which human beings in every society must adapt — and this is especially important to tramps. A frequent qualification made by informants was: "It depends on the weather, the time of year — from June to September you can sleep anywhere." One reason for a nomadic way of life is to escape the extremes of climate — in fact, some tramps traveling south for the winter are referred to as "snow-birds," and those traveling north for the summer are "rebels." During the heat of the summer a man may seek a cool place to sleep and prefer a weed patch over a paid flop. In any case, a man assesses the weather, his own needs, and then selects a flop — but this is not always as easy as it sounds since the choice may lead him directly to jail.

I went and got a jug and it was kind of cold in my room so I went down on the waterfront and sat in the sun. Sure enough I fell asleep in the sun rather than going back to my room and the police picked me up and took me back to jail — gave me thirty days for drunk.

All seven values used by informants to define sleeping places were related to the degree of protection they provided. There are always exceptions to these definitions — such as when the flophouse is not heated and the weed patch is! These exceptions are known to tramps and police alike and some law enforcement officials in Seattle knew of the following place, which was used by many tramps, and could make arrests easily:

On University Avenue — there under the bridge. There are the big city steam pipes and they're nice and warm. You can get under there and adjust your room temperature by moving away from them or getting closer to them. You might be the first there in the night and when you wake up in the morning it's like a bunch of snakes all coiled up, stacked closed together, trying to get to that heat 'cause it's pretty cold.

The major problem faced by these men, and clearly shown in the values on this dimension of contrast, is protection from wind, cold, and moisture. It is not too difficult to get out of the wind and the moisture, but finding heat or preserving body heat is not as easy. Tramps have an extensive knowledge of which material makes the best bed as well as the places such material may be discovered. Dry leaves, paper, dry branches, dry grass, cotton from old car seats, dry rags, cardboard, old coats, clothes stolen from clotheslines, and old mattresses are used for preserving body heat. Paper is the most useful material in most cases:

It's best to make a bed of newspapers and cover up with newspapers. You can put cardboard on top unless the wind is blowing. Then you put newspaper next to you and a sheet or blanket under and over it. Put the paper at a cold spot like next to your shoulders.

The best places to sleep provide heat and also shelter from the rain, wind and snow; some of these show the keen ingenuity of tramps. A sand house (one kind of railroad flop) contains sand to be used in trains to increase friction on the railroad tracks during icy weather. It is transferred to the train through a funnel, but in freezing weather if there is moisture in the sand it will freeze and not transfer easily and so it is heated. Tramps have learned that such a place provides a warm and not too uncomfortable bedroom. During cold weather a brickyard always contains stacks of bricks recently removed from the kiln, which give off warmth for several days. In urban centers heat is produced by a variety of means and some always seeps out of windows, doors, and other places. The man who gathered papers and slept in the bushes for fear he would be arrested if he walked to his rented room was warmed by heat coming out of the garage used for county police cars! Steam pipes which run underneath buildings and streets give off heat. "Crummies," or cabooses, are often kept heated for those who travel in them at the end of the train — or if they are cold they can be heated by building a fire in the stove. Churches are kept warm since it is often less expensive to maintain heat than to allow a building to cool when not in use. These and other sources of heat are known by urban nomads and on more than one occasion they have meant the difference between life and death in their adaptation to the weather.

The sleeping habits of these men provides a rich source of information about their life style and drinking behavior is functionally related to where they sleep. Drinking of alcoholic beverages to become intoxicated is institutionalized in the culture of urban nomads. They have defined alcohol as in many non-Western cultures, where it is a symbol of social solidarity and friendship and where group drinking and collective drunkenness is an acceptable aspect of the culture.[2] The most important primary group among tramps is the "bottle gang," and a tramp will almost never turn down a request from another man who asks to "cut in" on his bottle. Though these men drink in ways which are "excessive" as defined by the larger culture, they are not always drunk and many experience months of sobriety each year. Some tramps are not heavy drinkers, although most informants reported that nearly all tramps drink. Two dimensions of contrast which define sleeping places point to the significance of drinking behavior: the extent of intoxication and restrictions on drinking. The latter is the most important for our consideration.

Every society schedules behavior both in time and space. In American culture it is appropriate to drive fast, expose much of one's body, sleep on the ground, and drink alcoholic beverages at *some* places and at *some* times. The basis for such restrictions may be moral, legal, religious, or social and the sanctions which are used to limit such behavior in time and space vary in their severity. A man who sleeps on a public beach in the summer sun would receive less attention than the man sleeping on the grass in his front yard on Christmas morning. Neither would receive the censure reserved for the man found sleeping in an alley on Skid Road or in a stairwell — in fact, to sleep in such places could very likely result in going to jail for breaking the law. Many of the laws can be used against a tramp who sleeps or even walks about in places defined as *public*, places where behavior is more circumscribed. The following is not an uncommon experience:

You know, you talk about being picked up for drunk — I got picked up on a screwy deal one time. I was up in Bellingham, been working on the railroad and had to ride a freight over here to Seattle and I guess those bulls saw us coming out of the Great Northern yards — it used to be hot there. I was walking right by the yards down there and I had a card to go to work and these two cops came over and stopped me and I tried to explain to them that I was going to work. They took me and put me in that jail there. I pled not guilty and laid there for three days in the drunk tank. And do you know what kind of charge they had on there? *Idling!* Yes — idling, that was a form of vagrancy. I got up before that judge and told him, I says, kind of funny any more you can't even walk down the streets of Seattle. I told him I had a job and was receiving $102 every two weeks from drawing my rocking chair. Judge looked at those two cops and they just turned red in the face and he said, "Case Dismissed!" Held three days there on a charge like that — idling.

Although most people are aware that American culture restricts drunkenness to certain times and places, they are surprised to discover that the act of *drinking* itself is also restricted. The places where one may drink without violating the law are limited, in general, to licensed premises such as taverns, night clubs, restaurants, and more private places such as homes. Because of the life style of tramps, it is difficult for them to maintain a drinking culture and still conform to these norms.

Bars, taverns, and other licensed public places are open to tramps and many of them do much of their drinking there, but being there often involves considerable risk as well as hardship if they are without money. Bars have many functions for tramps other than drinking; it is here that a man may peddle goods for money, beg, find employment, and, most important, seek human companionship. In a bar he meets other tramps and, as they drink together, they often begin to "perform" — a word which covers a variety of behavior patterns such as talking, fighting, dancing, singing, etc. Such performances while drinking are acceptable to other tramps, and often to those who own the bar, but they may disturb those around them in the bar or police who check such places. Then, too, a man may run out of money or other means to secure additional drinks and if he isn't steadily purchasing drinks he may be asked to leave or face arrest. Waitresses and bartenders often take action against a man who drinks in a bar but runs out of money. Most men keenly felt the inequity of laws which defined certain places as proper for drinking but restricted the *way* they drank even in such spots:

Isn't it a man's personal business to live the way he wants? He's got a right to live and enjoy life like that — that should be his privilege as an American to live that way. Who the hell is the law to tell you that you can't drink — after all the bars are open! Those bartenders and waitresses will tell you to get the hell out of there — to stay awake and order something or they may pretend they are going to call the cops. They might call a bull and grab you by the neck and pull you out — even drag you out the door. And the bulls they'll come in the taverns and stuff, maybe a guy's been there only an hour, maybe he's been in there half a day. He's been drinking and he's still able to be served a drink, but yet they'll come in and get you and drag you off the stool and arrest you for being drunk in public or drinking in public. And every son-of-a-bitch in there is drinking. I don't see that law — when they can get you for being drunk in public, and what the hell does people go in the tavern for if they ain't gonna drink beer or something?

More than one third of the sample reported they had been arrested for drunk in a bar or even in their own room. One man stated, "I had just put in 26 hours of work with only time off to eat. I went to sleep in a restaurant bar and was hauled off to jail for drunk." Another said, "I was arrested in Lillian's Tavern because I fell asleep." Bars and taverns, then, are places a man may sleep and drink, but he must guard his behavior carefully and many risks are involved.

If a man is short on money and wants to avoid the risks of a bar, he may choose the other alternative and seek a more "private home" for drinking, as described here by some tramps:

There are certain men like myself that've got bedrolls stashed in different places. . . . I'll tell you — you'd be surprised! I'll take you down to certain places not far from Skid Road . . . some sleep in empty hotels and old condemned buildings. Some sleepin' under the bridges and different places and they sleep there for years — some all winter and they'll sleep out. . . . If you're outside a small town or something like that or a division where the railroad changes crews they'll build shacks along the river or something like that or lean-to's along the railroad. . . .

I get a bottle and look up my friends on the waterfront . . . some of them would be panhandling down there. We don't drink down there because it is dangerous — you have to be careful of rag pickers. If you are under the bridge down below Pike Street Market you are safe —

the police don't walk down there, just too lazy. Most generally three or four of us will be drinking together, sitting around talking about what we are figuring on doing. If we finish off the bottle, one of us makes a run, if we have the money. The one that had the money would go to the liquor store, the closest one is on Western Avenue. If it wasn't open then he'd go to the grocery store. After 2 A.M. our bunch is usually ready to sleep or go back to the hotel — it all depends on how drunk we are. We have our bedrolls stashed out, I've got three stashed where they won't get wet and nobody will find them.

In the morning we have coffee and if we aren't going to work we go down and sell a pint of blood at Occidental and Second — at $5 a pint. Some places you can give it three times a week but they test you. If you've got high blood pressure or your pulse isn't right you can drink red port wine and your blood pressure and pulse will become normal. The girls at the blood bank, if they know you are kind of shaky will say, "Here's 75 cents, go down and get yourself a bottle and drink it and then come back." That's why a lot of fellows will take one or two shots of wine before going to give blood. I'll go in on Monday and Thursday — we work it so someone else in our group goes in on Tuesday and Friday. Some of us will panhandle, others might get a spot job — but anyway we come back to our hangout the next night and someone makes a run for a bottle. Sometimes we go to the hotel, but if it is too hot in the hotel we go down under the bridge to our hideout.

The urban nomad is caught between two definitions of his life style. Flops, in a sense, are considered by tramps as homes, places to visit, drink, and sleep. In some places they may even cook and wash their clothes, always remaining alert to the possibility of arrest for violating the norms of the larger society — norms which condemn those who sleep and drink in public places. Though the following behavior would have been appropriate in a state park or campground, these men found that it was not allowed:

There was four of us and we had a job over in Eastern Washington — near Entiat. We got about $75, maybe $100 worth of groceries and asked the guy at the harvest when we gonna go to work. This guy said, "Well, I'll have my cabins cleaned up in the morning." We carried everything across the railroad tracks, you know by the big creek, and here I'm comin' across the tracks, there's the highway patrolman standing right in the middle of the railroad tracks. "Hey there," he says, "What you got?" "I got three quarts of milk, a gallon jug of water and a pound of hamburger." Well, he busted me for vag. I had money, all those groceries, had just quit one job and was going to

120

work the next day! That didn't make no difference. They went across and got the other guys then. Here's all of our meat and everything — looked like they had drug it through the dirt, rocks and everything on our eggs. They took all four of us to the jail. Oh, we had wine and beer and if we had been drinking they put a drunk charge on us, if we hadn't been drinking they would put a vagrancy charge on us. We had enough money to bail out, but they wouldn't let us bail. They put us in jail there for three nights and there was no place even to get a drink of water in that drunk tank. All there was in there was a Prince Albert can to get the water comin' into the toilet if we wanted a drink. And that's where we spent our time . . .

Seventy-two per cent of the sample indicated they had been arrested in Seattle for the crime of *drinking* in public. This does not reflect the actual number of arrests for this crime since often the police will arrest a man for drinking in public and when he is booked at the jail the charge will be changed to public drunkenness to facilitate processing in the courts. Though many Americans drink on the beaches, at football games, on picnics, and on camping trips, their behavior is overlooked and tolerated by the police. The tramp, on the other hand, is offensive to the rest of society — in particular, he threatens the values and security of our more respectable identities. Drinking in public, or drunkenness, is illegal, but the real crime of these men is that they do not work regular hours, they dress in old clothes, they bathe less frequently than most other people, and they sleep under bridges and in alleys. When they drink in bars they are arrested because their behavior and appearance are different. When they drink in one of their other flops, they are arrested because it is not an appropriate place to sleep or drink. The urban nomad is caught between two worlds: his own poverty and life style, and the law enforcement patterns of the larger society.

SECURITY

Most of the dimensions of contrast which tramps use to define flops serve to increase their security while sleeping and drinking. By defining sleeping places according to the risk involved in drinking, a tramp knows whether he can engage in this behavior without being bothered. By specifying what types of people can interfere with one's sleep a tramp can predict who will discover him in each particular flop and what the consequences of that discovery will be. If a farmer finds a tramp sleeping in his haystack the chances are small that the police will be called. The same is true if a man is found by someone sleeping in a harvest shack or apple bin. The semiconscious nature of sleep reduces an individual's ability to cope with threats from the environment so that choices made before going to sleep to maximize one's security are of utmost importance. One dimension of contrast shows vividly the importance of these strategies and also indicates the sophisticated knowledge that tramps have of their oppressors; it has been called *security*.

Three variables, in combination, provide a man with the necessary information about the relative security of a particular flop. A sleeping place may be fairly well *concealed* from those who might pass by:

You know where they got this little private club, down the end of the block, toward Alaska Way from the Bread of Life, that little dock back there? There's garbage cans back there, but they're paper cans, not garbage. They're clean. And many a night, you know, in the summer time, I'd go in there, turn the barrels over, and put a pasteboard box there, and turn that barrel and stick my feet in it, and maybe I'd stick my head and shoulders in this damn pasteboard box, well I was out of sight. I'd lay there with half my body in a garbage can and the upper half in a pasteboard box. Until someone kicks that can or tries to load it and you better get out! Well, that way no one knows.

Next, a sleeping place may be *protected* from intruders by means of locks or other physical barriers:

Used to be a junk yard up past the Millionaires . . . had that tow service. You could pick out your own car you wanted to sleep in. I had one in the corner. You'd see as many as 50 to 75 tramps, early in the morning come piling out of those cars. If you get into one you could lock it up. I had this wing window there, I'd close it. Guy would try the handles but never try the wings. Had my overcoat and blankets stashed down there. I mean it's a pretty good place to sleep. They never did bother me . . . no policeman around, no night watchman.

Finally, a flop may be in a *public* place where a tramp can act in such a way that he blends with the social environment — in a sense he becomes invisible by appearing to be engaged in appropriate activities:

If it's very late at night I know there's a very poor possibility of anyone wanting to take a bath, so I just sleep in the bathtub. If I hear someone really rummaging around, I kind of run water, swish it around or something like that. Once in awhile people will be irate and I get out and go up to the next floor.

Tramps usually seek a place which is concealed and protected — "Look for the safest place where they couldn't find you," — yet even these are often open to public view and so it is necessary to use strategies to appear invisible. Tramps believe that it is desirable to blend with their environment because being *visible*, in itself, often leads to arrest. It is drinking, begging, sleeping, urinating, and being drunk *in public* that affronts the dominant society. Their nomadic style of life has an *exposed* quality about it which contrasts with the seclusion which urban culture affords the rest of its members. These more respectable urban dwellers are, more often than not, doing the same things that tramps do, but their behavior takes place within the safety of their own walls. Tramps live in houses without walls, dwellings which leave them vulnerable to the view of all others and so they strive to reduce this visibility by becoming shadows which do not attract attention.

Many men felt they had become "marked" — almost as if an insignia had been sewn into their clothing or a brand had been burned into their flesh. This is one of the greatest fears among those men who have not acquiesced to the revolving door and one of the major reasons for their mobility. To become a marked man is to be known, recognized, and identified as one who should be arrested:

Other times you get picked up when you least expect it. You might be all dressed up and really not looking for any trouble at all and you just happen to be in the wrong place at the wrong time — not particularly drunk at all, but they *recognize* you. You're talking to somebody or someone comes up who has been picked up before and asks for a quarter and you are in the process of giving it to him and the police pick you both up. The cop doesn't know which one is giving to the other — but you're all in there and it has happened when I haven't had a drink at all.

123

In the sample, 20 per cent of the men indicated they had been arrested in Seattle when they had not been drinking at all. In addition, 60 per cent had been arrested when they had been drinking but they felt sure they were not drunk. Whatever the "actual" incidence (and this figure will vary depending upon which perspective is taken), tramps believe that this does happen often and there is always the possibility of arrest no matter *what* they are doing! In order to stay out of jail they must not only conform to the city ordinances, but they must also make themselves invisible. Although men are drawn to other tramps for companionship and sharing of drinks, they also know that such association may be their undoing:

I have been pinched by Seattle police while not drinking but by talking to friends that have been drinking. They picked them up and took me also. Now and then I have been picked up while not drinking but trying to take some friend home off the street.

One of the best ways to keep from coming under surveillance of the police is to walk — in a business-like manner, without hesitation, without stopping to talk to anyone — just keep walking. Many men reported that it was when they stopped on the street to do something that they were arrested:

In 1966 I was walking along First Avenue with an acquaintance and I stopped to say something to another acquaintance who was also pinched at the same time.

The following man, a recent arrival on Skid Road, who had been arrested several times for public drunkenness, found that the combination of being recognized and stopping on the street to talk to a woman was enough to result in arrest again.

In 1968 I was walking down the street and there were two bulls on the corner. One had picked me up previously on a drunk charge. I stopped to talk to a lady who worked at Boeing where I used to work and asked her about a job and she gave me a phone number of her supervisor and said, "Well, call him up, there may be a job available." I left her and went on down the street and the two bulls each walked up and took one of my arms and marched me into an alley nearby and said, "Look, we don't want you to talk to women on the street around here." I said, "Well, she worked where I did and she was giving me this phone number," and I took it out and they took it away from me and tore it up. One of them hit me in the stomach and then they took me in on a drunk charge and booked me for being drunk.

Sitting is even more dangerous than stopping for a moment on the street because the visibility factor is so greatly increased that, as one man put it, "A person with alcohol smell on his breath is automatically took to jail — it has happened many times in my case." Several men reported the following incidents:

In 1962 there were two times when I was not drunk at the time of arrest but merely sitting down on a bench in town.

About June 18, 1968, I was sitting on a dock, just going to take a drink out of sight when they took everybody in sight to jail in the wagon.

I was sitting in Pioneer Square when the paddy wagon drove up and arrested twelve people — some drunk, some sober. Another time I just walked by the paddy wagon and they told me to get in. I had just got off the bean bus come back from the harvest and was going to my room to wash up.

A tramp who is sitting on a bench or a dock often considers such a place as his own territory — a flop where he can catch a few winks and perhaps enjoy a drink with a friend. Tramps feel that the police view a man who is not mobile — who appears to have no destination — as a good candidate for the bucket. They may even attempt to keep him walking or get such a person out of their assigned beat by using physical force. An experience not uncommon for some tramps, who have allowed themselves to become visible, is to be kicked and threatened so they will move on. A tramp is mobile not only over wide areas of the country — he must be mobile within the city, or suffer the consequences. "A cop told me to take a walk and I didn't move fast enough to suit him and he kicked me in the ass." In the sample, 34 per cent of the men reported that a beat cop in Seattle had kicked them in the ass and told them to get off his beat. One man recalled:

I was eating in a Skid Road cafe when this bull noticed me. I had been home for two months and just got off the bus. He said, "I'm tired of seeing you around here — keep off my beat!" He aimed his kick for my rear end but kicked me in the thigh instead and I limped for three or four days.

125

One symbol tends to heighten the visibility of a tramp more than any other: the presence of a bottle. It is not always an easy matter to determine whether a tramp should be considered drunk by legal definition. If a man should later plead not guilty to the charge, the officer must appear in court and he will need to demonstrate that the arrest was legitimate. Bloodshot eyes, unsteady gait, and the smell of alcohol are used as evidence in court — but the presence of a bottle is especially valuable since it is tangible and may demonstrate to the judge that if the man was not fully drunk, it would not have been long until he would have been. If a tramp is found with a bottle, he knows that his chances to beat the charge in court are slim and so he will more than likely plead guilty to the charge. As one man said, "All you have to do is be in a crowd where there happens to be a bottle and let the police see the bottle!" Other men reported, "I've been arrested many times from 1961 to 1968 when I wasn't drunk but they pinched me with a full or part bottle — or just on general principles." And, "I was just going from a bar next door with a jug to my room when they arrested me — that was in 1967 and they robbed me that time too." Others may not have been arrested but have had a bottle, which was hidden in their clothing, destroyed — perhaps an effort by the police to reduce the incidence of crime. About 10 per cent of the sample indicated that a Seattle policeman had taken a jug from their clothing and poured the contents over their heads, or broken a jug they had in their pocket with a night stick. One man recalled, "I've had them pour it out in the alley." Others reported: "In 1965 an officer saw me leaving the tavern putting the jug in my belt. He broke it with his club and told me to get lost." "In 1966 I was sitting in the stairway of an old hotel. A bull came around and took my bottle, poured it on me and told me to get lost." This kind of experience is not only humiliating — it requires that glass and alcohol be cleaned from the clothes — but it also destroys what the tramp may be depending on to keep from getting the "shakes" or alcohol withdrawal symptoms. He may have junked for half a day or sold his own blood in order to earn enough for one bottle, only to find it destroyed. In every attempt to blend with his environment, the tramp knows that he will not always succeed — his visibility may not be adequately hidden and he must then suffer the consequences.

One way, then, to increase security is to become invisible, a fact which might have been observed or discovered by direct questions but which emerged here as one dimension of contrast for defining flops. A statement of the underlying semantic principles for one important area of culture, as sleeping places are for urban nomads, also reveals many other themes and values in that culture. Their periodic poverty is important because it limits their choices for sleeping and also brings them into contact with the police. Their drinking behavior influences much of their lives and becomes a symbol to outsiders of their "true condition," one which justifies their incarceration. A very important strategy for making life more secure is to decrease visibility; this tells us a great deal about the arrest record of those who are constantly in jail on public drunk charges. Most tramps would agree with one man who summed up his own recurrent arrests over a five-year period in Seattle, "It happened when you're around they take you in for just being there!" One of the best ways urban nomads have discovered to keep from *being there* is to "pick up your bed and walk. . . ."

CHAPTER FIVE

Making
the Bucket

Why do urban nomads encounter the police, get arrested, plead guilty, and do time in an almost never-ending cycle? These men *do* violate local ordinances which prohibit drunkenness, drinking, begging, sleeping and urinating in *public*. They are suspected and sometimes convicted of petty larceny, shoplifting, carprowling, and other misdemeanors, *but what they do is much less significant than who they are*. These men do their life sentences on the installment plan because they have been discredited and stigmatized by other Americans. They are not seen as fellow human beings nor as citizens; in fact, they are not even perceived as criminals, but, rather, they are identified as *bums*. The concept of equal justice in American society applies to those who are considered equal, and, as Wilson has observed, it is difficult for the police not to consider tramps inferior:

The patrolman, however, sees these people when they are dirty, angry, rowdy, obscene, dazed, savage, or bloodied. To him, they are not in these circumstances "equal," they are *different*. What they deserve depends on what they are. "Decent people" and "bums" are not equal, except in some ultimate and, at the moment, irrelevant sense (1968: 36).

These men make the bucket because of the public nature of their life style and because they fail to make themselves invisible. A high-ranking police official in Seattle admitted that:

The election to charge them is purely a matter of election. If you stick strictly to the law, the language of the law, you aren't going to have good law enforcement and you will have some injustices. Most of the people charged with drunk could be charged with disorderly conduct and sustain it. We have now a considerable per cent of persons taken in and charged with drunk who have actually committed some other offense.

Equal justice for all under the law is the basis of the American legal system, but this principle does not apply to tramps. When other people violate the laws which are used to take urban nomads to jail it is easy to overlook such illegal behavior. Even the Chief of Police in Seattle can publicly acknowledge with equanimity that the police:

face a dilemma in prohibiting consumption of beer and wine in parks. Most persons accept the presence of these beverages at family picnics in parks (*The Seattle Times* 1969).

Many causes then, other than their criminal violations, prompt the arrest of tramps: where they sleep, how they behave, the need for trusties to work in the jail, the public nature of their life style, and more. But if they are arrested primarily because they are bums and tramps, we must try to discover how a man enters the culture of urban nomads and how he comes to have these disrespected identities.

No man begins life as a bum, nor were these men socialized into the world of tramps as children. Their experience is different from members of most other American minority groups and very different, of course, from members of primitive societies. At one time in their adult life these men had a variety of respected identities — they were fathers, husbands, students, sons, employers, and employees.[1] Many attended high school, some went to college. One informant who had been a tramp for several years was a graduate of Harvard University. Others had owned businesses or worked at

129

skilled trades. Almost one-half of these men at one time had maintained a family. Some were receiving pensions from previous employers. How did they learn to be urban nomads? What forces were at work to encourage them to assume the identities of tramp and inmate? Why did they learn to survive in urban America by constant travel, and in a subculture where drinking and begging are accepted ways of life? The processes which led these men to abandon their former identities and life styles and acquire new ones in the culture of urban nomads are exceedingly complex. And, although a number of studies have been focused upon this identity change,[2] none has exhaustively described the influence of arrest and incarceration on this process.

The conception a man has of himself and his place in the world is, in part, socially constructed. Like the brick and mortar which go into creating a building, so the edifice of the human self is constructed, one building block at a time. Whereas new self-identities may be acquired throughout the life span, dramatic change in personality can only occur if these former identities are subjected to radical manipulation.[3] The jailing of tramps is not the only factor in their loss of their former self-conceptions and the acquisition of a new life style, but it is certainly one of the most important. Throughout the process of making the bucket their former identities are ravaged, like old buildings being torn down brick by brick for an urban renewal project. We have already examined their new identities in jail (Chapter Three), and also some of their encounters with the police while in the community (Chapter Four). Space and time are two other aspects of human existence which help to structure the self, and the way tramps define them in jail is especially crucial for the changes in their self-identity which occur there. In this chapter we shall introduce the major stages a tramp goes through each time he makes the bucket and show how these are tightly interwoven with the spatial aspects of making the bucket. In Chapter Six we shall see how the experience of going to court helps to convince a man that he is really a bum after all, and then in Chapter Seven we go on to show what it means to these men to "do time" and how it motivates them to live as urban nomads. In Chapter Eight it will become clear how the experience in the bucket not only strips away former identities but also helps these men erect new ones on the site where they became alienated from themselves. All these factors — identity, interaction, space, and time — are important for our understanding of how these men are socialized into the world of urban nomads through their experience with the law enforcement process.

One of the difficulties in analyzing the influence of such experiences upon the self is the tendency for outsiders to misread their *meaning*. Some have maintained that the jail is helpful to these men and they couldn't mind it too much — after all they *are* bums and being in jail is better than sleeping in an alley. Others have responded with horror to some of the facts reported here, but the important thing to understand is how *these* men perceive their experiences in the bucket. Goffman has pointed out that, in this type of study, ". . . cognitive processes are invariably involved, for the social arrangements must be 'read' by the individual and others for the image of himself that they imply" (1961:47). Reading this image is not an easy task and is, furthermore, one which may be hindered by making "objective" observations. I seldom visited the jail personally and did not go through the revolving door experience because it would have colored the study and resulted in more of an "outsider's view." If we are to allow members of minority groups to define their way of life, to tell us how they "read their experience," we must *listen to them,* rather than simply observe and describe them from a lofty objectivity which is always biased by the researcher's cultural background.

Tramps organize and identify the significant experiences which they have in jail by means of a complex dialect of English. Their language is a rich repository which holds the key to our understanding of their culture, both inside and outside the bucket. If we can decode this aspect of their culture we will be well on the way to reading what the law enforcement process means to them. Language orders experience in many different ways, one of the most basic of which is to label events and objects in the environment at different levels of generality. We saw earlier how there were different kinds of trusties in the jail, that *trusty* was a cover term which included nearly sixty different kinds of identities which tramps assume when they work inside the bucket. These terms are ordered on the principle of inclusion, a relationship where one term is included in another term: a bindle stiff is a kind of tramp and may be referred to as a tramp. A taxonomy in any language may be based on other types of relationships; terms may label not only specific *kinds* of the same experience but also different *parts* of the same thing and different *stages* of a more inclusive event. In discussing the jail with informants they often responded with statements such as "the drunk tank is part of the bucket," or "a stand-up cell is part of a time tank." Taxonomies which are based on the relationship in which one term is *part* of a more inclusive term have a different logical relationship than those in which one symbol is a *kind* of a more general term. It is beyond the scope of the present work to discuss in detail the differences in these or other types of ordering principles. These various types of cognitive structures enable the individual to anticipate events and experiences; they provide for a more secure world and enable one to adapt to that world.

The different parts of the jail are shown in Table 5.1, providing a taxonomic definition of the spatial dimensions of the bucket. The Seattle city jail is located on the sixth and seventh floors of the Public Safety building near the center of the city. Tramps usually use the word "bucket" when referring to this place. The terms in Table 5.1 were elicited by asking, "What are the different parts of the bucket?" Though this taxonomy is exhaustive at the higher levels of generality, many more specific parts of the jail are not included. Space and time are interwoven in the experience of these men, and this relationship is more important than a careful analysis of space alone. The entire process of arrest and incarceration is referred to as "making the bucket," and one of the phrases most often repeated among tramp informants is "when I made the bucket last time." "I made the bucket so often in San Francisco that I came to Seattle but I started making the bucket here also" is typical of the phrases used by these men.

The experience of "making the bucket" is one which occurs often in the lives of most tramps — in fact, if a man hasn't made the bucket he isn't even considered a tramp! As a series of events

132

which occur in a temporal sequence at specified spatial locations, making the bucket has a ritual quality about it. Just as religious ceremonies are a series of events and actions which have symbolic meaning and occur over time, so the places, actions, and symbols which a tramp experiences as he moves from one stage of making the bucket to the next make up a ritual, or, a *rite de passage*.[4] The actions, times, and places are intertwined in a complex array of symbolic meanings which ceremonially tell the urban nomad and those in his world that he has been stripped of his former identities and should believe the truth about himself: that he is a common drunkard, a bum. We shall focus here upon the ways in which the language of tramps orders their experience throughout this rite and enables them to anticipate and prepare for what is ahead. A newcomer learns quickly from oldtimers who have been incarcerated often. The questions a tramp asks others when he arrives in a new city usually relate to the police, bucket, court, and judges. He must know the slight differences which occur from town to town, as well as the general outline of what to expect, in order to make the most of his next experience in this rite of passage which he knows will surely take place. When it does occur he will not only learn new details about the ritual, but he will come to have a new appreciation for himself, who he was in the past, and who he is becoming.

The stages of making the bucket were discovered by asking men "What are the different steps or stages you go through when you make the bucket?" and "What is the first stage, second stage, etc." The major steps in this ritual, the places they occur, and several of the more important actions which bulls can do to tramps are in Chart 5.1 (page 138). A man's experience with the revolving door begins when he is spotted on the *street*, taken to a *call box*, and finally ushered into a *police car* or *paddy wagon*. From there he is driven to the basement of the Public Safety Building and ushered by one or more officers to the *elevator* and taken up to the sixth floor, through a sliding steel gate, to the *booking desk*, and there he is thoroughly searched and the details of his arrest are recorded. His property is removed from him and stored in a property box. He is then taken to the *padded drunk tank* where he will be left

TABLE 5.1 TAXONOMIC DEFINITION OF PARTS OF THE BUCKET

The Bucket
- Seventh floor
  - North wing
    - Trusty tank (717)
    - Trusty tank (716)
    - Trusty tank (715)
  - South wing
    - Catwalk
    - Hallway
    - Utility room
    - Blanket room
    - Trash room
    - Laundry room
    - Bull pen
    - Trusty tank (706) "Big Six"
    - Trusty tank (705)
    - Trusty tank (704)
    - Time tank (709)
    - Time tank (708)
    - Time tank (703)
    - Time tank (702)
    - Time tank (701)
    - Holding tank (710)
    - Delousing tank (711)
  - Hospital area
    - Hospital ward
    - Treatment room
    - Hospital office
      - Clerk's desk
      - Nurse's desk
    - Doctor's sleeping room

TABLE 5.1 TAXONOMIC DEFINITION OF PARTS OF THE BUCKET (Continued)

The Bucket	Seventh floor			
	North wing	Trusty tank (718)		
		Trusty mess hall		
		7th floor office		
		Barber shop		
		Utility room		
		Bull's locker room		
		Clothing and storage room		
		Kitchen elevator		
		Hallway		
		Catwalk		
		Stairs to 6th floor		
	Court area	Stairs to street		
		Women's rest room		
		Men's rest room		
		Elevators		
		Court lobby		
		Court docket	Toilet	
			Benches	
		Courtroom	Judge's bench	
			Spectators' area	
			Prosecutor's desk	
			Clerk's area	
			Bailiff's desk	
			Witness area	
			Railing	

TABLE 5.1 TAXONOMIC DEFINITION OF PARTS OF THE BUCKET (Continued)

The Bucket

Seventh floor	Court area	Hallway
		Holding cell
Sixth floor	Time tank (635)	Toilet
		Shower
		Wash bowl
		Stand-up cell
	Time tank (636)	Toilet
		Shower
		Wash bowl
		Stand-up cell
	Time tank (637)	Toilet
		Shower
		Wash bowl
		Stand-up cell
	Time tank (651)	Toilet
		Shower
		Wash bowl
		Stand-up cell
	Time tank (653)	Toilet
		Shower
		Wash bowl
		Stand-up cell
	Time tank (654)	Toilet
		Shower
		Wash bowl
		Stand-up cell

TABLE 5.1 TAXONOMIC DEFINITION OF PARTS OF THE BUCKET (Concluded)

The Bucket	Sixth floor		
			Booking desk
			Stairs to 7th floor
			Interview rooms
			Catwalk
			Barber shop
			Elevator from basement
			Electric gate
			Bulls' gun lockers
			Utility room
			Bulls' rest room
			Blue room
			Phone booth
			Waiting room
			Runners' room
		Office	Clerk's desk
			Lieutenant's office
			Property room
			X-Ray, mug and print room
			Visitor's stalls
			Padded drunk tank (660) "rubber tank"
			Cement drunk tank (659)
			Padded drunk tank (658) "rubber tank"
			Cement drunk tank (657)
			The hole (blackout cell)
			Padded cells (4)
			Investigation cells (8)

137

CHART 5.1 STAGES IN MAKING THE BUCKET

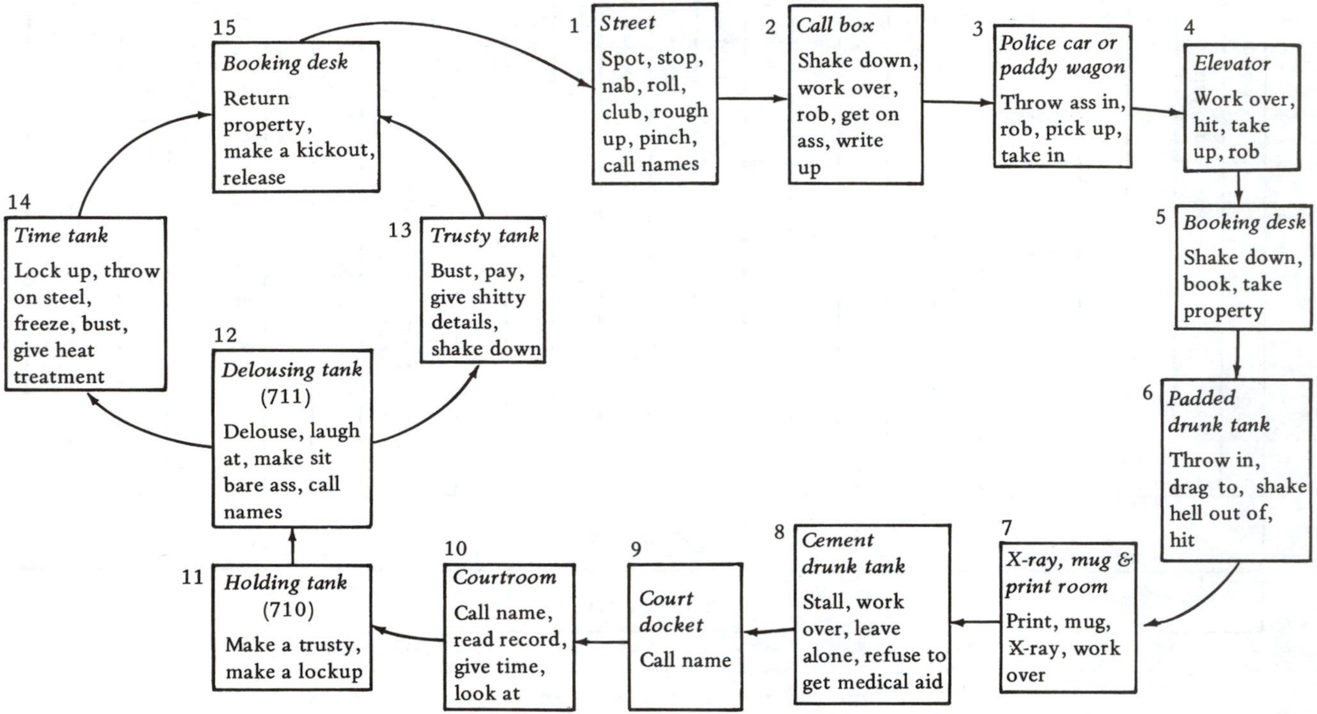

1 Street
Spot, stop, nab, roll, club, rough up, pinch, call names

2 Call box
Shake down, work over, rob, get on ass, write up

3 Police car or paddy wagon
Throw ass in, rob, pick up, take in

4 Elevator
Work over, hit, take up, rob

5 Booking desk
Shake down, book, take property

6 Padded drunk tank
Throw in, drag to, shake hell out of, hit

7 X-ray, mug & print room
Print, mug, X-ray, work over

8 Cement drunk tank
Stall, work over, leave alone, refuse to get medical aid

9 Court docket
Call name

10 Courtroom
Call name, read record, give time, look at

11 Holding tank (710)
Make a trusty, make a lockup

12 Delousing tank (711)
Delouse, laugh at, make sit bare ass, call names

13 Trusty tank
Bust, pay, give shitty details, shake down

14 Time tank
Lock up, throw on steel, freeze, bust, give heat treatment

15 Booking desk
Return property, make a kickout, release

138

for several hours to gain some semblance of sobriety if he is drunk, or simply to wait if he is not. He is then taken to the *X-ray, mug, and fingerprint room* where other details of his identity are recorded. After this he is placed in the *cement drunk tank* — a large room intended to hold 35 men — and there he will wait until one of two things happens: either he bails out with $20 or remains until time for a court appearance at some later date. On the day he will be arraigned in court he is aroused early and taken to the *court docket*, a large room with steel benches where he must wait until court is in session. At 9 o'clock each morning, Mondays through Fridays, the Seattle Municipal Criminal Court begins by hearing the drunk cases. About twenty-five men are called out before the judge and informed of their rights; they return to the court docket and, one at a time, are called out, asked to enter a plea of guilty or not guilty; then, on the basis of their past record, they are sentenced. This action takes place in the *courtroom*. If a man does not receive a committed sentence he is allowed to leave, returns to the sixth floor of the jail to recover his own personal property, and walks out a free man. If he is given a committed sentence he must wait for several hours until all inmates have been to court; then he goes to the *holding tank* on the seventh floor (710) where his status and identity within the jail are determined as either a trusty or a lockup. After this decision is made he is taken to a *delousing tank* where he will remain naked for several hours while his clothing is being deloused. Then lockups will go to a *time tank*, usually on the seventh floor, and there they will be held until the date of their release; trusties will be taken to the *trusty tank*, which is not locked during the day. They will have more freedom than the others but must work for the jailers until they complete their sentence. There are some occasions when a man may not spend his days in the time tank or the trusty tank. These occur if he is busted for misbehavior to a less desirable place within the bucket, which will be discussed in a later chapter. The tramp then begins to serve out his time, working day after day, or laying it out in the cell until his sentence of ten, twenty, thirty days, two months, three months, or even six months, is completed. When he has served his time he will be taken back to the *booking desk*, where he becomes a "kick-out," his property is returned, and he will be released. He then goes back on the street to begin again, perhaps in a few hours, perhaps in a few days or weeks, to encounter policemen who sooner or later will make an arrest.

Although the same events may take place at different stages of this ritual, some events are more likely to occur in one place than another. A man will probably receive a thorough search or shakedown when he is first brought to the call box, again when he is booked at the booking desk, and again, if he is a trusty who works outside, each time he returns to jail. A man may be hit by an officer on the street, at the call box, in the elevator, at the booking desk, and while he is in one of the drunk tanks, but this action is very unlikely to occur during the later stages of making the bucket. Though these events will be discussed at times as if they occurred only at one point in the process, similar actions may occur again and again at different stages.

The importance of a man's experience in making the bucket is especially crucial in what it tells a man about himself, the way in which these events symbolically portray an image to the man of *who* he is and *what* he is becoming. Very often those who inspect a local jail, such as the one in Seattle, examine the quality of these experiences from the outsider's point of view; they seek to determine whether the food and material comforts are adequate, or whether medical attention is sufficient. What they often fail to fully recognize is the subjective experience of the men involved and the psychological and social alienation which takes place again and again throughout their lives. What do the events in this ritual say to a man about his personal worth, his integrity, and his identity?

STAGE 1: STREET

One of the most important ways in which members of any society learn a new identity is by being labeled by others, especially those who hold power over their lives. A child who is told by a parent that he is a good child will grow up to consider himself a person of worth, whereas one who is repeatedly condemned and told he is stupid will come to have an image of himself which incorporates these symbolic definitions. Not all labeling activity by others is significant. But, when a man's concept of himself is shaken because of his own behavior and loss of control over doing those things which society considers important, he is especially vulnerable to the labels which others use for him. A man who is being drawn into the culture of urban nomads is clinging to his former respectable identities, but his ability to maintain them has been deeply undermined and, when those who are officials in the larger society label him, it is difficult to withstand such verbal attacks upon the self. When a man first encounters the police on the street he is often addressed in a way which infers or implies that he has little personal worth. In the sample, 53 per cent of the men indicated that bulls had used insulting language to them personally, often on the street and at other times within the jail. Although 40 per cent of the men indicated this had never happened in the city of Seattle, nearly half of the sample had been arrested fewer than five times in this city and may well have had the experience in other places. A man might be with a group of other men, one of whom receives the personal insult, but he himself is able to read the message and what it implies about him, understanding that he is classified with the man who has been so labeled. The kinds of insults reported by informants fall into three classes: discrediting labels, threats, and insults based on other personal identities, such as race.

The discrediting labels most often involved the concepts of "bum," "wino," "drunk," and "tramp." One man recalled, "That bull said I was just a wino and a bum that wasn't worth being tossed in a shit ditch." The label of tramp is often used in a manner which implies the inferiority of such an identity. "Get going you fuckin' tramp. Can't you hear your own name, ass-hole?" Many other discrediting labels such as "you wino son-of-a-bitch," "ding bat," "fucking dehorn," "drunken bum," "cock sucker," "Skid Road bastard," "fuckin' tramp," and "phoney ass," were among those reported by the informants. Tramps who encounter police on the street, or who must interact with the police in jail, experience many threats, such as, "Shut up or we will put you in the pads and beat the shit out of you." These are used early in the encounter and quickly establish the power relationship between bulls and tramps. Those men who have been arrested only a few times or have not been personally insulted have observed others experience this type of labeling and know they can expect it to happen. One man reported:

Two cops escorted a well-dressed drunk man to the call box. On the way one held him while the other took his wallet from a hip pocket and put it in his own pocket. All the time the man was protesting and they threatened to slug him.

A man may also be stigmatized in his interaction with the police by having other aspects of his identity thrown up before him as evidence that he is only a bum. This may be his physical condition, his drinking, his racial background, or his friends. One man recalled that the arresting officer had said, "You winos don't remember anything. Hey there, fuckin' tramp, what's that sore on your hand, syphilis?" A bull may insult a man by reinforcing his identity as one who cannot quit drinking: "Well the bull that lets you out has said he would see me sometime tonight to pick me up for drunk again." The worst threats and discrediting labels appear to be reserved for those who have a racial identity which is sometimes not respected in American culture. For example, "They made fun of me because I was a Mexican, and they made fun of the Indian girl I was with. They called her lots of names and me too." A black man recalled:

Yes, the last time I was pinched this one bull kept telling me what they were going to do to us black SOB's if we tried to start any shit in Seattle. He say he just couldn't wait to kill him a nigger, and I know a lot of Negro men that these same things have happened to. They even call you these names after you get to the jail if it's at night, and the rest of the bulls just laugh while this is going on.

The city of Seattle has a large population of Indians and many find companionship in the Skid Road district and often get charged with being drunk in public. In many ways they are considered beneath others. One man recalled, "That bull called me a fucked-up chief and stated that liquor rights should never have been given to these fuckin' Injuns." Another recalled an officer saying to him, "They didn't play cowboys and Indians long enough; they should have killed all of you bastards off." Tramps sometimes find it hard to understand why they receive such abuse at the hands of the

142

officers when their only crime is an illness and the only person they are hurting is themselves. One man summed up this attitude:

Many times they have said things to me that make me sick and ashamed of them, not me. I ask myself, "Are these the men the people hire as guardians against crime?" That these same officers can spend so much of their time abusing poor damn fool drunks instead of doing what I think they should be doing — crime protecting our women and kids, things like that, a drunk mostly only hurts himself.

Whatever the reasons for this labeling behavior, most tramps are aware that it goes on and come to the same conclusion as the man who stated, "In many cops' minds a drunk isn't human."

The relationship between tramps and bulls is intense not only at the time of arrest and while they are in jail but extends over a long period of time. A man who is in and out of jail often and has many arrests may find that, aside from his peers within the culture of urban nomads, his major contacts with other persons in American culture are with the police; when they label him in these ways he begins to sense within himself that he is not fully human, and the process of alienation from himself is furthered. As he moves on through the latter stages of making the bucket and has experiences which strip him further of his respected identities, these names will haunt him, and though he may struggle within himself to deny their reality, they inevitably come to replace the self-conceptions to which he tries to cling.

STAGE 2: CALL BOX

Personal and social identity are structured not only by the roles we play and the names we use, but also by objects of personal property. In American culture this is especially important; a person comes to think of himself in terms of his home, car, clothing, and other things which are "mine." The English language provides us with ready-made ways of extending self-referential terms, such as "I" "me," and even names to include the objects we own. During socialization children may learn the possessive case before they learn to refer to themselves as the subject of their action. Their growing sense of identity develops by attaching themselves to their possessions: "my toy," "Sheryl's blanket," and "that bed is mine" are all expressive of the growing sense of self-awareness. Studies in non-Western societies which have tried to eliminate ownership of private property suggest that it may be impossible to maintain a very strong sense of selfhood without it. Spiro's study of an Israeli kibbutz showed

with respect to private possessions, at any rate — that the child is no *tabula rasa*, who, depending on his cultural environment, is equally amenable to private or collective property arrangements. On the contrary, the data suggest that the child's early motivations are strongly directed toward private ownership, an orientation from which he is only gradually weaned by effective cultural techniques (1958:375–376).

It was significant that the motivation to own at least some personal property was especially strong during the early years when children were acquiring their identity as separate human beings. The men considered here are on the verge of losing their identity and cling to their possessions, even though they are very limited in number. Part of the meaning of the concept of tramp is bound up with owning a car or carrying a bedroll with one's private property stashed in it. Rings, watches, money, wallets, identification papers, address books, and clothing help to give form and structure to *who* one is, and their loss, especially when a man has only a limited number of these items, is significant. Although these losses may occur throughout the ritual of making the bucket, the first of them often takes place at the call box.

When a man is arrested by a policeman on his beat he is taken to the call box where a paddy wagon or police car is summoned to take him to jail. During the interim he undergoes a thorough search and may lose some of his belongings; in the sample, 23 per cent of the men indicated they had been robbed by a policeman while he was shaking them down at a call box. One man recalled:

I was robbed of $15 by two police that was working the beat in Chinatown. I was taken to Jackson and Maynard to the call box, while the one police called for the wagon the other took $15 from me. As I argued with him over the money, he said, "What are you going to do about it?" While this took place the wagon drove up and I was taken to jail. I told the desk officer what had happened and he told me there was nothing he could do about it, that was the last of it. There was nothing more I could do, as I'm sure being picked up for drunk no one would believe this would happen.

Because of their mobility, tramps often carry most of their possessions with them. A man may be working in Florida and decide to travel to Washington and he will carry his money with him. Another may be traveling from Seattle to Portland to Spokane, and back to Seattle on the Northwest circuit with all of his money in his pocket or sewn into the lining of his shirt. Some men make the harvests in Eastern Washington during the summer and return to Seattle with several hundred dollars on their person. Tramps believe that robberies by the police and jackrollers are likely to occur especially around the first of each month when the older men receive their pension checks, and that property may be destroyed if it is not usable: "They took my payroll check and tore it up and threw it in the gutter because I didn't have any cash." When the wagon takes them off to jail, they hope against the odds that their possessions will be in their property box when they are released, but this is not always the case, as one man recalled, "They took a watch and ring from me in 1968 and told me it would be in my property at the jail. I never got them back." Tramps do not always know if their money is taken on the street or later from their property, but 33 per cent of the sample reported they had personally witnessed the Seattle police rolling, clipping, or stealing from a drunk or someone who had been picked up for drunk. One man stated:

This happened in October 1967. This fellow was working with me and he cashed his check in a bar on First Avenue. We had a couple drinks and got up to leave. As we were leaving these two bulls were standing on the corner. When we got to them they made us put our hands on the wall and proceeded to go through our pockets. When they finished the other guy asked for his money. They looked at each other and asked, "What money was he talking about?" Then they told us we'd better take a walk or go to jail for drunk.

The tramp who loses his money finds that his very self is changing as he loses the few remaining symbols of his identity.

In addition to property dispossession, a man at the call box is almost always robbed of his autonomy at a deeper psychological level. His world, his very home, has been invaded by someone with the authority to treat him in a manner which hardly serves to remind him he is innocent until proven guilty. The street corners on Skid Road where call boxes are located have a meaning for tramps different from that held by others in American society. They are not merely dingy public places, they are the "living rooms" and private meeting places for urban nomads. A man who has recently arrived in town will hang around a street corner hoping to meet an old friend or find a new one. When a man is required to place his hands over his head and allow a bull to invade his clothing and other domains of privacy systematically, at the same time threatening him, it is done in the full visibility of other tramps. A person is thus exposed to indignities in the presence of his colleagues and required to submit to what tramps define as a personal affront, made more reprehensible because it occurs in the presence of peers. The man who is being shaken down with no means of defense is unable to portray to his friends the desirable image of an independent human being. Goffman has noted that such experiences:

disrupt or defile precisely those actions that in civil society have the role of attesting to the actor and those in his presence that he has some command over his world — that he is a person with "adult" self determination, autonomy, and freedom of action (1961:43).

STAGE 3: PADDY WAGON OR POLICE CAR

The trip to the jail usually takes place in a paddy wagon or police car. Some men may be apprehended by officers driving a wagon or car and thus bypass the first two stages of the ritual. In either case he is placed in the vehicle: "The bulls threw my ass in the paddy wagon." Although the drive to the jail may only involve a few blocks, a man does not always get there after he is picked up in one of these vehicles; 23 per cent of the sample reported the police had stopped them or picked them up, taken their money or other property, and then let them go. A young Indian boy wrote the following letter to the Seattle Chief of Police while he was at the alcoholism treatment center:

December 6, 1967

Dear Sir:

One Sunday night on the 15th of October, 1967, I was picked up by two Seattle police in a squad. I got picked up between Main Avenue

146

and Pine Avenue on First Street. The time was between 9 P.M. and 4 A.M. While riding in the squad car one of the police asked me where I was from and I told him Alaska. The next question was where I was staying and I answered I hadn't found a place yet so they took me to an alley behind the Alaska Fertilizer building. I told them I still had my luggage and tools at the Greyhound bus depot. They asked me how long my luggage and tools were there, and I said about a week and a half. They wanted to know if I still had money to take out my property and I said, "yes." Questioned by the two cops about why I didn't take them out I answered, "I have no place to keep them." And then the cops took my three dollars I had left and the bus locker keys nos. 12 and 16. They said for me to wait for fifteen or twenty minutes and they would be back with my tools and luggage. I waited a long time and they never showed up. I wasn't booked that night. The following Monday I went to work at my job. I do not know what those two police looked like because it was dark.

It took courage to write this letter, since tramps are aware of the retaliatory action which may occur if they complain about this type of treatment. They feel that the officers know they will seldom say anything about such incidents because they are not arrested on such occasions. This is considered to be an *involuntary payoff* to the police. Only 6 per cent of the sample reported they had ever made a *voluntary* payoff. One man recalled:

The beat cops asked me, "How much money do you have" So I told them, "Ten or twelve dollars." They said, "Well, what would you rather do, give us the money or go to jail for thirty days?" I gave them the money.

Other tramps would say, "No, actually you don't pay off, they take it from you." "In 1965 they took a shopping bag with purchases of food and clothing and let me go but kept the bag. Either take off or go to jail." "In 1968, they picked me up in a prowl car and took me down on Skid Road back in an alley and searched me, took my money, drove me around for awhile, and then let me out way down on Skid Road in a back alley. They drove off without returning my money." "They stopped me and asked for my I.D. Then take my money and tell me to get lost before I go to jail."

Our interest here is not so much in the actual incidence of such experiences which are almost impossible to verify by legal means. The culture which urban nomads use to organize their behavior and anticipate the future has arisen because enough tramps have experienced these losses for it to become general cultural knowledge that they do occur. The strategies which tramps use to make themselves invisible when they sleep (discussed in Chapter Four) are also used to protect their personal property. Like chameleons who change color to blend with their environment and avoid their enemies, tramps are careful to conceal any hint that they have valuable possessions. Some men reported they would dress in old clothes "like a bum" in order to avoid becoming a candidate for jackrollers and thieves. A man who is thrown into a paddy wagon or police car knows what can happen, knows that his money might be taken, and knows that he must use every skill he has learned to protect what remains of his meager property and the identity it symbolizes.

STAGE 4: ELEVATOR

The elevator from the basement of the Public Safety Building to the sixth floor where the jail is located holds important and treacherous implications for the tramp. He is entirely cut off from the view of everyone except the police — not even a disinterested passer-by can influence what takes place. The special hazards which must be reckoned with in the elevator are summed up in the phrase, "they work you over." Although it is a short trip, the tramp knows that the time in the elevator can be extended easily if the bull pushes the stop button between floors. As the elevator slowly rises, the reality of imprisonment sweeps over the tramp with an immediacy which suffocates the self-assertive wishes he may still have harbored. The two bulls at his side like uniformed bars of a cell, must not be considered human beings to whom he can respond because any reaction besides a plastic passivity may be interpreted as resistance which demands a counterreaction. The tramp may have been worked over in the elevator on previous occasions; if not, he certainly has heard of the experiences of his fellow urban nomads. He has learned a rich vocabulary for talking about the ways the police may physically assault him. Thirty-five per cent of the sample indicated they had undergone at least one of the following kinds of treatment by the police in Seattle; the bull may:

> *Rough you up*
> *Hit you*

Take shoes to you
Club you
Shake the hell out of you
Work you over
Slam your face on something
Split your head open
Bounce you off his knee
Drag you someplace

Because tramps have many names for these experiences, it was necessary to phrase questions carefully to include a variety of terms or to use a cover term. If the questions had been asked early in the research, prior to the discovery of these verbs, it would not have tapped the range of experiences tramps have with the police. The variety of ways a tramp can be worked over may occur at any time during the stages of this ritual but they tend to cluster during the early ones: on the street, at the call box, in the wagon, in the elevator, and at the booking desk. Although being worked over symbolically reminds a man that his body, the most intimate part of his self-concept, is vulnerable, it has another important meaning. Like rehearsal before a dramatic performance, it forcefully instructs the tramp to play the part of a dependent and passive actor within the bucket, and if a person refuses he may have the following kind of experience: "Me and the fellow I was with and two cops were on the elevator. This fellow I was with talked back to one of the cops and the cop slugged him three or four times." The significance of such events early in the ritual has been discussed by Goffman who states:

Staff often feel that a recruit's readiness to be appropriately deferential in his initial face-to-face encounters with them is a sign that he will take the role of the routinely pliant inmate. The occasion on which staff members first tell the inmate of his deference obligations may be structured to challenge the inmate to balk or to hold his peace forever. Thus these initial moments of socialization may involve an "obedience test" and even a will-breaking contest: an inmate who shows defiance receives immediate visible punishment, which increases until he openly "cries uncle" and humbles himself (1961:17).

All encounters which strip a man of the rights deemed inalienable in civil society remind him that he must be compliant. The longer

149

a man has been in the world of tramps the more he learns to respond as if he is an animal whose will has been broken by its master. Labels, threats, physical abuse, and thefts of property in themselves are hard for any man to take, but more significant is the implicit message in these actions: they clearly identify for the tramp those who hold power over his life at that point in time and during the coming months he may spend in jail. If he refuses to acknowledge this deference relationship further steps will be taken, as they were with the man who recalled:

In 1967 he shook me down, took my wallet, looked in it, took eleven dollars. Put my wallet back and I said, "Since when do you look for a gun or a knife in a man's wallet?" He split my head and it took four stitches.

When a man reports, "Two of them picked me up bodily and heaved me face first into the paddy wagon," he is not only complaining of physical abuse, he is saying how he feels about being treated as an object and being forced into giving up the control over what happens to him. If a man's will is not broken on the street or during the trip to the jail, he knows it probably will be at the booking desk if he shows any intention of something less than complete compliance.

STAGE 5: BOOKING DESK

When the elevator door opens a man sees, to his left, the gun rack where the officers will deposit their weapons, as if to imply that they have no further means of hurting him while he is behind bars. Before him is a row of closely spaced steel bars which lurch into motion with the sound of a buzzer pressed from behind the booking desk. As the steel gate opens he is ushered across a waiting area twenty or thirty feet in diameter to a high counter with several windows. A booking sheet and property record are completed in quadruplicate for each man: these include his name, address, nationality, occupation, place of arrest, the charge against him, and a list of the personal property that is taken from him. Although there is a space for the prisoner to sign and verify the personal property taken, 69 per cent of the sample indicated they were not usually allowed to do this. They admitted they sometimes could not remember because of intoxication, but this feeling arose primarily because they were never given a copy of the property slip as a receipt. Ninety-eight per cent of the sample indicated they had *never* received such a receipt in Seattle, a practice which was common for most other jails in which they had been. A study of the Seattle Police Department in 1968 by the International Association of Chiefs of Police corroborated this fact: "Personal property such as money, watches, etc., are removed from the prisoner but the prisoner is not given a receipt" (1968:486). The Chief of Police in Seattle further confirmed that it was not the policy to give receipts and explained the reason: "Property receipts were given to prisoners years ago but the practice was discontinued because inmates stole the receipts from one another. The Chief said the present system has been in effect for more than 17 years" (*The Seattle Post-Intelligencer*, 1968). Without a receipt a man cannot prove how much money he has had and thus is a ready victim of thefts from his property box while in jail, an experience reported by many men but also confirmed by the International Association of Chiefs of Police study:

As previously mentioned, prisoners are not given a receipt for their personal property, money, or valuables at the time of booking. In the future, each prisoner should be given a receipt for his personal property at the time of confinement. . . . The property room is always open and is readily accessible to all assigned personnel and trusties working in the area. The security measures for money and other personal property of prisoners are considered inadequate and measures should be taken to correct this deficiency. The door of the property room and all individual metal property boxes should be secured and entry to this room restricted to designated personnel from the service and supply section. . . . There have been instances of cash missing from money containers and the shortages have been made up by voluntary contributions of assigned personnel. Provision is also made for the accounting of money received by prisoners while confined for the purpose of posting bail, paying fines, or for the prisoner's personal use to make commissary purchases. A receipt for all moneys received in this manner is executed, one copy to the sender of the cash, and one to the property room to be placed in the prisoner's property box. The prisoner is informed but no receipt is given to him (1968:491–492).

Although our main concern is to describe the cognitive world of tramps and how they perceive the law enforcement process, it is interesting to note that at some points they are in agreement with what an outsider might consider a more "objective" point of view.

When tramps were questioned about thefts from their property boxes, 40 per cent reported their occurrence. Many others admitted they were drunk and thought their money had been taken from the property boxes but could not confirm this fact since they had not received a property slip. One man recalled: "In 1968 I know for sure that I had $3 in cash but only had $1 when I got out. But no way of proving this because no property slip." Another man recalled:

I was in jail and had no money and there was a fellow who owed me $12 and so I wrote and asked him for it and told him to send it registered letter. I got the letter but the money wasn't in it. When I got out I didn't have no money in my property box. I said, "I've got a registered letter here saying I was sent $12. I'm not leaving until I get it." The bull said, "You don't have no money." The sergeant came by just then and came and asked what it was and looked at the letter and went back to the property box and then came out and said, "Oh, here's your $12. It was in the wrong property box."

One man arriving at the treatment center after spending some time in the Seattle city jail awaiting transfer reported that:

I was robbed of 60 cents and I'm sure because (the staff from the treatment center) came over and looked at my property slip and it said $1.20. He called this to the attention of the booking desk bull and he said, "Well, You've only got 60 cents here," and said that was all there was.

Ten per cent of the sample had been working as trusties in the jail and reported they actually had seen the police steal money from drunks being booked or take money from their property box. Although this is a small percentage, it must be remembered that some men in the sample had never worked as a trusty and many who had were not in a position to observe this behavior. One man said, "In 1968 I seen a bull taking change out of a prisoner's box and using it for cigarettes on machines." Another man recalled:

Four times I was coffee man for the officers and could watch all the bookings and the crookings. I have saw them book a man, put his property box away, ten minutes later go get the box, step behind the rack of clothes, take the money out, put the box back. Sometimes split with another bull. When they count the money they put a little on your slip and the rest they take. I have saw one, in fact, count money four times waiting for clearance, and then he shoved $50 in his pocket.

Tramps are most keenly aware that at every point they receive different kinds of treatment than those they refer to as "citizens" or "up-town tramps." A well-dressed man is seldom robbed, beaten, or cursed because he is likely to cause a problem, and if the police make a mistake and take property from a man who is not a tramp they may have experiences similar to the following:

I was uptown and there was this well-dressed guy got picked up, too, and he had a suit on, I mean, he wasn't no tramp. So when we went down to get our property he was just ahead of me, but he told me in the tank, he says, "They wouldn't let me make a phone call." He had $220 bucks in his property and they wouldn't let him make a phone call or bail out. He said, "Well, I'd better have my $220 and my $500 Longine wrist watch and my gold pocket watch. They'd all better be in there." Well, it wasn't. There wasn't a bit of money in there. He didn't have a dime. Well, boy he argued with them. And they said, "Well what in hell you trying to do — get smart with us? You get too damn smart we'll put you back in that tank." He said, "I don't give a damn how long you put me in the tank, I got $220 and two watches and I aim to get them. I'm not leaving here until I get them." Well, nobody knew nothing about them, no property slip and nothing marked down. So he stayed there and I left and said, "I want to see you when you get out," and he said, "I'll see you down there." So, about 10:30 or 11:00 he came walking down First Avenue, and I said, "Well how did you make out?" He held up his arm and said, "Well, there's my wristwatch." He showed me his pocket watch. He said, "I got my $220." I said, "Where was it?" He said, "I had to go downstairs to the first floor to get it. I asked them down there how in hell they got ahold of $220 and two watches when I had them in my pocket when I got upstairs?" Well, nobody knew nothing, there was nothing signed, no officer's name or a thing. But he got his two watches and his money. Would they ever do that for a tramp? No!

Whenever tramps get together one of the topics of conversation is the strategies employed to keep money from being lost at the booking desk. One man told of his Indian friend who was arrested with a large sum of money:

I had a friend of mine who had just come down from Alaska and he got picked up and was in a group that I was at the time of booking. He had $3,700 on him. And when he came into the jail he was in line waiting to be booked and became aware of what might happen. Suddenly he began to scratch himself all over in a very nervous way. The officer said, "What's the matter with you?" and my friend said, "I've got the seven-year itch. I just came down from Alaska to see a doctor." Because of this they wouldn't touch him. They put him in the drunk tank and allowed him to bail out the next morning without ever removing his property.

Although tramps sometimes discount experiences reported by other men at the hands of the police, some are in a position to make observations which are considered more reliable and reinforce the validity of personal experience. When a man is robbed or worked over at the booking desk, a trusty may observe this and then will tell his friends, who pass the word quickly on to others. The networks of communication among tramps in jail and on the street are well developed. The man who learns of the latest injustice and is getting out of jail the next day will tell his friends on Skid Road, not just to complain, but also to augment their store of information about what to expect the next time they are arrested. The more frequently a person observes violence in jail, the more certainly he comes to believe that it is a myth that a *tramp* is considered innocent until proven guilty. One man observed:

I have personally saw them grab a man from behind while two holding him and choke him to the floor and drag him to the drunk tank; I have saw two hold a man up to the window and because he was drunk and wouldn't answer questions another jailer stood there and punched him in the ribs six or eight times until he fell to the floor. I have saw the jailers take money from drunks at the window, put it in their pocket.

An older Indian informant who had been around Seattle for many years reported:

I was on as night coffeeman in the jail and I saw the bulls dividing up money they had taken from a tramp after they had booked the guy. Once they were booking a man and slammed his face into the booking desk. And then they called me over and I had to wipe up the blood. The man's nose would be bleeding and his lip would be bleeding from where his teeth hit the booking desk and they would take him to the doctor the next day or so and tell him he had fallen down. I do think that picking up drunks saves them from getting killed, but they give them too much time.

154

Another man recalled:

Two fellows were being booked for drunk, and one for interfering with an arrest. The one that was stupid drunk was talking as only a drunk can and after they had booked them he started to walk over to sit on a bench and one officer grabbed him and shoved him into the wall and down he went and started to cuss. They both grabbed him and started to hit him in the face a couple of times and then about six times in the stomach and then they put or dragged him to a padded cell.

When this kind of incident occurs in the presence of other inmates, some waiting to be booked and others working as trusties, it is a reminder to them, as well as the victim of this violence, to keep their place, never step out of line, and never speak out against these injustices.

The booking desk has one further significant effect on these men who are undergoing an identity change and that is *creating a "record."* One of the critical factors in determining the treatment of a tramp who repeatedly makes the bucket in his arrest record. Every individual has a unique history and seeks to portray an image to others by concealing some information about his past and disseminating other historical facts. When a man's record becomes too widely known, especially those things which are socially defined as failure, he may be able to maintain self-respect only by traveling to a new city where his past is not known. At the booking desk he is asked about his past arrest record at the very moment he is creating a new one. The record made at the booking desk is, in a sense:

a violation of one's information preserve regarding self. During admission, facts about the inmate's social statuses and past behavior — especially discreditable facts — are collected and recorded in a dosier available to staff (Goffman 1961:23–24).

This record then becomes part of the court file on each man and is used to determine the severity of his sentence. Later it may be much more widely disseminated, as explained in the study made by the International Association of Chiefs of Police:

Under the open-door policy of the administration, Record Bureau personnel feel obligated to provide any information which the news media may desire. They also readily give information to what must be considered unauthorized personnel such as credit corporations and businesses in the area (1968:417).

The man who is attempting to maintain regular employment or to resist being drawn into the world of the tramp may find that his record alienates him from the rest of society and, more importantly, from himself as a worthy, respectable human being. Any success at passing as an average citizen, whether it be for employment, housing, or friendship, may crumble when others discover his "record." Although *he* may know that many of his arrests were simply due to his visibility in the Skid Road area, it is not easy to convince others that this was the case.

STAGE 6: PADDED DRUNK TANK

From the booking desk it is a short distance down a hallway to the padded drunk tank. A thin layer of cork covers the floor to cushion the body as one sleeps off a state of intoxication or awaits the next stage of the ritual. Most men have very few memories of this tank because the time spent there is brief or they are too drunk to remember what transpired. The only instance reported where a man was returned to the padded drunk tank occurred when an inspection was made in the jail. A young merchant seaman, who was 29, had arrived in Seattle and was arrested several times. While waiting for his appearance in court this incident occurred:

> I was in the cement drunk tank with about 40 guys. They had some visitors coming through the jail and they took several of us out of the cement drunk tank and gave us each two blankets and put us in the padded drunk tank. It had a rubber floor. They brought us in food, they heaped our trays with stew for dinner at 4:30, and the visitors came through and everything looked great.

Tramps are aware of such subterfuge and it is one of the reasons they believe no one can discover their plight and you "can't change city hall."

STAGE 7: X-RAY, MUG, AND PRINT ROOM

On most journeys through the revolving door the processing which goes on in this room — photographing, fingerprinting, and X-ray — are routine, but tramps know they cannot relax their vigil, they

156

cannot allow themselves to digress for a moment from the path toward total submission, or they will quickly be reminded of their subordinant position vis-à-vis the bulls, as one man discovered:

There was a cop in there I'd never seen before. They take your picture and they take your fingerprints and X-ray. They sat four of us down on a bench, John and I and one or two others, and they called us in, you know, one at a time. I had a cigarette in my hand, I guess, so I turned around to put the cigarette out and then came back in and this cop said, "What in the hell are you walking around for?" Well I said, "I was putting out my cigarette." He said, "Get up there and take that X-ray." So I went over to that X-ray machine and stood there for ten seconds and then I got up and started to go to the door again and because he was pissed off anyway he pushed my face into the X-ray machine. When he did that and I turned around to complain to him he figured I was going to swing on him, which I might have, I don't know, but at any rate he hit me and broke three of my ribs. He was a big cop. He's sober and I'm drunk and he bust three of my ribs and I wore a belt for that for about six weeks. That was early in 1968. You know they don't like to hit you in the face. They'll give you the body punch so it won't show, if you know what I mean.

The mug, print, and X-ray room is like a watershed in the rituals we are considering. Any man who has been through this process more than once knows that the poor are separated here from the not-so-poor. After a man is sober enough to be processed in this room, he also is sober enough to post a bail of $20, walk out of the jail as a free man, shaking off the experience of the last few hours, and feeling secure because he has been immune to the stigmatizing influence of these first stages in making the bucket. He does not have to lie in the drunk tank for several days. He does not have to appear in court as a bum. He does not have to go through the interminable waiting in holding tanks or be deloused. Most important, he does not have to spend the next few months paying a debt to society for appearing drunk in public. He has bought his way out for $20. He has purchased a clean slate, a new sense of self, an *immediate* opportunity to assert himself and release all the pent-up hostility he may have felt toward the system — all for only $20. And he can continue bailing himself out forever if he has the resources or friends who will pay. But what does this separation based on monetary qualifications say to the poor? What does it symbolically tell the man who sees others post their bail, who tries to phone a friend or bondsman for the needed money, only to fail again and enter the drunk tank with the knowledge that he could have been free if he had not been poor — a poverty which may have been incurred only a few hours earlier at the hands of his captors? One well-educated tramp summed up the message that this has for urban nomads:

I think the alcoholic or the drunk is considered to be the lowest human form in the jail and you can't help being used. There is a tremendous hiatus between $20 and six months in jail. Most everyone is capable of earning more than $20 a day. It doesn't take that long to sober up. And this is the only charge they have against him. The drunk can be arrested six days a week, every day of the week. It will never cost him more than $20 to remove himself from that jail. And so, are you a landowner or are you a peon? That's about what it amounts to. It's completely unfair. There is just no conceivable explanation for it.

STAGE 8: CEMENT DRUNK TANK

Until he is finally placed in the cement drunk tank a man may harbor the hope of escaping at least a part of the ritual of making the bucket. He may be released on the street, the police car may not take him to jail, he may have enough money to bail out, or he may find a friend who will post bail for him. These hopes are almost entirely extinguished when he is thrown in this drunk tank. Old memories and feelings now sweep over him. Back again! Back again to take up his other life as an inmate. He knows what to expect for he has seen it all before in other jails, if not this one: the cold cement floor which will leave him bone sore; trusties running here and there in their service to the bulls; the grey walls which seem to reflect his own drab image of himself; the great gulf between him and those who might give support to his crumbling identity; the pill pusher warily dispensing his envelopes of aspirin; and then on beyond to the court where he knows with certainty that his guilt has already been established. He knows that time will change its shape and form to become an onerous task to be done, no longer a valuable possession to be spent.

Events have moved rapidly for the tramp who has gone through the first stages of the ritual. From the street to the call box, into a paddy wagon and up the elevator, through the booking desk process and on into the padded drunk tank for a few hours of sleep, X-rays and pictures follow in quick succession. And then suddenly, as the heavy door closes on the cement drunk tank, time seems to wind backwards. The number of days spent there will vary from one arrest to the next depending upon the day of the week. If arrested on Tuesday, a man will spend one day and night in the tank, going to court on Wednesday. On weekends it is a different story. More than 90 per cent of the sample reported that the longest period they had waited in this drunk tank before going to court was two days or more. When a man is arrested on Friday morning he must wait until Monday's court session, or even longer if there are holidays in the coming week. During February, 1968, there was a holiday on Monday, followed by election day on Tuesday, and finally the first court session of the week was on Wednesday. The longest periods the men had spent in the drunk tank are:

1 day	7%
2 days	13%
3 days	34%
4 days	31%
5 days	9%
Over 5 days	6%

One man described his experiences:

Well I've been in there when they stack them up like cordwood. I was in there once on a weekend of the 4th of July when we laid there Friday, Saturday . . . and they bring these guys in there, they throw the son-of-a-bitches in there with you, bugs running all over them. They feed you like a bunch of cattle in there, why if they did that to a bunch of dogs in the humane society, Christ Almighty, people would scream bloody murder.

Another recalled:

That drunk tank is really bad. Whether a person is guilty or innocent when he is picked up he is thrown in that drunk tank. There's no blankets, no beds, there's shit and piss all over the floor. You're thrown in there with guys who are diseased and sick and if you get in there on a Friday you stay in there for two or three days.

159

While he lies on the floor in this tank a man will often ponder his experiences of making the bucket. He remembers the times when he met a friendly cop who helped him to his room or allowed him to go on down the street to find a flop for the night. He thinks of the times he has been handled with care and gentleness even though arrested, and the times he has seen men who are drunk turn on a cop with a broken bottle; he knows their work is not always easy. He recalls the times his money was *not* missing from his property and hopes it will be there this time. He remembers the favors done for him by jailers on previous occasions and wonders if they will be as kind again. Such experiences seem to remind him for a moment that, after all, he is not guilty until he has had his day in court, but such fleeting thoughts quickly fade with the awareness of the cold cement, the days which lie ahead, and sometimes he is forced from his reverie by more brutal reminders, as one man who recalled:

In 1963 one time I was in the drunk tank asleep on my stomach in front of the door. I was back far enough away from the door so it wouldn't bump me when it opened. All of a sudden — Boom! Something landed on me and knocked the wind out of me. They had tossed a colored guy right in on top of me. He cussed the bulls, and they came in with black-shot-lined gloves and took him out. He was brought back in about four or five hours with his jaw wired together. He looked all beat up. They had broken his jaw and had beaten him up and then had taken him to the hospital. I saw him later and he was still beat up and his jaw wired together for three or four weeks.

The cement drunk tank is not a comfortable place to spend several days. There are no bunks in this room, meant to hold about 35 men, and only one toilet and wash basin. Only 3 per cent of the sample reported ever receiving a blanket. The lights are left on 24 hours a day and there is nothing resembling privacy, but the most abhorrent part of this experience is the crowding, which makes it impossible for a man to protect himself from being contaminated by others. One man described these conditions graphically:

They'll take a man and throw him in the damn drunk tank, maybe 70 in there, some of them's got TB, some of them's got something else. Got one damn cup to drink in. When a man is drunk, he can lay on that concrete, if he's drunk, he'll go to sleep. But I think it should be made that when a man gets sober to take him out of that damn place and put him in a decent place where he can sleep anyway. But if

160

you've got a holiday, say Monday is a holiday, you get in on Friday nite and Monday is a holiday, you lay right there on that damn concrete until Tuesday morning and you can imagine what you're going to look like when you go in front of the judge, needing a shave, dirty, clothes all wrinkled up to beat hell.

The number of men who are placed in this tank may range from two or three to nearly one hundred. Those who had actually counted the number of men during a 24-hour period reported an average of 69 inmates (66 per cent had made such a count). In order to get a better estimate regarding the degree of crowding, tramps were asked if they had ever spent a night in the drunk tank when it was so crowded they could not lie down. Eighty-three per cent of the men reported this had been the case and nearly half of these said it happened most of the time. One man recalled:

That's all right if you're a young fellow, you can take it. It's miserable but you can take it. Sometimes, I don't know what the reason for it is, it doesn't make sense for you at all, but I've been in there when there is standing room only, in one of those concrete cells, for two or three days. There's barely room to sit down. You certainly can't lie down without putting your face in someone's dirty socks or something like that. And this is when there are two or three other tanks available that are completely empty. There's no reason why they don't take half of them and put them in another one, except they don't want to bother to clean it up.

The loss of such bodily comforts and personal privacy "reflects a loss of self-determination, too, for the individual tends to insure these comforts the moment he has resources to expend" (Goffman 1961:44). The physical discomfort in itself is not unbearable; after all, tramps have slept on cold hard cement before without a blanket. The thing which is so devastating is that one is being treated as an animal, is being robbed of what he feels should be his right, is being told symbolically that he is not a human being worthy of respect and better treatment. He has lost control of his life, and the drunk tank reminds him of this as nothing else could. As he lies there waiting for court, the stripping process reaches a crescendo.

In order to maintain a sense of reliance, esteem, and integrity the human self is constantly reorienting itself to physical and social reference points. Extreme sensory deprivation has a devastating effect upon the personality because it cuts the individual off from the most immediate features of his environment which locate and define the self. Though each new stage of making the bucket further deepens the unsettling experience of being arrested, the drunk tank is especially crucial because it cuts the tramp off from the rest of society by setting up an almost impenetrable *communication barrier* between those in the tank and those outside. This gap is all the more devastating because, unlike the bars and locked steel doors which are visible, the communication barrier is intangible and its existence is denied by outsiders. When a tramp reaches the cement drunk tank he has a great need for assistance. His mind is filled with questions about the threads of his life outside the bucket: Where is my car? Who will notify my employer so I will not lose my job? What will happen to my clothes and other belongings when the room rent is not paid tomorrow? Where are my glasses? How will I explain this to my family and employer? Who will believe I was robbed by the police? How can I get in touch with an attorney? Who could I get to bail me out? If he is going to get information and assistance in answering these questions he needs help from someone outside the jail. He has other immediate questions which are often more pressing: How can I get a cigarette? What will I do when I start getting the shakes? Will I go into delayed DT's? What is left in my property? Where are my identification papers? Can I get some medicine for my chronic ailments? Can I make a phone call? Can I get a pencil and paper and even a stamp for writing a letter? As these questions pour through his mind, the man in the drunk tank has already learned there will be difficulties in answering them. One man summed up the meaning of this communication barrier when he said: "They do all in their power to degrade you mentally and physically as a human being. No outside contact. If you haven't got money you are dead in the water."

The communication barrier is made up of a complex chain of people a man must get to act on his behalf. Those who can offer assistance for the most critical needs are the farthest removed from him. Chart 5.2 shows the major links in this communication chain: A man's most immediate needs are often for cigarettes, food, and information about the state of his property. He has lost control

CHART 5.2

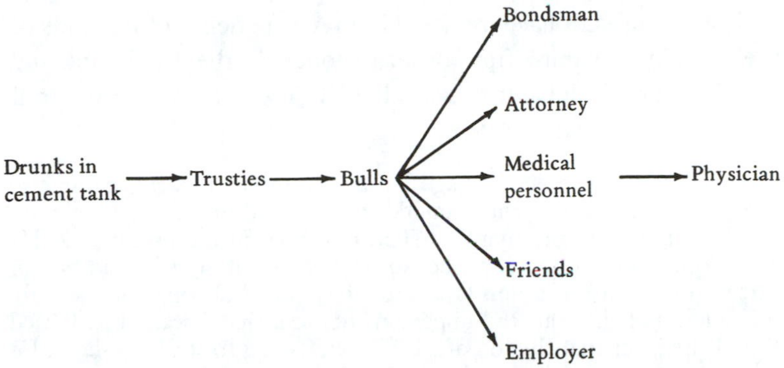

```
                                                    ,Bondsman
                                          ,Attorney
  Drunks in                    Medical
  cement tank  ──► Trusties ──► Bulls ◄    personnel  ──► Physician
                                          `Friends
                                           `Employer
```

over all of these items. Although food is served three times a day it is never enough and he may have arrived in the cement tank just after the last meal of the day was served and so must wait from 5 P.M. on one day until early the next morning. If he has been able to smuggle some money into the drunk tank in his clothing he can pay a trusty fifty cents or a dollar to "hustle" him a cup of coffee or get something from his property, but he can never depend on this. Some men have given trusties as much as ten dollars, and after waiting for them to return with cigarettes, coffee, and change, find only that they have disappeared with all the money. The man who has a request which must be carried to the bulls is also in a difficult position:

You cannot get tobacco, cigarettes in your property, under any circumstances, and they take all cigarettes and matches when you go in. Any request you might have is either refused, stalled, or you are told to ask some other particular individual, whom you will never get to see. About all the contact you have is with a trusty. Even though he might want to help you he can't and is so scared of being busted that he won't take a chance on doing anything. Even to telling an officer you want to see him. You have no record of your possessions.

The trusty must be on guard not to talk with the drunks or bother the bulls too much or he will suffer the consequences. As one former trusty reported, "I did the rest of my sentence in the drunk tank myself for talking to the drunks, giving them cigarette papers, tobacco, and matches."

If a man's money is stolen by a trusty who promised to bring him cigarettes or coffee, he cannot complain to the bulls since it is against the rules to have money. He may experience other kinds of theft or physical abuse from other prisoners in the drunk tank and even here find it difficult to get adequate protection from the staff of the jail. One man recalled:

I remember about three years ago I was working in a logging camp and had just come to town and I ended up in the drunk tank. I woke up and I caught some guy trying to steal my shoes in the drunk tank. He was taking them off my feet, see, so we got into it, and he had two or three buddies in the drunk tank, and I started hollering for the bull, the jailer, and they put the finger on me, see, that I started it. I tried to tell the jailer that the son-of-a-bitch was trying to steal my shoes. I'd sobered up by that time and that big jailer, he says, "You come out here." He took me over into an empty tank and I knew what was comin' then. He slammed the door shut and he walks up to me and says, "You think you're pretty tough, huh?" I seen it coming, you know, and held my breath and he hit me in the guts as hard as he could. He didn't even knock me down, I just stepped back two or three feet and he kind of looked at me, you know, and that was it. He didn't knock me down the first time, so he left me alone, and I said, "What in hell did you do that for?" He didn't answer me but if I had swung on him, which I could have done, well then they'd have brought in two or three more, you know, and really whipped my ass.

If a man calls a bull he may be misunderstood, but sometimes the bulls will not respond even if they do get a message from a trusty about some problem in the drunk tank. One man summed up the feelings of many tramps when he said:

Most jailers are *"too busy"* to bother when called. I saw a man die in the city drunk tank when he fell and cracked his head. Saw a man die in the next bed at the city jail — *no attention.*

The jailers usually check the drunk tank periodically and a man might talk directly to a bull at these times. However he makes contact, directly or through a trusty, he often finds they will not listen to his problems. Some tramps felt that both trusties and bulls were selected for their lack of sympathy with others and this made it even more difficult to gain their help. One man made the following observation:

They put overbearing trusties in charge and officers being disciplined for a wrong he committed while on outside duty by being made a jailer. These men then take out their disappointment on prisoners.

Such an observation was also made by the International Association of Chiefs of Police survey:

In earlier days, it was believed that a strong arm and sadistic temperament were the qualifying characteristics of a guard or jailer in a penal institution. This situation has not changed radically in some communities, but in others either an enlightened public, or legislation, has forced the upgrading of personnel and programs in local custodial facilities. . . . There are no official departmental standards of selection for sworn personnel assigned to the city jail. If, in fact, there are any prerequisites at all for positions in the facility, the standard is that the officers so assigned have become a disciplinary problem within another division of the department or the officer concerned has allegedly developed a personality conflict with his superiors. . . . The usual disciplinary problem of those now assigned is reported to be that of drinking. It would appear that the city jail, with the high percentage of inmates confined under conditions involving the use of intoxicants, would hardly be an appropriate assignment for sworn officers who have clearly demonstrated that they have a drinking problem themselves (1968:476).

If the bulls are not sympathetic, a man believes he may be able to contact a bondsman, attorney, employer, or friend who will help extricate him from the jail. He still can bail out since he has not been to court, but if he is to get money, it must be from his property or from some outsider. The man who has asserted himself at any point or "bucked the bulls" has increased the chances he will not get money from either source. One man reported,

In 1968 I had money to bail out but they wouldn't let me because I refused to sign a property slip when I couldn't have a copy of it. When I ask him to let me bail out he told me I was still drunk.

The men in the sample were asked how many phone calls they were allowed to make when waiting for court in the drunk tank. They gave the following responses:

None:	10%
One:	85%
More than 1:	2%
It depends:	3%

Although most men agree that there is the privilege of one phone call, 32 per cent of the sample reported they had been refused permission to make a phone call while they were in the drunk tank. The reasons, as perceived by these men, were varied: "The bulls

were too damn busy when I asked in 1962, 1963, 1967, and 1968."
"I asked to make a phone call to bail out on and they wouldn't let me." "I asked to call my daughter and was rudely refused." "The bull says he don't have time, but the trusty tells us they are drinking coffee and playing cards. This happened in 1968."

The man who does not conform to such customs as regular employment, family living, and a permanent place of residence with an address, finds the privilege of a single telephone call next to useless. The call may be allowed at a time when those he wishes to contact are not available. If he tries one time and they are not in, he has lost contact with the outside world for another day at the very least. This problem was summed up by one man who stated:

The one phone call is allowed late in the evening and almost invariably you are unable to contact your party. That is considered "tough shit" by the bulls and you may not have another chance for another week depending on who is on duty.

A man may need to contact several people until he finds one who will bail him out, get his money, pay for his room, get his clothing, or assist him in some other way. Some had the feeling, as Mr. Tanner noted, that they were being held *incommunicado*. This communication barrier not only keeps one from satisfying certain desires, but by keeping a man cut off from the rest of society it reaffirms the alienation that has begun to grow — an alienation from himself as well as others.

The man who is in the drunk tank waiting to go to court is probably in greater need of medical care than at any other time while making the bucket. He may be suffering from malnutrition, withdrawal symptoms after a protracted period of intoxication, or injuries from the earlier stages of this ritual. During the research there were many debates among community leaders in Seattle regarding the quality of medical care in the jail. A physician who had some responsibility for the jail hospital described the treatment as adequate:

Every prisoner is seen at least once per day. In the jail the doctor makes the rounds at least once a day. In the morning all the inmates are lined up and they go before the doctor and he sees if anything major is wrong with them. They go to court and after court they can come and see him. Evening rounds are sometime between 6 and 7 o'clock. The jailer can call the doctor out any time during the night. At 7 in the morning they are lined up and passed before the physician. The only difference in treatment at some other kind of treatment center is that they are not behind bars.

Another physician felt that the jail provided an almost ideal situation for alcoholics: "All things now are provided in jail — emergency medical treatment and interruption of drinking." These views were in direct contrast to those of the inmates. In the sample, 46 per cent of the men indicated they had needed medical care when they were in the drunk tank but had not received it. A man's symptoms may be minor, like those of the man who said, "I had a bad cold and asked for cough syrup and was only given an asprin." Others had more serious problems: "I had a broken thumb. I could move it a little so I was declared OK." "In January, 1968, I had the DT's and was thrown into a padded cell for three days. Still in DT's I was taken to court and given a suspended sentence." "I had an alcoholic seizure and was merely allowed to lie there until it was over." When asked to evaluate the quality of medical care in the jail, the men in the sample gave the following responses:

Very good	1%
Better than average	1%
About average	26%
Below average	16%
Very poor	56%

The discrepancy between the views of inmates and others who had knowledge of the treatment procedure is best understood by understanding the communication barrier. Medical personnel or physicians may give the best of care to those they see, but they are probably not aware of the ones they are not allowed to see. The tramp in the drunk tank knows he must often get through the trusties and bulls before he will get any medical care. They report that, "The bull always says to wait 'til morning before court time," or "I could not get an officer to let me see the doctor." One man pinpointed the problem when he stated,

Those worthless trusties wouldn't give information to the police when a drunk was really sick, and the trusty only laughed about it. I would think the police should see that the cells are checked every half hour.

A man who is not himself sick may observe others who fail to get needed care and such experiences tell him a great deal about how he is defined socially:

On more than one occasion I've looked at men go into DT's, and those bulls just ignore these people, sometimes as long as 30 minutes. I don't know if they are lazy or just too mean to help a sick man.

Several types of medical personnel work in the jail. The man who makes rounds in the morning and evening is sometimes only a medical student, not a fully qualified physician. If one is seriously ill and sees a nurse or medical student, they must, in turn, refer him to a physician who might have to come from another part of the building. At each point in this chain of communication, each person attempts to stop the message and keep from "bothering" those who are above him. The trusty limits messages to the bulls, the bulls to the medical personnel, and they in turn limit the ones which finally get through to the doctor. One research assistant who made observations in the jail related an example which illustrates this problem:

The next patient I saw with the doctor was a rather young Negro, about 19–22 years of age, and he had a rather deep and infected cut between his little finger and his ring finger. Apparently, I learned later, the nurse had seen him earlier in the afternoon and absolutely refused to treat him or to let him see the doctor until he had taken a bath — exactly how long it took him to take his bath and get back to see the doctor I'm not sure, but I'm sure it was a matter of at least an hour or two — this infection had already spread to the back of the hand where it showed it had pain and swelling.

A man who is lying on the drunk tank floor, alone and isolated in the middle of the night, when he begins to be aware of symptoms within his own body, feels the isolation more than anyone else. He knows he will probably have difficulty in reaching the doctor, and even then he may not get adequate care. One man eloquently expressed this feeling:

Late one night in the drunk tank my heart began palpitating and missing beats. The bull took me to the dispensary and awakened the doctor who scoffed at my complaint and said I was making too much noise for such a little man, and anyway that I brought it all on myself. So back to the drunk tank I went.

One more complexity in the communication gap devastatingly affects the normal relationship between a physician and patient in our society. Tramps are usually poor and when they go to jail they are often without any resources except their own ingenuity. Almost any item they get can be turned into money or something to trade for food, cigarettes, and other commodities. A full description of their skills along this line is reserved for a later chapter, but the medicine dispensed by the physician is especially significant. One man summarized the way in which tramps sometimes use this medicine:

Speaking of survival in jail, there are various ways, of course. If you come in with some money, of course you have commissary twice a week. That way you can get 8 packages of cigarettes and 8 candy bars, a toothbrush, toothpaste and that's about the limit of what you can buy and of course postage stamps. Now these cigarettes, 5 cigarettes is roughly worth 10 cents, and so is a candy bar, and so is Bull Durham worth 10 cents. These are all trade items, that's provided you have commissary. If you do not have commissary you have to find other means, if you wish to have more than two packs of Bull Durham a week. One of these means is that when you first come in you might be very nervous, shaky, and very uncomfortable, particularly if you've been on a concrete floor for the first few days, and just eating coffee and toast before court, no soup at all at the midday waiting for court, and at the end of the day you are pretty well shot. In any case you are shaking for the first few days from nothing more than malnutrition, and so one asks the doctors who come around twice a day, once in the morning about 7:30 and then at about 7 o'clock at night. They make the rounds of all the cells. At that time you might ask him for some librium, or some phenobarbitol to quiet you, or whatever you might be able to get from him, cold pills even, but the wise drunk who has no money at all will just go through the whole thing cold turkey, suffer though he will, he will save his pills and trade two quarter-grain phenobarbitol for a package of Bull Durham, or 1.25 mg. librium for a pack of Bull Durham. This is more or less the going price. And so, for the first three or four days, he'll be collecting from the doctor because he will still be shaking. Some of them will even do push-ups or something like that before the doctor comes, just to be shaking and sweating. Rather than taking these things themselves, because they are essentially alcoholics and have gone through it cold turkey so many times they can handle it. You build up your Bull Durham to last you as long as you can. Of course, eventually, on weekends when relief doctors come in, if you haven't seen them before, you can get even more even though you've been in for three weeks.

Thus, a man in the drunk tank, and in other parts of the jail, may be trying to get the physician to give him pills that he can trade to others for cigarettes, candy bars, or other food. The medical staff learns to suspect the complaints of the inmate and the inmate learns to con the medical staff. When a leading physician in Seattle states, "I find it hard-put to think that any other facility is going to be able to offer better care, other than the bar bit, than in the jail," he may be speaking in good faith but he fails to understand how the very structure of the jail destroys the usual doctor-patient relationship, so necessary for adequate medical care.

Earlier in this chapter we stated that making the bucket is like a rite of passage for these men, drawing a man out of one society and thrusting him into another, at the same time transforming his self-concept. We have examined events of the first eight stages: on the street, at the call box, in a paddy-wagon or car, in the elevator, at the booking desk, in the padded drunk tank, in the X-ray, mug, and print room, and in the cement drunk tank. A single trip through would be an unsettling experience for most Americans, but for these men it has a powerful ritual quality because of the repetitive, timeless character of the entire cycle. In city after city across our land there are thousands of men at this moment being inducted into the tramp world by making the bucket. The details of the ritual vary from one city to another but the effect is the same: a man is alienated from himself and the rest of society as he is stripped of his former identities and labeled a bum. The vacuum created by such alienation sets the stage for being further degraded and then motivated and taught to live by the culture of urban nomads.

CHAPTER SIX

They Make You
Feel Like a Bum

Time drags its feet in the drunk tank. The hours creep by, turning slowly into days and nights to be endured. The men think
about food, count the hours until they will appear in court, rack
their brains for someone who could bail them out, swap experiences of other jails, listen eagerly to newcomers with word from
outside, and wonder where they will travel when they are released. Uppermost in the minds of most men are thoughts of
"beating their drunk charge." A newcomer may soon learn, as one
informant put it, that " 'you can't beat a drunk charge' is a common expression in Seattle." He also learns that though this is a
common expression, it is not altogether true. Various strategies are
used to "beat the charge," with the relative success weighed on a
scale that runs from a few hours to as much as six months in jail.
In the past this has even stretched out to be a full year in jail for a

171

single offense. Before we return to the next stages of making the bucket, it would be well to point out the ways a man learns to lessen the effect of being convicted for public drunkenness since the strategies he may use are germain to the experience tramps have in court.

These strategies form a domain in the culture of urban nomads which may be called "ways to beat a drunk charge." The terms and phrases which make up this domain were not all elicited from informants in the same way as the domains previously presented. The terms and the resultant componential analysis were discovered by carefully analyzing field notes related to this domain. Many published analyses of domains, such as kinship, are constructed in this *post hoc* manner and require verification, and, though I have the feeling from long acquaintanceship with informants that this analysis does reflect their view, such an assertion has not been tested with question frames in the interview situation. The members of this domain which make up a contrast set are shown in Table 6.1. The man who constantly makes the bucket learns to order much of his life in ways which will enable him to avoid arrest, and, if he fails in that, to limit the influence of jail on his life. By knowing the ways to beat a drunk charge with their relative degrees of cost and risk, he can at least make an informed choice. As we discuss the next two stages of making the bucket, these strategies will be our subject.

STAGE 9: COURT DOCKET

The drunk tank on the sixth floor of the jail opens its heavy door about 8:00 each morning, Monday through Friday, for the drunks to file out, down the hallway, through the main lobby past the booking desk, up the stairs, and through a maze of corridors to the court docket. This room is much like the cement drunk tank except it is smaller and is filled with rows of steel benches where the men await court. On most days, just before court begins, a counselor for the alcoholism treatment center appears to explain their program and how a person can qualify for it. Most men are sitting sleepily on the benches or lying on the floor, some still fighting the pains of a hangover or withdrawal from a long drunk. The waiting and wondering are sharply interrupted when a small speaker box

TABLE 6.1 TAXONOMIC DEFINITION OF WAYS
TO BEAT A DRUNK CHARGE

Ways to beat a drunk charge									Make a statement					
Bail out	Bond out	Request a continuance	Have a good record	Use an alias	Plead guilty	Hire a defense attorney	Plead not guilty	Submit a writ of habeas corpus	Talk of family ties	Talk of present job	Talk of intent to work	Tell of extenuating circumstances	Offer to leave town	Request the treatment center

begins to bark loudly from one corner of the docket. The officer in charge lines up the men as each hears his name and ushers them into the courtroom. They move in groups of about twenty-five into the small area to the right and front of the judge's bench, barricaded from the rest of the courtroom by a railing. They are crowded into this space and told where to stand by the officer, where they remain, lined up three deep, pressed together, holding their hats in their hands, heads down, waiting for the judge to speak.

STAGE 10: COURTROOM

As the men stand waiting for the judge to tell them of their rights, their thoughts may flash back to other times they have stood in

173

this very spot, much as Mr. Tanner's did while he was serving time in jail:

Judges are notoriously capricious, careless, and at times could care less when sentencing a drunk. The good magistrate commands my admiration for the consummate ease, dispatch, skill, and judgment he exercised Tuesday morning. Never, but never (it beggars verbal description) have these astigmatic orbs witnessed a more electric or superb judicial travesty. I felt like doing a Finnish fling when on Tuesday the judge said, "I'm going to help you Mr. Tanner — 30 days." I tried to conceal my joy and queried, "May I use the phone and have some writing paper?" "Why certainly, the officers will take care of minor requests such as yours." I replied, "I beg to differ. . . ." "That will be all, Tanner. Next case."

Such thoughts will soon be interrupted by the calm voice of the judge:

You men have all been charged with drinking in public, drunk in public, or begging which are in violation of the ordinances of the city of Seattle. The maximum penalty for these crimes is $500 fine and/or 180 days in jail. You have a right to plead guilty or not guilty. You have a right to consult a lawyer before you enter a plea of guilty or not guilty. If you want to consult a lawyer you must pay for your own attorney. The court does not have provisions for this. If you wish a continuance, please indicate when you return to court. On a plea of guilty you waive your rights to appeal to a higher court. On a plea of not guilty your case will be continued for trial at a later date. Now return to the court docket and when you are called in you will enter a plea of guilty or not guilty. If you wish to make a statement you may do so.

The "rights speil," as Mr. Tanner fondly dubbed it, takes less than a minute to complete. The men are then hurried back into the court docket to listen for their names again. Though current practice is to inform the men of their rights, that has not always been done in this court. Under present practices oversights do occur and when there is a large group of men, some may be arraigned individually without being called out in a group and informed of their rights. The court has a very large task in hearing the drunk cases — during 1967, this court handled 17,367 cases; 11,265, or just under 65 per cent of the case load, were "Drunk in Public." The number of men appearing in court on this charge averages about 70 persons per day.

When a man hears his name for the second time he returns to

174

the courtroom alone. He faces the judge's bench, separated by the railing and the prosecuting attorney for the city of Seattle who says, "You have been charged with the crime of public drunkenness, how do you plead?" If a man enters a plea of guilty, and over 90 per cent of them do so, the prosecutor reads his prior record to the judge who will sentence him according to a pre-set formula based on his record. A man may plead guilty or not guilty, ask for a continuance, make a statement, or request he be sent to the alcoholism treatment center. What he does now sooner or later will lead to a decision on the part of the judge which tells the man how effective he has been in beating the drunk charge. Like players in a game of chess, the tramp and law enforcement officials engage in carefully planned strategies. Although most of the game is played out in the courtroom itself, it involves much of the life style of tramps. The moves made by tramps sometimes occur months before the countermoves by police or judges. In order to understand how tramps define and evaluate what happens in the courtroom we must examine all the "ways to beat a drunk charge."

When a man makes the bucket and he has money, he will usually *bail out*. A phone call to an employer or a call for the purpose of "hustling a friend" may result in the needed $20. If these avenues of escape are closed, he may try to *bond out* by negotiating with a bail bondsman for the needed money at a fee of ten or twelve dollars. Since, in Seattle, he must then return to court and receive a suspended sentence, few men go to a bondsman unless, as in Mr. Tanner's case, they are being held for a trial at a later date; bonding out is a better option in some other parts of the country than in Seattle. Some men are unable to reach an employer or friend prior to going to court, and so they may *ask for a continuance* on their arraignment. The judge will usually grant this, moving up the arraignment several days; then the accused returns to the drunk tank or holding tank where he will attempt to contact someone who can supply him with the money to bail out. Most men will not ask for a continuance unless they are quite sure of a source of money on the outside. Once their arraignment has taken place and they have entered a plea of guilty or not guilty, they cannot post a bail.

The best way to beat a drunk charge is to *have a good record,* a strategy which has wide ramifications for the life style of tramps. In some courts there is one sentence for anyone guilty of public drunkenness, but in Seattle, as in many cities, there is a sliding scale determined by a man's past record. As he stands before the judge, the defendant's record is reviewed from the Common Drunkard File by the prosecutor who reads it to the judge. Those with relatively recent records are sentenced on the basis of the policy set up for "first offenders" shown in Table 6.2. Whereas this is the present practice, this policy is new and, as recently as 1966, men were receiving sentences of six months for drunk convictions. A man who has a long history of convictions is treated as a "prior offender" and will receive long sentences for each conviction, unless he can stay out of jail for six months; then he begins again with a suspended sentence. In order to quickly recognize those who are prior offenders, they are given a five-day suspended sentence on their first offense after a six-month absence, then 20 days for the next three offenses, then 30 and 60 days on subsequent convictions. There is, however, some unpredictability about this sentencing procedure; if a man has been in and out of jail constantly during a four-month period, the judge may give him a *major suspended* sentence of 60 or 90 days. This is done by the

TABLE 6.2 POLICY FOR "FIRST OFFENDERS"

Offense	*Sentence*
First	2 days suspended
Second	10 days committed (may be suspended if 30 days have elapsed since first offense)
Third	20 days committed
Fourth	20 days committed
Fifth	30 days committed
Sixth	30 days committed
Seventh	30 days (if these seven offenses occur within a six-month period, 60 days)
Eighth	30 days (or up to 90 days depending on the case)

judge to give the man another chance to get his drinking behavior under control and a serious warning that he must change his way of living, for if he is arrested again he will have to serve the new sentence as well as the one suspended for the last offense.

Most tramps are quick to learn the pattern of sentencing in a town, either from experience or from other men. They are then in a good position to beat the charge in the most economical way. If a man is new in Seattle and arrested, he learns that he will get a "kickout" or a two-day suspended sentence; he may have $20 with which to bail out, but decides to save it for other needs since he knows he will be released as soon as he goes to court. Tramps learn to keep track of their record and the sliding scale used by the court and then calculate the number of days they will probably get for each offense. One long-time tramp commented on the Seattle court practice:

The judge has a system, even though he's kind of unpredictable. He usually gives first a two-day suspended, then five days suspended, then twenty days, twenty days, thirty days, thirty days, and then sixty days. So when a person goes into court and he's waiting to go to court he knows what he's going to get. If he's going to get thirty days, he says, "I have thirty days hanging."

Whenever tramps are discussing previous experiences in jail and court they explain them by making constant references to how many days they had hanging. It is impossible to understand the actions a man takes, such as bailing out, asking for the treatment center, or pleading guilty unless it is also known how many days he had hanging.

The judge apparently gives sentences of increasing severity, with an occasional major suspended sentence, for two reasons: to reduce the recurrence of a man's drinking sprees, and help him regain his health. Tramps, on the other hand, know they are arrested for many reasons besides their drinking behavior; it is their life style, only one feature of which involves drinking, that brings them into court. Though the punishment imposed by longer sentences may motivate some men to abstain from public drunkenness, it has a much more significant influence for most tramps: *it motivates them to travel*. The life style of urban nomads, with its drinking

177

rituals, provides men with a group of friends wherever they go, men who accept them as they are. If a man stops drinking and sharing drinks, he cuts himself off from the most valuable of all resources, human companionship and acceptance. In order to improve their record in court so as to reduce the amount of time they will do on their next conviction, tramps choose another alternative — leaving town. With each succeeding arrest in Seattle a person's record becomes more tarnished and the number of days he has hanging increases, and every tramp knows this slate could be completely erased by leaving town for six months! One may only go as far as Portland for a few months in the spring, then make the harvest in eastern Washington for the summer before returning to Seattle in the fall with a clean slate. When we consider the category of men called urban nomads, criss-crossing the nation on freight cars or continually traveling from one place to another by other means, it is important to realize that in the town where their trips began each man probably had many days hanging.

The suspended sentence is even more important because of the way in which it increases the mobility of tramps. When a tramp receives a suspended sentence of 90 days, he has escaped doing time but only for the moment; back on the street he walks with the knowledge that he now has probably doubled the number of days he has hanging. If arrested again he will serve the suspended and the new sentence consecutively. After Mr. Tanner had been in Seattle a little less than a year he finally left — and this was his major reason:

I was pinched in Seattle on March 10 and the good judge gave me sixty days suspended sentence. Next time in his court I would have gotten that sixty plus additional so I blew town. I think I'd better get back to Minneapolis or anywhere.

In an earlier chapter it was shown that these men define their identities inside and outside of jail according to an underlying value of environmental anchorage; as tramps they are far less anchored than most other Americans and as inmates they are far more anchored and restricted in their mobility. After a long incarceration a man is motivated to engage in unrestricted mobility as an end in itself; he wants to enjoy his freedom to the utmost since he has just experienced extreme limits on that freedom

Tramps also travel from one place to another because they become "marked men" who are arrested over and over again because of their very presence in the Skid Road district. There is an intimate relationship between mobility and other features of their life style which involve drinking: alcoholic beverages function as a social lubricant at all levels of American society, but they fulfill this need in a special way for urban nomads. Nomadism creates a unique kind of loneliness in an individual, and when he arrives alone in a new town he seeks to find others of his own kind to reduce such anxieties. Almost the only place where he can find acceptance, friendship, and sociability is on Skid Road and in the bars located there. Bars are categorized among tramps in a variety of ways, but especially in terms of what one may find there in the way of friends, female companionship, and work opportunities. For urban nomads, bars function as churches and clubs, employment agencies and dating centers, begging places, drinking and eating places, and flops. Most of all, they are a place to find friendship, even if it is only of a fleeting nature. In a Skid Road bar one is not restricted in his behavior, he can "perform" in ways appropriate to this subculture and know he will be accepted; from other tramps he can freely get information about jail and court and employment. One tramp who wanted to control his drinking behavior clearly saw the relationship between mobility and drinking; he was about to be released from the alcoholism treatment center and commented:

My biggest problem when I get out next week is traveling. When I get in a strange vicinity I head for a bar. If I want work, I go to a bar; that's where they come to hire a man.

Skid Road and its bars, in addition to being a place to solidify new-found friendships with a drink, is also where most arrests for public drunkenness occur. And so we have come full circle: *urban nomads visit Skid Road and its bars because they travel; they are arrested because they live and drink in this area of town; and they travel because they are arrested.* They are indeed induced by American law enforcement agencies to be mobile!

Some of the strategies used to beat a drunk charge are linked together. A man who requests a continuance does so in order to be able to bail out; similarly, a person who *uses an alias* does so to have a good record or escape the one he has created over the past months. As one informant stated, "If they have no previous arrest for a name they usually give a kickout. You've got to beat them some way!" Eleven per cent of the sample said they had used an alias and 35 per cent had known others who had done so. The results are not always the same, and there is some risk involved. The man who uses a fictitious name probably has a record in this jail and court and so runs the risk of being recognized; as one man said, "I have been here for forty-five years and I would be a fool to try." Thirty-three men reported the consequences of using an alias and half of these said it led to a kickout or two-day suspended sentence. The others stated that it resulted in doing more time than one would have received under his own name! One man said, "I was successful as were some others, but some were caught and did *extra* time." Others reported: "If it is found out before the hearing additional time is given, or if he is deservant of a kickout he is given time for the alias." "Some get away but usually they get caught when they go to get their property." "Some have done this and made it; they were gambling on being kicked out the next day. Others were given time for misrepresentation." A man who decides to use this strategy must do so when he is being booked and cannot have any kind of identification on him to contradict his verbal statement. It sometimes leads to embarrassing situations:

They know this or I wouldn't mention names. One Friday Sanders gave the name Johnson as he had time hanging. They called for Johnson many times Friday, Saturday, and Sunday. Monday morning when they called Johnson for court the officer who knew him spotted Sanders and told him he ought to kick his teeth in. Sanders had forgot what name he'd used!

The most widely used way to beat a drunk charge is a passive one — *plead guilty* and hope for the best. Ninety-four per cent of the sample reported they usually pleaded guilty to a drunk charge even when they felt sure they were not really drunk at the time of arrest. Almost 97 per cent of the drunk cases heard in this court result in convictions. Tramps firmly believe that "you can't beat the charge," "you can't win the case," and it doesn't make any difference what you plead, "you are guilty anyway." Most men felt they actually had "no other choice," and it is this feeling that leads them to see this, and other courts, which hear drunk cases, purely as kangaroo courts. Most men also believe they will be rewarded by the judge if they take this passive role and plead guilty. One man stated, "In my opinion you get a lighter sentence"; another said, "It's the best out."

Another important reason given for pleading guilty is that there might be additional punishment if you do not. This could manifest itself in any number of ways. Often it means that one returns to the drunk tank to await trial; more than 30 per cent of those who reported pleading not guilty had waited in the drunk tank for their trial, some for more than ten days. Twenty-seven per cent of the sample had, at one time or another, entered a plea of not guilty, although only four men reported they had been acquitted. One man stated:

The judge told me if I didn't think I was guilty to plead not guilty, which I did. He moved my case ahead 30 days and I spent 30 days in jail, was found guilty and sentenced to 30 days!

It is important to remember how these men feel about the drunk tank and the sense of isolation there. It is an almost unbearable thought to stand in court and know that if you plead not guilty you will return to that place. A man pleads guilty because he can be sentenced soon and start "doing my time." The uncertainty of waiting for the outcome of trial, and the fact that the days you wait for trial may be "dead time," not even counted as part of the sentence you finally receive, are all perceived as punishments for entering an honest plea and they provide sufficient motivation to enter a plea of guilty. Sometimes the sentence given after the trial is over is not even as long as the days spent waiting for the trial! "I stayed in jail twelve days waiting to go to trial and when I did go I was found guilty and given five days. So you can see you just can't win." One who pleads not guilty also runs the risk of offending the arresting officers who must take time to appear in court as witnesses. One man recalled:

I pled not guilty lots of times and they had to appear against me and so they lost a little time and they got mad. Every time the wagon went around and they seen me, to jail I went.

Another said: "If you plead not guilty you have the arresting cops against you so you can't win anyway!"

Finally, men plead guilty most of the time because they believe the courts are in collusion with the police against them. "All a cop has to do is say you were drunk — the judge never goes against a cop!" The American criminal justice system is based on the assumption that a man is innocent until proven guilty and this premise has very significant ramifications for the integrity and self-identity of anyone accused of a crime. He is not placed in the highly vulnerable position of having to prove his innocence — that is assumed; he also has the right to hire *a defense attorney* whose skills not only make it more difficult to find a man guilty, they also throw up a protective shield around the self. Tramps are well aware that hiring an attorney would be an effective strategy; in fact, 56 per cent of the sample said if the court provided a defense lawyer they would avail themselves of his services. On the other hand, if a man had the money to hire a lawyer he could also have bailed out and thus would not have needed one, so while tramps are aware of this means to beat a drunk charge, they never use it. Tramps not only know the assumptions and rules of our legal system, they also know that the law enforcement agencies violate these rules as far as they are concerned: they are assumed to be guilty rather than innocent; they are rewarded for pleading guilty even when they are innocent; they have no way to provide themselves with a defense attorney; and they are punished if they go against the system by pleading not guilty. The network of protections for the innocent are stripped away from the process of criminal justice for these men and in their place is an overwhelming tide of pressure coercing them into violating their own integrity by agreeing with the verdict of the system. He is asked to speak against himself on those occasions when he feels sure he is not guilty, and he knows he must comply because the immediate consequences will be worse than if he defends himself. Mr. Tanner's case beautifully illustrates the consequences of trying to fight the system. Yet the long-range consequences may be devastating: the act of publicly and repeatedly repudiating himself increasingly alienates the man from himself, creating an inner vacuum obliterating his true identity. When he thinks of speaking out in his own defense, when he considers the alternative of pleading not guilty, he remembers that "a drunk's word doesn't mean anything." The days in jail which result from pleading guilty are a minor inconvenience when compared to the effect this process has on the crumbling identity of these men.

Rarely, some men do tell the judge they are *not guilty*. Sometimes this has been effective, as with one man who stated that in Portland, "I waited a week in jail before I was called before the judge again. I was given a dismissal because the arresting officers didn't show." One or two other men reported they were released when the judge actually found them not guilty, but more typically they are found guilty:

My case was postponed until the following afternoon. The arresting officers appeared and tried to make a bad matter worse — said I was breaking the furniture and disorderly — plain outright falsehoods because they were put out by having to appear.

On two occasions I pled not guilty but was found guilty — the presiding judge said, "I have to take the officer's word."

If a man is going to *submit a writ of habeas corpus*, as Mr. Tanner did, he must first plead not guilty and then appeal the conviction to a higher court. The waiting period is long enough to convince most men they should not try to fight the system by this means.

One option usually open to a man in attempting to beat a drunk charge is to *make a statement*. Only 16 per cent of the sample reported they had, on at least one occasion, asked to make a statement in court and not been allowed to do so. The tramp learns which factors influence the judge as he sentences a man to jail for public drunkenness, and his statements reflect these concerns. The following questions which judges asked defendants were recorded from court sessions and reflect the kinds of issues to which the men's statements will respond:

Have you ever been arrested before?
How long have you been in Seattle?
Are you employed?
Are you interested in help?
Do you have a drinking problem?
Are you married?

Do you live with your family?
Can you control your drinking?
If I suspend your sentence can you find a job?
Are you permanently employed?
If I give you an opportunity will you go pick apples?

Equal justice for all under the law is the maxim of this court, yet when we consider to whom the judge gives sentences to and who escapes them, we must conclude that some men are more equal than others. The legal system of America and the criminal justice practice are based on norms and values which are in contrast to those of the urban nomad. Judges are socialized into the dominant society and learn to dispense justice on the basis of those values. This practice means essentially that the man with the *most resources* is rewarded. Unto whom much is given, little shall be required. As a man moves into the world of tramps he loses many of the things which middle-class Americans consider important: steady employment, wife and family, interest in working, and a sedentary existence. The man who has retained any of these resources has a better chance of escaping incarceration than others. We may see how this principle of inequality works by considering each of the major ways to make a statement, which, in turn, are ways to beat a drunk charge.

The man who still has family responsibilities may *talk of family ties* in an effort to get a suspended sentence. He is aware that being a responsible family man is one of the things which separates urban nomads from the rest of society, and any indication that he is still trying to keep from being a bum will carry weight with the judge. One man's case may show what might be done:

Prosecutor:	How do you plead?
Mr. Dancy:	Guilty, with a statement.
Judge:	What is your statement?
Mr. Dancy:	My wife is sick and I desire that you suspend the sentence so that I can take care of my wife.
Judge:	How long has she been sick?
Mr. Dancy:	About ten days.
Judge:	Do you have a job?
Mr. Dancy:	No.
Judge:	Who took care of her while you were in jail and drinking this time?

| Mr. Dancy: | Well, she took care of herself. |
| Judge: | (To the bailiff) Will you please check about Mr. Dancy's wife and see whether she's sick or not and we may suspend the sentence later if this is the case. But now you are sentenced to 20 days in the city jail. |

(Total time: 2 minutes)

Although many men *indicate they have a job*, unless it is a rather permanent one or unless there are some other extenuating circumstances, they are still likely to get a sentence. One man was persistent in the following case:

Prosecutor:	Mr. Smith, you have been charged with drunk in public. How do you plead?
Mr. Smith:	Guilty.
Prosecutor:	Previous record, two days suspended on September 20, just five days ago.
Judge:	Do you wish to make a statement?
Mr. Smith:	I have a job at Snoqualmie Falls and I have money to get there, and if you suspend my sentence I will go there.
Judge:	When did you last work?
Mr. Smith:	It was last week, and then there were three days when they had no work. Please, judge, if you will suspend my sentence I'll leave.
Judge:	Well, you are back too soon.
Mr. Smith:	I'll lose my job.
Judge:	I will have the bailiff verify your work conditions and I will consider it, but for the present you must spend ten days in the city jail.

Another case was more successful:

Prosecutor:	Mr. Blue, you have been charged with drunk in public. How do you plead?
Mr. Blue:	Guilty, with a statement. I asked the officer to lock me up to sober me up.
Judge:	Have you ever had any assistance?
Mr. Blue:	Yes, Alcoholics Anonymous.
Judge:	Are you going back?
Mr. Blue:	Yes, I have a job, I request you suspend my sentence.
Judge:	I'll check on that. I'll suspend your sentence if you get help and a job. Ten days suspended sentence if he has a job.

Many men have been observed who were sentenced although they made such statements as: "I want to hold down my job. I would like to go back to it." "I'm employed and I want to go back to work." "I would like to go back to work. I am a seaman and I expect my papers to be coming in any day. I've been working at another job." Beating a drunk charge by telling the judge about an *intent to work* is most effective when coupled with a willingness to leave town, as in the case below:

Prosecutor:	Mr. Brown, you have been charged with drunk in public. How do you plead?
Mr. Brown:	Guilty.
Judge:	When were you released?
Mr. Brown:	Last Saturday morning. Could I have a break? I want to go pick apples. Last time, I got out of jail and walked around to where the bus was to the apples and when I got to the bus I was waiting in line to get on and the patrol car picked me up.
Judge:	Will you go pick apples if I give you an opportunity?
Mr. Brown:	Yes, I will!
Judge:	30 days suspended.

Many men make statements which tell of *extenuating circumstances,* at least from their point of view. They may deny they were drunk or report on some aspect of their life style which leads to arrest as in the following case:

Prosecutor:	Mr. Lawrence, you have been charged with drunk in public. How do you plead?
Mr. Lawrence:	Guilty.
Judge:	What is his previous record?
Prosecutor:	He received 20 days on August 18, a little more than a month ago, for the second time.
Judge:	Do you have a drinking problem?
Mr. Lawrence:	No sir, I was baby sitting. I stayed up all night the previous night and then I went and dozed off in a tavern.
Judge:	Are you an alcoholic?
Mr. Lawrence:	No, sir.
Judge:	Doesn't your jail record make you feel you have a problem?
Mr. Lawrence:	Well, I always sleep in a bar because I work nights or something of that sort.
Judge:	30 days in the city jail.

(Total time: 1 minute 50 seconds)

Such claims as "I was asleep in my car," or "I just got out of the hospital and I've been taking pills. I had a couple drinks and fell asleep but it was the pills that made me fall asleep," are commonly

186

heard in court but they do not often lead to a suspended sentence. At the least they offer a meager opportunity for a man to attempt to restore his damaged self-respect for having given in to the system and pleaded guilty.

One of the ways of making a statement is to *offer to leave town.* One man stated: "I would like to return to my family in Portland where I live. I will go there to my job." Combining several strategic kinds of statements another man said: "If you can give me one break I can go the pea harvest. I'm ready to go with three others right now. If you can give me 180 days suspended sentence, I'll leave town." In such cases men are offering the judge the only thing they have left in life — their mobility.

During the past few years, a new strategy for beating drunk charges has been added to the list of those which have been available in Seattle: *request the alcoholism treatment center.* In the state of Washington civil commitments may be made for insanity but not for alcoholism so that, when the treatment center opened its doors, the only way for a man to gain entrance was to be committed to jail as a drunk and then be transferred by the judge to serve his time at the treatment center. A typical and often repeated discussion between judge and defendant at the time of arraignment about the alcoholism treatment center follows:

Prosecutor:	Mr. Grant, you've been charged with being drunk in public. How do you plead?
Mr. Grant:	Guilty.
Judge:	What is his past record?
Prosecutor:	He had a previous offense in August and another one this month also, in September.
Judge:	Do you have a drinking problem?
Mr. Grant:	I believe I do.
Judge:	How long has it been out of control?
Mr. Grant:	The last few years. I would like to get help at the new treatment center.
Judge:	You will have the opportunity to be interviewed and we will continue your case for one week.

When a man is considered a good candidate by the judge, he then continues his case, waits for him to be psychologically and medically examined, and finally recommended by the treatment center staff for acceptance. If he is acceptable he will then be sentenced to the treatment center for four months. Sometimes a man is anxious for treatment but does not indicate appropriate interest and goes to jail instead:

Prosecutor:	Mr. Pace, you have been charged with drunk in public. How do you plead?
Mr. Pace:	Guilty.
Judge:	Do you have a drinking problem?
Mr. Pace:	We all have drinking problems but I've worked on mine.
Judge:	Have you had any help?
Mr. Pace:	Yes, I went to Alcoholics Anonymous, but their rules are too stringent. They wouldn't allow working any night job or overtime. I talked to the probation officer and he said try to take their advice.
Judge:	Do you want assistance or do you want to continue as you are?
Mr. Pace:	It depends on how strong the treatment would be.
Judge:	We have a new treatment center but it's only for those who want help and will cooperate with the program. If you don't want to you can go back to the city jail.
Mr. Pace:	Well, I would like to go if their program isn't too stringent.
Judge:	There can be no conditions on your going there. The sentence is 30 days in the Seattle city jail.

The treatment center is viewed by some men as an easier place to do time than in jail and in a sense they "beat their drunk charge" by going there. They may even combine it with other strategies as one man who volunteered for treatment on the basis of the following calculations:

If I'd done my time in there (jail) I might have been back in there doing time now. I think I'm ahead coming out here (treatment center) because I had 60 days hanging and might have gotten another sixty days on the next sentence.

He was to spend four months at the treatment center; then he planned to leave town for two months and then he would begin again with short sentences when he returned to Seattle. Going to the treatment center was a way to help him create a good record for the future!

The major ways of beating a drunk charge form a contrast set and may be defined componentially. This definition is given in

Table 6.3 and shows most of the criteria the men use to calculate the cost and risk of each particular way to beat a drunk charge. The semantic criteria set forth in Table 6.3 show with startling clarity the overwhelming importance of some strategies. Having a good record, for instance, involves *no cost* and *no risk* to the tramp — all he has to do is keep traveling! Mobility is a small price to pay when compared with twenty dollars a man does not have or the prospect of months in jail. Though there is some risk in the outcome if a man pleads guilty, there is a *grave* risk in the outcome, in offending the bulls, in getting more time, and in doing dead time for those who plead not guilty! Some have considered these men to be passive and dependent and one might easily gain such an impression from observing their behavior in court. The important thing from a tramp's point of view is that his very survival depends upon portraying such an attitude to those who hold his life in their hands; perhaps only a fool would carefully calculate the risks involved in pleading not guilty and then continue to do so. Tramps are not fools and they wisely play the role of the passive individual, pleading guilty to a crime of which they may be innocent, in order to partially beat the charge. The degree to which they are able to reduce the consequences of arrest is infinitesimal

TABLE 6.3 COMPONENTIAL DEFINITION OF
WAYS TO BEAT A DRUNK CHARGE

Strategy	Risk of outcome?	Risk offending bulls?	Risk getting more time?	Risk doing dead time?	Money needed?
Bail out	No	No	No	No	$20
Bond out	No	No	No	No	$20+
Request a continuance	Yes	Yes	No	Yes	Yes
Have a good record	No	No	No	No	No
Use an alias	Yes	Yes	Yes	No	No
Plead guilty	Yes	No	No	No	No
Hire a defense attorney	Yes	Yes	No	Yes	Yes
Plead not guilty	Yes	Yes	Yes	Yes	No
Submit a writ of habeas corpus	Yes	Yes	Yes	Yes	No
Make a statement	Yes	No	Yes	No	No
Request treatment center	Yes	Yes	Yes	Yes	No

compared to the freedom of those who have bailed out, but in a world where most everything is in short supply, any way to soften the impact of this ritual is desirable.

Consider how these men feel. They are arrested for the public nature of their life style; those who live in better parts of town and behave in similar ways are not. They are robbed and roughed up because they are tramps; other citizens are not treated this way. They are kept in jail for days after each arrest awaiting court because they are too poor to bail out; those with money are released in a few hours. They are brought into court and arraigned with no opportunity for a defense counsel; those with wealth may hire an attorney. They are induced by the system to plead guilty to escape the consequences of using other means which require self-assertion; those with money never even face this dilemma because they have bailed out. With these contrasts in mind it is with ironic disbelief that the tramp views the sign hanging over the judges bench: EQUAL JUSTICE FOR ALL UNDER THE LAW, and it is no surprise that 64 per cent of the men in the sample reported they did not feel that the Seattle Criminal Court provided them with such justice. But there is a deeper and perhaps more significant aspect of the court experience which concerned most men.

Those in our society who define these men as alcoholics, bums, or common drunks often believe that they have "reached bottom" and lost all respect for themselves. They appear in public in a condition which offends other people and many would find it hard to believe that they are concerned about the image of themselves they portray to others. My first observations in the court aroused feelings of shock and pity for the men who appeared on public drunkenness charges; they were unshaven, unkempt, poorly groomed individuals who appeared to be the dregs of humanity. It was a long time before I was to discover that they may have spent five days and nights in a crowded cement drunk tank with no possible opportunity to prepare themselves personally for their appearance in court. The men in the sample were asked, "What do you feel is the worst thing about appearing in court on a drunk charge?", and though their answers were varied, they consistently fell into the following major categories:

The public humiliation	53%
The waiting, loss of time	24%
Facing the judge without any defense	17%
Loss of food, liquor, and physical comfort	6%

Those who felt the worst aspect of their experience in court was the public humiliation were especially worried about their physical appearance, which is always important for maintaining a viable self-image:

Your appearance, it is degrading to lay in the drunk tank over weekend and appear in court — no shave, no comb to even comb your hair, clothes all wrinkled.

It is as if the drunk tank were especially designed to desecrate a man before he is placed on exhibit in court:

A person is usually sick and dirty from laying on the concrete floor and to have to appear in front of a lot of people in that condition is very humiliating.

When men were asked to draw the parts of the jail, they pointed to the largest area in the court and labeled it "the spectators gallery." The fear that someone would be sitting in court and recognize them in this condition was present among many. Other comments about the worst part of appearing in court included: "You're not washed, hair not combed, look like a tramp in rumpled clothes," and "A person doesn't get a chance to groom himself for personal appearance so with a heavy beard you look like a bum after a couple days in the drunk tank." One man summed up the deepest feeling for most when he said the worst thing was simply "the degradation."

Very few tramps have become totally immune to the norms and values of American culture and they often feel guilty, especially when they are arrested for a long drunk. Some men reported that the most humiliating aspect of court was the way it intensified their feelings of shame and guilt without any opportunity to express this. One said, "It hurts my pride. It's degrading. You are on exhibition for everyone to see, not being able to express how sorry you really are for being drunk." In all these experiences — the public humiliation, waiting, facing the judge without any means of defense, the physical discomfort involved — tramps feel that underlying the whole process they are looked upon by the officials of the society as objects to be manipulated, as something less than human. The worst thing about court is being "herded around like a bunch of cattle — dumb animals." From the moment a man is taken to the court docket until he receives his sentence in court, he feels more like the victim of our legal institutions than their beneficiary. He may attempt one or more strategies for beating the charge, but these almost always end in failure and he quickly learns it is best to comply with the system. Yet, in so doing, the sense of alienation from oneself and others increases; he has moved even further away from those respected identities he had when arrested for the first time, and as he finally goes to the court docket and the courtroom he finds, as Mr. Tanner put it, that "you look and feel like a bum whether you are or not."

CHAPTER SEVEN

Doing Time

It takes about an hour each weekday morning to process public drunkenness cases in Seattle. Many men are arraigned, plead guilty, and receive their sentence in less than twenty seconds, and seldom does it take more than two or three minutes for an individual case. As the court liaison officer checks off each name, he hurries the men from the courtroom where everyone has been given something: another period of waiting, freedom, or time. Those who have pleaded not guilty or asked for a continuance return to the jail to await their trial or a second arraignment. Those who have requested help at the alcoholism treatment center must wait in jail for nearly a week while being examined and processed. Another period of waiting, for whatever reason, adds a certain amount of uncertainty to one's life and most men avoid it. Other men walk from the courtroom with a sense of exhilaration knowing they have avoided the later stages of making the bucket: they are kickouts who have received their freedom, and in an hour or two will be back on the street looking for old friends, joining a drinking group on Skid Road, or seeking a traveling companion for their trip to a town where their record is better than in Seattle. A third group leaves the courtroom with mixed emotions: on the one hand, they have a sense of relief because their immediate future has been decided; on the other, they are filled with deep resentment because they must now proceed through the last familiar stages of the jail experience. These men were given *time* by the judges, time which must be *done* during the days and months that lie ahead.

Time has captured the imagination and attention of Western scholars from many disciplines because, although an elusive concept, it is a universal and an exceedingly significant part of human existence. Time is so important in the culture of urban nomads that we would do well to analyze it briefly before returning to the last five stages of making the bucket. There are at least two types of temporal experience in jail: repetitive and non-repetitive.[1] Each day and week is viewed as a repetition of previous days, and time intervals are marked off with an elaborate vocabulary based on recurring events such as "mush time," "soup time," "pill time," "walk time," and "lockup time." Time is also viewed as something which is non-repetitive; it exists in limited amounts, may be used up, and, for tramps, it is something they must do. Every person in our society, rich or poor, possesses a quantity of time in this sense. In American culture time is a personal commodity, owned, and, to some extent, controlled by the individual — it has a qualitative value which is similar to money or other forms of wealth. We speak of time as something which belongs to us, "my time"; as something which can be squandered or saved, "I spent too much time doing that," or "I've got a whole evening just for myself"; and as something which can be exchanged for other values, "time is money." Since time is considered precious it is not surprising that those who have very limited amounts of money are asked to pay their debt to society with time. Tramps refer to this experience as "doing time" or "pulling time" and have many terms which denote the various aspects of this kind of time. Although our legal system tends to equate time and money, and both are accepted as

194

payments for the crime of public drunkenness, the equation takes on bizarre proportions for tramps.

We have already seen how the bail of $20 never changes, yet the amount of time required to pay for this crime does. An example from the life of a younger tramp clearly shows that time and money are not equal. Fred is a 34-year-old American Indian who served as an informant. He estimated that his income had been between $500 and $1000 during 1967. He has moved between 25 and 50 times during the past five years and held at least as many jobs. He was first arrested in Seattle during 1956 at the age of 24. Although he traveled frequently in the state of Washington and had probably done time in other jails, he spent most of his time in Seattle and, by his own admission, considered himself to be a homeguard tramp. Police records showed that from November, 1957, until June, 1968, he had been arrested 114 times for public drunkenness in Seattle. On 33 of these charges he had bailed out at a cost of $660; he had received a number of suspended sentences, but on 58 occasions he had been sentenced to jail. The total time to which he had been sentenced was 3,069 days or a little more than eight years, all of which could have been easily avoided for a little less than $120 per year in bail money. If, instead of giving him time, the judge had fined him $20 for each conviction and allowed him to work it off in jail at the going rate of nine dollars per day, Fred would have only received 130 days — a mere 4 per cent of the amount he was actually given!

It is no surprise, considering this kind of experience, that the concept of time as a non-repetitive phenomena is an important domain in the culture of urban nomads. The different kinds of time which make up this domain are shown in their taxonomic relationships in Table 7.1. These terms were elicited by asking informants, "What kinds of time are there?" The terms have meaning beyond doing drunk time in the Seattle city jail, as may be seen from a casual examination of them. In order to define these terms further, informants were asked to indicate similarities and differences among them, and this resulted in the discovery of several underlying semantic principles which organize this domain and which are shown in Table 7.2. These principles make up the

TABLE 7.1 TAXONOMIC DEFINITION OF TIME

Time		
Misdemeanor time	Jackrolling time	
	Vag time	
	Larceny time	
	Boosting time	
	Bootlegging time	
	Assault time	
	Begging time	
	Drunk time	
	Etc.	
Joint time	State time	
	Fed time	
Good time	Good time	
	Extra good time	
Dead time		
Hard time		
Easy time		
City time		
County time		
Road camp time		
Farm time		

196

TABLE 7.1 TAXONOMIC DEFINITION OF TIME (Concluded)

Time
Chain gang time
Hospital time
Suspended time
Own time
The other guy's time
Laying out time
Tank time
Trusty time
Short time
Solitary time
Flat time
Big time
Over time
Rabbit time

TABLE 7.2   DIMENSIONS OF CONTRAST FOR TIME DOMAIN

1.0 Time that can be done
   1.1 Yes
   1.2 No

2.0 Time controlled by others: they can give it to you
   2.1 Judges
   2.2 Bulls
   2.3 Physicians
   2.4 Other inmates
   2.5 No one

3.0 Time controlled by bulls: they take it away from you
   3.1 Yes
   3.2 No

4.0 Time controlled by inmate (after arrest)
   4.1 By inmate attitude
   4.2 By inmate earning it
   4.3 By inmate choosing it
   4.4 No control by inmate

5.0 Time related to crime committed
   5.1 Time given for type of crime
   5.2 Not related to type of crime

6.0 Time involving additional losses
   6.1 Loss of time only
   6.2 Loss of voting rights
   6.3 Loss of physical and/or psychological comfort
   6.4 Loss of days
   6.5 No loss

dimensions of contrast of all the terms which are at the highest level of contrast and are mapped on to the terms in Table 7.3. These dimensions of contrast are not sufficient to discriminate among all the terms in this set and two groups remain undifferentiated: (1) city time, county time, big time, and misdemeanor time; (2) trusty time and tank time. Additional dimensions of contrast, such as identity, length of time, and political jurisdiction could be used. More important, although these contrasts do provide a starting point for our understanding of time, they fall short of exhaustively defining these terms. Several will be examined briefly, before we look in more detail at the meaning of *hard time* and *easy time* in relation to the latter stages of making the bucket.

TABLE 7.3 COMPONENTIAL DEFINITION OF TIME
(HIGHEST LEVEL OF CONTRAST)

	Dimensions of Contrast					
Time	1.0	2.0	3.0	4.0	5.0	6.0
Misdemeanor time	1.1	2.1	3.2	4.4	5.1	6.1
Joint time	1.1	2.1	3.2	4.4	5.1	6.2
Good time	1.1	2.1, 2	3.1	4.2	5.2	6.5
Dead time	1.1	2.1	3.2	4.4	5.2	6.4
Hard time	1.1	2.2	3.1	4.1	5.2	6.3
Easy time	1.1	2.2	3.1	4.1	5.2	6.5
City time	1.1	2.1	3.2	4.4	5.1	6.1
County time	1.1	2.1	3.2	4.4	5.1	6.1
Road camp time	1.1	2.1	3.1	4.4	5.1	6.1
Farm time	1.1	2.1, 2	3.1	4.3	5.1	6.1
Chain gang time	1.1	2.2?	3.1	4.4	5.1	6.3
Hospital time	1.1	2.3	3.1	4.4	5.2	6.1
Suspended time	1.2	2.1	3.2	4.4	5.1	6.5
Own time	1.1	2.5	3.2	4.1	5.2	6.1
The other guy's time	1.1	2.4	3.2	4.1	5.2	6.3
Laying out time	1.1	2.5	3.2	4.3	5.2	6.1
Tank time	1.1	2.2	3.1	4.3	5.2	6.1
Trusty time	1.1	2.2	3.1	4.3	5.2	6.1
Short time	1.1	2.1	3.2	4.4	5.2	6.1
Solitary time	1.1	2.1, 2	3.1	4.3	5.2	6.3
Flat time	1.1	2.1, 2	3.2	4.4	5.2	6.4
Big time	1.1	2.1	3.2	4.4	5.1	6.1
Over time	1.1	2.2	3.1	4.4	5.2	6.4
Rabbit time	1.1	2.1, 2	3.1	4.4	5.1	6.1

The most pervasive feature of meaning for the different kinds of time is that they are something *to be done*. Almost any conversation among tramps about life in jail is filled with phrases such as "I was doing drunk time," "He was doing over time," and "I was doing laying out time to save money." The only term which is not used in this way is suspended time which is considered "time on the street." From the perspective of the outsider, tramps may seem to overemphasize time, especially *doing* time. Many of the terms in this set could be spoken of in other ways and, in a sense, it appears that this culture has taken a varied group of objects and events such as *city, county, trusty, begging, rabbit,* and *dead* and thrown them together with the concept of *time*. Time as something *to be done* has become all-encompassing, it has taken on such importance in the lives of these men that it becomes a basis for defining space (county, city), identity (trusty), actions (misdemeanor), bodily conditions (hospital), rewards (good), punishments (solitary), and psychological definitions of the entire jail experience (hard, easy). It is almost impossible, then, to understand urban nomads without taking into account what doing time means to them. One man summed it up this way, "When you're doing time you're paying a penalty. There's so much time you've got to do. It's a job to be done, but you're doing the time, not the work." In American culture we speak of doing work in the context of time and though the work may be disagreeable, time may drag, and we may put in our time, this is very different from doing time in the context of other activities. Time for tramps becomes objectified and enlarged in consciousness as they go through repeated incarcerations.

Making the bucket not only changes the place where men must live, restricting their freedom of movement in space; it also restructures their temporal orientation. It is transformed from a resource or commodity to a difficult task that must be performed, and from something which is largely controlled, scheduled, and organized by the self into something which is controlled by others. When we consider the importance of controlling one's own time we must recognize that time in itself has important ramifications for personal identity. A unique characteristic of man is his awareness of the temporal dimension:

It is interesting to speculate that knowledge of space, something I believe we share with much of the animal kingdom, relates to the development of self-powered locomotion. Because such locomotion can be considered an early evolutionary adaptation, so may the knowledge of space be considered a primitive stratum of consciousness. With the growth of man's mental powers, a more sophisticated adaptive machinery emerged in the form of the successive discoveries of future, past and present. This new and powerful tool which we recognize as man's knowledge of time, is coeval and necessary for the establishment of his personal identity. For, only through the combination of expectation and memory can he know in what cumulative way he is different from others. In turn, the discovery of one's personal identity is but a way of recognizing his self-awareness (Fraser 1966:589).

200

As a child's personal identity develops it is inherently linked to, and dependent upon, the time dimension. When a man embarks on the ritual stages of making the bucket, his identity is changed and he is thrust into a world where time first becomes extremely important, arising as a major feature of his consciousness, and then is restructured on a different basis. This restructuring involves changes of great significance, the transformation of time from commodity to task, and a reduction in the degree to which the self controls time. Several dimensions of contrast define the tramp's perception of this reduced amount of control. For example, *solitary time* is an experience which is controlled almost entirely by the bulls. One man reported, "This guy was busted to solitary in the blackout tank because he sassed an officer over a food tray. He said something like 'this slop.'" Another man stated it this way, "On solitary time you're being punished for more than your original crime." When a man does *dead time* he has even less choice over the matter. One man said, "The time you do in the city before going to court is dead time. Dead time would always be hard time. You can't get any credit for it. You only do easy time after you're sentenced." Another kind of time which a man may do in jails across the country is *over time*. One man reported, "I did over time in the South one time because the captain held us over to the next day to fill baskets for a party at Thanksgiving at the Fireman's Hall." One man defined over time this way: "You can do over time when somebody makes a mistake or there's a misunderstanding. The court officer might forget to write down 15 days suspended on a 30-day sentence if that's what the judge said." When a man escapes from some kind of minimum security institution — an alcoholism treatment center, city jail, or a place where he may have been doing road-camp time — he is referred to as a rabbit. If he is arrested again, as many of these men are, he may have to do "time on the top of the time you were doing before you rabbited." Sometimes *rabbit time* involves wearing chains, as one man reported about a city in Tennessee, "If you escape from the city jail in Chattanooga they put you in chains. I had to wear chains for 10 days on a drunk charge in Chattanooga in 1956." In Seattle the person who controls whether a man does rabbit time is the trusty officer in the jail. When a man is released from jail it is not always entered in the common drunkard file in court, making it difficult upon his return to court to discern whether he served the entire length of the previous sentence, and so it is a bull who actually has control over whether an inmate does rabbit time. As one man summarized, "That's the time you have to make up. The trusty officer who runs the jail keeps a rabbit book and makes you do rabbit time."

A man's control over the kind of experience he has, which he refers to as doing time, is not only limited by the police and judges but also by other inmates. When urban nomads talk about interpersonal relationships in jail they define them as related intimately to the time dimension. Every man must do *his own time*, but it is also possible to do *another person's time*. There are two ways to do this: first, if you worry about the other man and how he's getting on, how he will survive when he gets out of jail, you're going to do the other guy's time; if the other inmate bothers you, then you are going to be doing his time. One man reported, "A guy might say, 'Let me do my own time. Get the fuck away from me.' He'll say this if he's deep in thought and some guy comes up to him, this is what he'll say." If a man is successfully to endure the time he must put in himself he will avoid those who give him any extra frustration. This may well be because in the anxiety that is produced by stripping a man of his identity, labeling him with a new identity, and restructuring the time dimension while limiting his movement in space, his tolerance for frustration is lowered. One tramp summarized it this way, "A guy is doing the other guy's time along with his because that guy is crying a lot about his time — that kind of guy is really shunned in the bucket."

The control of one kind of time is very important to tramps because, among other things, it may shorten the amount of time they must do while in jail. Men refer to this as *good time* and it involves a category of different types, only two of which are listed in the taxonomy. One man summarized the meaning of this term when he said:

You get good time as a matter of course on every sentence. You can lose your good time. A trusty who is busted loses his good time; a lockup who's hard to get along with and is bucking the bulls loses his good time. Up to 20 days you don't get any good time; 20–29 days you get three days good time; 30–59 days you get five days good time; 60–89 days you get ten days good time; and for 180 days in jail you get thirty days good time.

When a man enters the Seattle city jail for thirty or sixty days he is keenly aware that all he must do to have the sentence reduced by a certain number of days is to stay out of trouble, conform to the rules, and keep from offending anyone. But this may put heavy burdens upon him. His life now is not only controlled spatially and temporally but the bulls are further controlling many small actions which could result in the loss of his good time. The judge can also take away a man's good time, and this is one of the reasons a man appears to be passive in the courtroom; any show of hostility may be interpreted by the judge as cause for taking away his good time. Time, in this sense, is used to motivate inmates to conform to many standards, both written and unwritten, that govern life in the bucket. A common practice in many jails is giving *extra good time* for a variety of activities. One man stated:

In Mississippi you get three for one by working it out. If you work, you get three days off for every day in. I got a half a day good time for snapping beans and peeling potatoes after my regular duties. Also you can get time off for doing work at a policeman's house, like painting, helping him build his house, or doing garden work.

The tramp who has not been able to bail out and has been sentenced to do time in jail may direct a great deal of energy toward control of his behavior to ensure he gets his good time. One way to get extra good time graphically symbolizes the stripping process through which these men go as they make the bucket — giving parts of their body. A man has given nearly everything he possesses and all he has left is his body and the shirt on his back. Before he gets out he will sometimes be given the opportunity to give blood. One man referred to it in this way: "Sometimes men refer to good time as blood time. If you give blood you get out sooner, it cuts your days off. If you had ten days you wouldn't do but seven for it." Informants reported that this practice had been formally eliminated in the Seattle city jail in recent years, but is still practiced in many other cities, for example, "In Atlanta they give you three days good time for giving blood, or you can do extra work for a judge or a policeman." In some jails, such as San Jose, California, and Portland, Oregon, men receive extra good time by giving skin. One tramp recalled the following experience:

I was in Portland one time when they asked for so many volunteers, "Who would like to volunteer for skin grafting on your back?" They take four strips. They first put a little alcohol on your back and then take off four strips of skin and two days later they take the bandage off, or if it doesn't heal very fast they wait. They use it for skin grafting up at the hospital. They give you five dollars for doing it and give you that in cash; and then when I was released three days early they said, "Your work record is good, you cooperated with the rules, and you donated skin." The guys know they will get good time and five dollars for doing it.

To understand the full meaning of doing time we must focus upon *hard time* and *easy time*, for these are undoubtedly the most important conceptions that a man comes to have about his days in jail. There are a number of synonyms for these terms such as "tough time," and "soft time," but the most frequently used terms are "hard" and "easy." The subjective sense of time passage varies from person to person and experience to experience; when one is doing time it tends to pass rather slowly. This in itself makes it painful, and as time slows down for the man in jail he is going to do hard time. One man observed that in jail, "Time seems to never end. The day seems forever. You do it a day at a time." If you think of the future, the date of release, it seems interminable. You must do it a day at a time. You cannot face being oriented toward the future because it is so painful. Time seems forever that way and the men develop a radical present-orientation. This is yet another aspect of the restructuring of time; in our society most people are future-oriented, looking forward to the accomplishment of goals rather than passively enduring the present moment, but, if a tramp who is doing time looks forward to getting out, the days are going to drag more slowly and he will be doing hard time. In fact, it is almost inevitable that tramps do some hard time on every sentence: "After a certain amount of time, the routine, eventually you are going to be doing hard time and looking forward to getting out." Hard time means many things, but at the very core, one does hard time if he maintains an active, goal-oriented way of life which involves a commitment to the future. He must learn to withdraw

204

into himself, to become inert, and assume a passive attitude toward life in the bucket:

A guy does hard time if he's on the go all the time, gotta gal buggin' him — then he's doin' hard time. The guy who's the nervous type — he can't sit still, he can't reconcile himself to the fact he has to stay, he does hard time.

Whereas the oldtimers know that a passive strategy works not only in court but also in jail, doing easy time is not always simple for newcomers and conforming or learning this practice presents great difficulties. One man told of his friend, "Jones is doing hard time out here. He doesn't sit back and wait for something to happen; he uses something to the hilt, like the phone." The first step in learning to do easy time, by giving up a goal-oriented life in jail, is to control the external evidence of an active response. Sometimes this is very forcibly learned, as in the case of one tramp:

This guy got in an argument with a guard during visiting time. He had a visitor and they drug him away from the window. The guard gave me his wristwatch and wallet and took this guy back in the padded cell and beat the hell out of him.

The man who has not spent much time in jail finds that it takes a great deal of energy to control himself and appear to be a passive, retiring individual. In a sense, he does hard time while trying to do easy time until he has mastered a passive response to life in jail. One long-time inmate observed, "The guy who you don't notice is really pulling hard time. He holds himself back to keep from causing himself more trouble." With each repeated incarceration a man learns a little more fully how to conform and accommodate to the demands of life in the bucket and thus do easy time. Passivity, in a sense, becomes part of his essential character, an automatic response, one which he no longer has to consciously control. Such a person speaks with the authority of an oldtimer who knows the stages of the bucket and can predict what events are to come, how he will be treated, and most of all, which strategies will reduce the painful effect of doing time:

There are different ways to do hard time. You can refuse to work, be locked up, or just get on somebody's shit list. Some individuals do hard time — time is just harder for them to do; others can take it as it comes. A guy can make it as hard as he wants.

An interesting relationship is set up between what a man learns in jail in attempting to do easy time and much of his life style in the other scenes in this culture. Repeated experiences in the bucket impress upon a man the importance of living one day at a time, keeping his mind centered in the present, and passively responding to all stimuli around him. To most Americans urban nomads on Skid Road and in other places appear to have a life style which is passive and lacks a future orientation: they live from day to day; they sleep wherever they can find a flop; they spend their money on one meal without enough left for the next; they drink when they feel like it, sharing their last bit of alcohol with a friend. Their way of life appears to involve a hand-to-mouth, present orientation. They also appear to be very passive — moving on when told, trying to make themselves invisible, seeking to stay out of trouble; in essence, they are sensitive to the demands of others, whether these be peers in a drinking group who are encouraging them to go on another drunk, or the police, bartenders, or others with whom they have contact. The man who makes the bucket early in his career as a tramp finds not only that his identity is changing but also that he is learning the basic values upon which survival depends, both in jail and on Skid Road.

It would be a mistake to believe that hard time results only from one's attitude and inability to monitor external responses carefully. The man who still has ties to the civil society is in greater danger of doing hard time than are others:

The guy with outside problems does hard time: a wife to worry about, bum checks that are coming back, bills that are coming in, a car he owes payment on and is afraid they will repossess, clothes that he's going to lose because he can't get to them.

Sixty-two per cent of the men in the sample reported that they had on one or more occasions lost a job because they did time on a drunk charge. Whatever their means of income, many of these men have rented rooms and paid the rent in advance. A large majority of men reported losing this money because they were given time. When asked if they had ever lost rent they had paid on a room because they did time on a drunk charge the men in the sample reported:

Many times	33%
Occasionally	27%
At least once	20%
Never	20%

These are the kinds of problems a man faces when he comes into jail; the fewer of these connections to civil society which he maintains the greater his chances of doing easy time.

Although tramps are usually poor, this does not mean that they have no personal property; some may even have sums of money that amount to hundreds of dollars. Many, because of their mobile way of life, keep this money in their rooms or carry it with them instead of using banking facilities. When arrested they may have money, clothing, identification papers, or other property in their rooms; if they can use a telephone or contact a close friend to take care of it for them, or perhaps persuade a policeman to bring it to them in jail, they may be able to preserve what little they do have. The men in the sample were asked if they had ever lost property or clothing which they had left in their rooms because of doing time on a drunk charge, and they reported:

Many times	31%
Occasionally	20%
At least once	23%
Never	26%

It is interesting that these losses involve not only money and personal property but also roles and identities. An individual is an employee, and a roomer, and one with personal identity symbols in his property such as discharge papers and union cards. Thus, he not only loses ties to respectable identities by doing time, but in order to make the time easy he must voluntarily cut himself off from the outside world, further alienating himself from those roles he formerly played and also from the rest of society. As one tramp put it:

A guy does hard time if he's a worry wart. If he's worrying about that outside — it's up to the guy himself, the only way to do easy time is to forget about that outside world.

207

This observation clearly shows the dual process of being cut off and losing ties to the outside world while simultaneously learning to become oriented toward the inside world of tramps and trusties. The very moment an individual is experiencing a dispossession of a number of roles upon learning that he must do time in jail, he is also being prepared to assume either the role of trusty or lockup in the next stage.

STAGE 11: HOLDING TANK

We have followed these men through many stages of a very complex ritual. Those men who receive a sentence walk back into the seventh floor section of the jail and are placed in the holding tank after the court session is completed. The trusty officer joins them there and some decision is made regarding the future role they will have in jail: trusty or lockup. The most significant factor in determining whether a man does hard time or easy time is this decision, since trusties have many advantages which lockups do not. One tramp summed it up in this way:

You are usually doin' easy time when you have plenty to eat, plenty of reading material, soft job, and you can watch TV. You're doin' easy time when the day is filled up. That's why work time makes your time shorter and easier.

Many men refer to work time as trusty time. Trusties stay in several different kinds of tanks which are unlocked during the day. As we saw earlier in the discussion of trusty identities, some have freedom to move throughout most of the jail and others even go outside to work. Their greater freedom allows them to watch television at certain times and, most important, they have access to food and other resources in and out of the jail. The basis for assigning men to either trusty or lockup is not altogether clear; it is difficult to determine the reasons why an individual may not become a trusty but the following are some of those reported by the men:

If there are not enough jobs, if you're too old and cannot work, if you do not receive enough time, if a man has rabbited from a previous sentence, and if a man was sentenced for a crime of a more serious nature.

208

Some men actually considered being a trusty as undesirable but found that they had to do hard time as a result of refusing the opportunity to work:

I went into 710, the holding tank, and the trusty officer was making the guys trusties. All the guys who had 60 days were made trusties and when he asked some of the others and they said, "No, I don't want to work." The trusty officer then said, "Then you lose your good time." And these guys lost their good time and they wouldn't even let them give blood, just because they didn't want to work.

STAGE 12: DELOUSING TANK

The time in the delousing tank generally lasts several hours, but most men felt it was the worst part of making the bucket. As soon as the assignments are made in the holding tank all inmates, both trusties and lockups, are taken a few feet down the hall to the delousing tank. There are sixteen bunks in this tank with a small passageway between the bunks, a shower, and toilet. The men are crowded into this tank and told to prepare to have their clothing deloused. The trusty officer has gone by this time and one or more trusties take over the process, ordering the men to strip off all of their clothing. The nakedness which the men must now endure is felt to be contaminating and degrading in itself, but perhaps at a deeper level it is the way in which it symbolizes the complete loss and stripping of every facet of life in civil society, just prior to assuming the identities of inmate within the bucket, that is most significant. Whenever delousing came up for discussion the comments were vitriolic, especially about having to sit "bare-ass," crowded into this small tank. The men in the sample reported on the largest group of men they had seen at one time sitting naked in the delousing tank:

15–25	27%
26–40	48%
Over 40	25%

One man said it was so crowded there was "standing room only"; another described the situation, "several on each bunk and some on the floor." Goffman has remarked that in this type of institution "the admission procedure can be characterized as a leaving

209

off and a taking on, with the midpoint marked by physical naked-ness. Leaving off, of course, entails the dispossession of property, important because persons invest self-feelings in their possessions" (1961:18). One man described the sense of defilement:

One machine with 30 men's clothes for delousing — some guys are better than looking at carnivals, wearing a couple of union suits, couple pair of pants. The clothes should be turned inside out where the seams show so the greybacks can't hide; some guys are filthy. If they're lousy and guys are so crowded together everybody's contaminated. Them clothes should really be in that machine for maybe three hours so nobody gets lousy.

One of the most frequent criticisms was this sense of being pol-luted by the lice carried on the bodies of other men while being exposed to their nakedness and allowing oneself to be revealed to others in such crowded conditions. One tramp recalled:

I'll tell you one thing, they got a poor system down there of delousing. Throw all your clothes in a big can, I don't know how long they keep them down in there, but sometimes they only keep them there 30 minutes; next time you're liable to be up there waiting two hours, but when they come back with those clothes they're lousier than they were before they put them in there.

The men in the sample were asked to estimate the longest period of time they had had to sit "bare-assed" in the tank while their clothes were being deloused, and they reported the following:

1 hour	18%
2 hours	25%
3 hours	36.5%
4 hours	14%
5 hours	6.5%

The complaints about the delousing involved not only the con-tamination of being exposed to other men and being forced to sit naked in extremely crowded conditions, but also the distasteful and damaging treatment of the clothing. When a man is poor, has very few possessions, and, as in the case of these men, has been dispossessed of everything except what he is wearing, these gar-ments are invested with much greater self-feelings than others

210

might suppose. In discussions, many tramps reported that they felt very keenly about their clothing and would not report for a job which had been offered to them because they did not have the proper attire. They are aware that the designation of bum is used for them largely because of their personal appearance and their clothing. While they were in court the state of their clothing, after they had lain in the drunk tank for several days, caused great embarrassment and concern. All these feelings about clothes reflect the fact that, as the self crumbles and men become further alienated from themselves, they cling more desperately to the last vestige of any material objects which symbolize, in some sense, their personal identity. Their clothing was not only stripped from their backs, but in the delousing process two further things usually happened. First, the clothes were dumped into a common barrel and carted off by a trusty, and thrown into a machine which was heated in an effort to kill any lice or other bugs. Seldom did the heat penetrate all the clothes nor was the barrel cleaned out while other clothes were being heated or cooked. One man described the situation in the following way:

I'll tell you, I walked out of that jail in worse shape than I was when I went in. They put your clothes in that garbage can and some of those guy's clothes are lousy. I'm not lousy but when they come out of that can — they don't wash the can out — the bugs fell off in that can.

On occasion, if a man has not yet learned the importance of submission, he may attempt to protect his clothing as well as his deteriorating self-image by resistance, but this seldom succeeds and may even lead to situations like the following: "I saw this drunk who had the hell choked out of him because he refused to take his clothes off to be deloused."

In addition to becoming infested with lice, clothing was either stolen or ruined during delousing. Forty-seven per cent of the men in the sample reported that they had had some good clothes ruined; one man described the general situation:

If your clothes happen to be the type of material that won't stand very much heat they aren't fit to wear when you get them back. If your clothes are not lousy when you give them to them, they are lousy

211

when you get them back. The clothes are dumped on the floor in the delousing room and the heat runs the lice from the clothes on top to the bottom of the pile where the heat doesn't reach them and gets the clothes lousy that were not lousy.

Those who reported having clothes ruined gave examples: "I had an Orlon jacket put in the oven and the lining melted and hardened." "A hundred dollar suit was completely shrunk out of shape." Others reported their jackets were burned, the pockets in pants were ripped, the buttons were torn off, shirts and underwear scorched, and one man summed it up, "The delousing process made good clothes look like old rags." This kind of experience emphasizes the process which is going on throughout the jail but which symbolizes and reaches the peak here of making the men appear to be ragged bums who should be treated with little concern. Many men also reported their clothing was stolen by the trusties who were probably making up for clothing that had been ruined when they came in. The entire process of being deloused is utterly degrading and makes men begin to feel they are no longer human beings. One man expressed the feelings of many when he said, "There were 41 of us by actual count, and the jailer even laughed about how much we looked like animals."

STAGES 13 AND 14: TIME TANK AND TRUSTY TANK

Differences occur in the daily routine of inmates depending on whether they spend their time as trusties or lockups, but no contrast is greater than that related to food, and no experience increases the amount of hard time a man does as much as that of hunger. One man said, "You can do hard time any place especially if there's poor grub or if you're sleeping on the steel." Mr. Tanner's diary provides us with an exhaustive description of the subjective experience of one man in lockup who was doing hard time — first, because he refused to respond passively to his environment, and second, because he had poor food. He wrote, "Food obviously is the dominant thought here, everyone continually hungry." The contrast may be seen by responses of men in the sample who had done time as lockups and trusties. Ninety-eight men responded to the question related to lockup food and 62 men responded to

212

the question pertaining to trusty food in the Seattle city jail. They evaluated the amount of food in each situation:

	Trusty	Lockup
All you can eat	1%	3%
Enough to eat	37%	2%
Not quite enough to eat	20%	14%
Never enough to eat	40%	43%
Starvation diet	2%	37%

A young tramp, who was a college graduate, gave this analysis of the great bitterness over food in the Seattle city jail:

What is shocking and what the inmates feel in regard to the food situation, especially those who know and who are working in the kitchen . . . it's really amazing how much meat they have down there, a tremendous amount of meat for the number of people in jail. But we don't see any of it. But the officers, for instance, it makes you kind of mad because you see them get a great big steak like this and the whole works for 35 cents. Everyone else eats so darn well, all this very good food and we get the chowder. The drunk, in general, is not really a criminal type and I don't know why a bank robber should be fed better than he is. Anyone in the county jail eats a lot better than in the city and the drunk is made to feel that he is on the lowest rung of society and he's treated as such.

Agreement was general on the amount and kind of food provided for the men in lockup. Mush time occurred at about 6:00 in the morning and the men consistently reported it included two pieces of toast or bread, one cup of black coffee without cream, and one-half bowl of mush with milk and sugar. Sometimes on Sunday morning a bowl of fruit replaced the mush. Soup time took place about 10 or 10:30 and included one quarter bowl of broth, two slices of bread, and nothing to drink. Soup time is an innovation in the jail since only two meals were served daily until several years ago. Some men reported they had discovered lemon rinds or other inappropriate items in the broth served at soup time. Chow time occurred about 4 or 4:30 and was usually a complete meal but the portions were so small one man reported it could be eaten while walking back to his tank. No seasonings were provided with any meal except breakfast when sugar was supplied for the mush. One man stated, "At 4:30 P.M. a dinner smaller than a TV dinner —

with nothing solid for breakfast or lunch a person would get progressively hungry and in fourteen days I was starved to death." When asked to describe the content of the evening meal, men reported such things as "small piece of liver or fish or hamburger, maybe peas or carrots," "a tray of beans or macaroni," "poorly seasoned lamb stew or ox joints."

The recent survey of the jail by the International Association of Chiefs of Police came to conclusions very different from those of the inmates about the quality and quantity of food. They ended their report by stating, "The entire food serving program, including the quality of food, and much of the equipment used, leave little to be improved upon" (1968:499). In contrast to the description of the menu provided by the inmates, this survey reported these typical menus (1968:498–499):

Breakfast:	Dinner:	Supper:
Hot cereal	Pea soup	Hamburger
Scrambled fresh eggs	Wieners	Gravy
Bacon	Sauerkraut	Beets
Hash, brown potatoes	Carrots	Potatoes
Toast, oleo	Potatoes	Bread, oleo
Milk	Cake	Hot tea
Coffee, sugar	Bread, oleo	
	Hot cocoa	

In actuality two cultures operate within the jail: those of the inmate and of the staff; they grow side by side but are separated by an impenetrable barrier. The study of the police department done by the IACP said, reporting on their survey methods, that: "During the course of the survey, consultants conducted extensive interviews with police executives and middle management and subordinant members and employees of the department" (1968:3). Nowhere do they indicate that inmates were interviewed, nor was their perception of the situation to become an important part of this survey. They conclude with an interesting observation about the food situation: "The average cost per meal for feeding prisoners during 1966 was $0.1512 per prisoner. The professional employment of a steward is the major reason for this nominal menu cost" (1968:499).

214

The inmates and tramps who spend much of their lives in the Seattle city jail, of course, would give a different opinion as to the reason for this nominal menu cost.

The experience of doing hard time as a trusty or lockup is related to many other facets of life in the bucket. It results, in part, from failure to maintain a compliant attitude toward the social and physical environment, failure to live a day at a time, inability to force any thought of the future from one's consciousness, losses of personal property and jobs on the outside, poor food and other discomforts on the inside, and losses of personal clothing in the delousing process. In addition, within the jail is a system of rewards and punishments which contribute directly to the experience of doing hard or easy time. An individual who is selected as a trusty often considers this choice as a favor, but the men reported other kinds of favors which friendly policemen had performed for them. Any diversion, such as watching television, contributes to easy time:

One guard was in the right mood during the New Year and he personally saw to it we could watch some of the football games. It was quite nice of him, otherwise we would never have seen them. The guards at the city jail are pretty fair as having so many repeaters.

Sometimes a man perceives that a policeman is doing him a favor when it may very well be part of the policy, as in the case of a man who said a bull had done him a favor by letting him "make a phone call and getting something for me out of my property." Actually, only 23 per cent of the sample reported they had ever had a bull do a favor for them while they were in jail. When asked what these favors were they indicated such things as "had a check I couldn't cash and he made my bond," or the man who reported:

The officer had me released for six hours to get my clothes and property taken care of at the place where I was living. Also had busted my glasses previous to arrest and was released five hours to get some reading glasses and to finish taking care of some other things. This I really appreciated very much as otherwise I would have lost all my clothes and would not have had any money to get commissary or no glasses to see with.

Other men had had officers give them cigarettes, make them trusties, allow them to make extra phone calls, or, if they were working

215

in the blue room, give them extra food to eat from the meals of the officers. Not all these favors are an unmixed blessing, as with one man, who said: "If you call it a favor, by cashing a bank draft and charging 10 per cent for it — it happened twice in 1968." Another man said that a bull cashed two $10 checks for him but he had to give him the amount of one of the checks.

Though rewards are sought and favors are gratefully accepted from many policemen, the men are aware that they are granted only if one maintains a submissive attitude and, even at that, favors are few and far between. The men are much more alert to the possibility of punishment which may come in the form of withheld privileges, extra physical torment, or being busted. These punishments hang over the head of a man, constantly reminding him that while he is in jail he must be on guard to conform to the slightest wish of the bulls and restrict any thought he has for self-assertive behavior. In jail men have the privilege of writing letters, making a phone call each week, getting out of their cell for a brief period of exercise, and using the money in their property to purchase candy and cigarettes through the weekly commissary. These privileges are not equally available to all men and they may, in themselves, contribute to hard time. When asked for spontaneous comments about aspects of the police or jail one man said he disliked "the censorship of mail and only being allowed to write one letter per week on one side of one sheet of paper, and even then I could not write if I could not buy stamps." Visiting and letter writing are two privileges which enable a man to maintain ties with the outside world, and if he does not conform in the proper way to life in jail he will find both of these privileges withdrawn.

A second kind of punishment involves additional physical or psychological torment. The men usually refer to this as being put on "the bull's shit list" or having "a cop on your ass." One man recalled, "Even a trusty may·do hard time if a cop is on your ass." Fifteen per cent of the sample reported they had been put on the bull's "shit list" for various reasons: "I refused to polish a cop's shoes," or "because I told him I was going to call the Civil Liberties Union about the sadistic treatment," or "by not calling him officer." Sometimes a man finds that he is in trouble with the officers in jail for reasons of which he is unaware and concludes it is "because he hates drunks," or because the police have "a natural dislike." Sometimes a trusty doesn't do his job well and gets on the bull's "shit list" and receives additional psychological torment, at least, if not some other punishment.

Several forms of group punishment are meted out to an entire tank because of the misbehavior of one or two men, or simply because the officer is out of sorts one day. The first kind of group punishment is referred to as "the heat treatment"; 31 per cent of the sample reported that a bull had punished those in the tank by closing all windows and keeping the tank too warm. One man said, "For five hours during 1968 the jailer closed the windows a little too close for 14 men to be able to breathe, so someone opened them back up by reaching through with a towel and pulling. The officer then closed them up tight and took our commissary rights for one day." Another man said, "During 1968, someone asked to have them open and the bull got ornery and locked the windows because he was too damn lazy to open them and he left them shut all day." Fifty-four per cent of the men reported they had a bull freeze them and other prisoners by opening the windows and making the tank too cold. This kind of experience is referred to as "freeze treatment." "On April 1, 1968, the windows were open on a cold day for five or six hours. I asked the jailer to close the windows but no action was taken." The freeze treatment may come during the delousing period if the windows are left open; one man said he received the freeze treatment during "delousing, naked, no cover, subject to colds. That was in 1966." Others find the freeze treatment may go on day after day like the man who said, "It happened twenty days and nights in winter. I was released with pneumonia." Sometimes the freeze treatment takes place in the drunk tank; one man reported, "In 1968 they left the windows open all night. We were laying on the cement without any blankets."

Extra physical punishment or bad treatment may occur not only at the hands of the bulls; 32 per cent of the men in the sample reported that they had been treated badly by the nurses or doctors in jail. One man said:

I was insulted by the nurse and once upon having some cracked ribs was taped on the wrong side because the nurse would not listen to me when I told her which side I was injured on and she taped the wrong

217

side and told me that I was not a doctor, and how did I know where I was injured. Then two or three days later when I got to see the doctor again and he took me out of the cell and taped the right side which was injured. But I had to lay on the drunk tank cement floor for three days with the cracked ribs before trial in court and I was in pain all of that time.

Favors, as well as ill treatment, may also come from the nursing staff.

One nurse who was working there would bend over backwards to treat you for any ailment but the other two are like most of the doctors, as far as they're concerned you don't exist. If you are sick or hurting in the morning the two nurses mentioned tell you to see the doctor on his rounds at night. When and if he makes it he has a pocketful of asprin and tells you to see the doctor in the morning.

Sometimes it may be a very small thing:

For seven days running I asked for nail clippers and was always promised but never allowed to use them. The nurse thrust a needle completely through the vein while taking a blood sample.

It is not only the actual physical discomfort which is conceived as torment but the attitude of the medical staff that is perceived as hostile by the men. One man summed this up by saying about one nurse: "She is rough and overbearing, she seems to enjoy the pain of others, she talks to you as if you were a dumb animal."

The final kind of punishment is *being busted*. Almost any person, whether lockup or trusty, can be busted to another, less desirable, place within the jail. In order to understand this we must have a greater understanding of the structure of space in the bucket. A man may be busted to six distinct places within the jail for misbehavior, for getting on the bull's shit list, or for some unknown reason (see Chart 7.1).

Fifteen per cent of the men who reported they had worked as trusties in the jail said they had been busted from trusty to lockup, that is, from the trusty tank to a time tank. One man said, "In 1966 I had half of a razor blade under my mattress and the jailer busted me for this." Sometimes a man will do hard time after being busted as a result of his effort to make the time he's doing easier:

This historical event took place in the year 1968. I tried to sneak back in the mess hall for another round of meal, although I had slipped

218

CHART 7.1 PLACES TO BE BUSTED
WITHIN THE JAIL

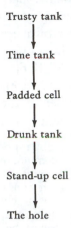

Trusty tank

↓

Time tank

↓

Padded cell

↓

Drunk tank

↓

Stand-up cell

↓

The hole

into it several times what I thought unnoticed a guard called me aside later and politely informed me I was relieved of my duties as a trusty. I was locked up in lockup.

A man must not only be careful to avoid actions violating the rules but must be very careful not to allow any negative attitude to show. One man said he was busted from trusty to lockup for "silent insolence." Another said he was busted for "personality clash, for not copping out and stooling on fellow prisoners." A trusty may not be busted directly to the time tank but instead may pass over one of the places lower on the scale and go directly to the drunk tank or one of the even less desirable places. A man does time in the drunk tank after he has been sentenced by being busted or by personal choice. Only 5 per cent of the sample reported they had ever been busted to the drunk tank, although 34 per cent knew of other inmates who had been returned there. One man reported:

I was reported to the day officer by a head trusty. He said I wasn't working fast enough and the head trusty's word was taken without my being given a chance to defend myself. I was doing 30 days at the time and half of that I did in the drunk tank in 1966.

Another man reported being busted to the drunk tank because "I kept asking for medical treatment and this is what I received to keep me quiet." Another said, "The nurse had this man busted on word from another trusty which was not true pertaining to his work in the dispensary and he did 35 days there." Yet another re-called, "In 1966 I knew a colored man who did 150 days spent in the drunk tank for not shaving." A man comes to realize by ex-ample of others, or from his own experience, that speaking out against any of the inequities in jail is a dangerous thing to do. One man knew of another who "did 18 days in the drunk tank because he raised hell about some of his clothes being stolen when they were being taken to be deloused by the trusties in 1966." Another had been threatened for simply observing certain injustices:

I was a trusty and worked as night runner. Our working area is right next to the booking desk. It's a common occurrence every night for the cops to rough up a drunk. In some cases they are dragged to the padded cell area where five or more cops can get in a few licks without being seen. On one occasion we were chewed out by the sergeant for watching such an act and were told to stay in the runners room or be busted. I've witnessed at least twenty beatings by Seattle police.

Some men will do time in the drunk tank at their own request in order to do easy time. Eleven per cent of the sample reported they knew men who had asked to be placed in the drunk tank. A man does this because he wishes to have the extra food which those who are too ill and cannot eat will leave there for him, or to avoid having to control his behavior carefully as he must when he is a lockup or trusty. One man reported he knew of a man who went to the drunk tank by his own choice "because he could not get along with the city guards and he spent about three months there."

One of the worst kinds of punishment reported by the men was the stand-up cell. Many men did not know of this place or had never seen it themselves, but several others had been placed in this cell, had seen men doing time in it, or knew those who reported such experiences to them. One man made an observation which explains how the stand-up cell is part of a time tank:

In 1963 or 1964 I was being held on the sixth floor in the women's side, because the jail was so crowded. I was in on a drunk charge. One night I was in a cell across the hall and there was a man who had been raising hell, kicking the bars and making noise in another sixth-floor cell where he was kept alone. Two bulls came back and they stuck him in this stand-up cell. There is a steel sliding door going into the tanks, and also a curved door with bars on it so there is a double door going into each of the tanks on the sixth floor. They slammed the inside curved bar door, and then slammed the outside steel door shut and left him in there a couple of hours. It's not actually a stand-up cell but it is used for that purpose. A man is in such a small area that he could not bend his knees.

Less than 10 per cent of the sample had been placed in a stand-up cell or knew of anyone who had been put there. One man who had been placed there reported:

I didn't feel that I was drunk enough to have been arrested in the first place and I was trying to convince the officers of this when one hit me and split my left eye over the brow and when I started to bleed I sort of lost my head and tried to fight back. That was in 1959 and they put me in a stand-up cell for approximately four hours.

Another man told of his friend:

One time there was a big man from Carolina who was put in a stand-up cell. He'd been in there, I don't know how long, but they wouldn't even let him take a shit so they gave him his food in there and he ate his mush and shit in the bowl.

The lowest level in the hierarchy of places to which a man may be busted was reported by some men to be the hole; others called it the "black-out cell," or "solitary." Very few men reported the existence of such a place, but no questions were given to the sample to discover the proportion of men who knew of it or who had been placed there. One man described it:

There was a small Indian man who I knew and he got in a fight with a bull at the booking desk. They cuffed his hands behind his back and worked him over and then put him in the hole and left him there for two days. He said he passed his time by doing push-ups. They stripped him naked, he had no clothing, and the hole is a little concrete cell about six foot square. There was no light and he was fed bread and water.

Most men are keenly aware that the possibility of being busted is ever-present. It may be initiated by other trusties, the medical staff, or the bulls. The men feel they must constantly watch their behavior and never step out of line in order to avoid this. They feel that if they make too many requests, even for such things as medical treatment or the use of the telephone, they may be busted. One man summed up what could happen:

A trusty can be busted to lockup for saying the wrong thing to bulls, for being disrespectful, like saying, "Go to hell," for smuggling newspapers, food, salt, coffee, sugar, or magazines into the jail. A man can also be busted for being caught trying to rabbit or for not doing his job.

Several factors should be considered in discussing the rewards and punishments which are perceived by the tramp in jail as a means of controlling his behavior. First, it is not the actual incidence of these punishments which motivates their behavior, but the threat of their use which worries them. The man who does hard time is often the one who is aware of these possibilities and is seeking to control his behavior. He may feel the need for medical treatment or a telephone call but, in his effort to avoid contact with officers, which may lead to being busted, he does not act on his need. One man summed up the effect the threat of punishment had on the inmate:

Well, one thing a man does not do in jail is talk unless he is spoken to. There is a constant fear of loss, because loss is a penalty. One way to penalize a man is simply to ignore him as he rattles the bars of his cage or the cell. For instance, a man might be going into DT's and need some medical attention, and so to attract attention of the guard he will shake the cell bars very loudly, because he is desperate for some kind of help, and he'll be penalized by simply ignoring him.

Second, most men felt there was a great deal of unpredictability in the punishments they might receive. This depended on the vagaries of the officer's moods, something a man did, and especially which officer one encountered. One comment expresses a belief widely held among the men: "The most likely way to get into trouble is by offending the ego of the staff and you do this by insulting them openly and by swearing at them under your breath." As a man seeks to order his life in the bucket in order to do easy time the sense of alienation and frustration increases, motivating him to seek a new identity and to search for escape from those things which will bring hard time.

STAGE 15: BOOKING DESK

Whether a man is a lockup or trusty the days do pass until the inmate is doing *short time* — only a few days remain on his sentence. For some, the last few days are easy time, filled with the knowledge

222

and expectation of release. For others, it is not so easy because their minds become filled with memories of the outside and they plan for the days ahead. One such individual said:

I'm getting shaky and anxious because I'm on short time. I did eighty days on drunk one time, they added a $70 fine for traffic and when it got down to five days, I couldn't take it. I got my gal to bail me out. Short time is hard time and the last few days are the hardest to do.

Eventually the morning arrives when a man knows he will be escorted from his cell, lay aside his identity as a lockup or trusty, and become, for a few hours, a kickout. That day will come sooner if he gets his good time or has earned some extra good time by giving blood or by some other means. The tramp who has few resources will leave the bucket in the same clothing with which he entered it, the same clothing he has worn continually for weeks or months if he was a lockup. The day he becomes a kickout may come earlier than expected if the ranchers in eastern Washington need men to pick fruit; then he will get an "apple kickout" or "pea kickout." If his release date happens to coincide with Christmas or some other national holiday that, too, may result in an early kickout. The time at the booking desk is brief; a man's property is returned, and if something is missing, it may be disturbing, but he will not quarrel, for the street beckons from outside the Public Safety Building. After being discharged he walks to the elevator and rides quickly to the ground floor, walks out of the building — a free man who will now take up his life as an urban nomad in other scenes of that world. If he came in a novice, he goes out with his identity changed — and with each experience of making the bucket that change will be more complete until he may find one day that there is no turning back to his previous life in civil society. Others may see him as a bum — he will see himself as a tramp who lives by the rules of the urban nomad culture.

The jail is perhaps the most important scene in the life of tramps. It is here they find the remaining shreds of respectable identity stripped away as they become participants in an elaborate ritual — that of making the bucket. Identity change takes place for these men as they are labeled "bums," cut off from former roles and identities, treated as objects to be manipulated, and coerced

223

into being acutely aware of the new definitions of social interaction, space, time, and identity which are part of the jail. The description of this rite of passage reflects the way urban nomads read their own experience. It has a ritual quality about it because it is an often repeated sequence of highly patterned events. Its structure, as well as what each stage means to those who go through them, was not created in order to organize the data — rather they were elicited from informants. The questions which were asked *of* these men were first discovered *from* them — and tramps were queried in their own language to avoid their expertise at translating their world into terms used to describe our world. Those who go through this experience often are thoroughly cut off from their former selves and alienated from the rest of society, which now views them as bums or common drunkards. Within the lives of such men there develops an *identity vacuum*, which is backed by powerful motivations to fill it, not only because of the losses, but because the inactivity, restraint, and oversensitivity to the jail staff create pressures to act, to become, and to gain a new sense of personal identity and a new set of values to replace what has been lost. The novice who repeats this experience several times may first seek to escape it by traveling to a new town, but once there he usually goes to Skid Road for ready acceptance. Sooner or later, for many men, the world and culture of the tramp becomes a viable alternative to that which has been lost in this ritual. In that culture he may still be alienated from the rest of society — but *not from himself* or others like him. He will find acceptance as well as adaptive strategies for survival as an urban nomad. But, more important, something else has been going on simultaneously during the days in jail — he has been learning the attitudes, values, and skills required for survival in this new culture.

CHAPTER EIGHT

Freedom
to Hustle

Misdemeanor inmates have no collectiveness. Subtle form of coercion used by jailers to have inmates practically run the jail — feed, clean up, wash cars, do cooking, run errands, hospital orderlies, gun range, substations. Paid help supervise. Every city has its regulars. Have more and better food, freedom to *hustle* more restricted prisoners. Some have been in so long they are almost part of the force. Should have honorary badges. Will do a favor for a price or to a pal who may return same. Otherwise you are solely out of luck.

Mr. Tanner

We have followed these men through a complex maze of experiences which they speak of as "making the bucket," a ritual which picks them up and manipulates them like pieces of dust blown by the wind. Things happen to them and they are the recipients of the action of others: they are arrested, shaken down, worked over, booked, thrown in the drunk tank, given time, made into trusties and lockups, deloused, busted, robbed, and kicked out. As indi-

225

viduals they are bereft of resources — extremely poor, unable to bail out, possessors of a criminal record, and with few friends who can offer help. Their jobs have been lost, their clothing has been defiled, their wills have been broken, and their identities have been spoiled. It would be difficult to imagine a situation in which men could be more destitute, and because this is how they read their experience their primary response is passive endurance. We have described in detail the stripping and deprivations which lead to doing hard time; we may have left the impression that this is their only response. Is there no other way to stand up to this situation without being knocked down again? Have these men lost every bit of initiative and self-assertion so that they no longer respond to life with verve, creativity, and the pride of accomplishment? Although it is true that they accommodate to the process, warily try to make themselves invisible, and seek to endure the pain, this is not the whole story, and we shall now examine other important ways they have of responding to repeated arrests and incarceration. Many things a man does in jail are routine — he eats, sleeps, washes, cleans up his tank, talks with other inmates, thinks about the past, and plans for the future. If he is a trusty he works at one of the nearly sixty different jobs to which he may be assigned. Some men argue with the bulls, attempt to rabbit from the jail, make statements to the judge, request assignments as trusties, or, in some other way, assert themselves. Any discussion of life in the bucket is filled with constant references to these and other activities such as "slipping," "bucking the bulls," "keeping one's eyes peeled," "sticking your neck out," and "stashing something." Most activities are aimed at getting out of jail, beating the drunk charge, or alleviating the intensity of hard time. Many men will do favors for other inmates by sharing cigarettes or matches, bringing extra food from the kitchen, slipping the daily newspaper to a man in lockup, making a phone call for a friend, or standing point to warn another inmate that a bull is approaching. Perhaps the most important actions a man learns in jail are labeled as *hustling*, and we shall seek to describe what tramps mean by this term, what activities it involves, why they engage in hustling, and how the ability to hustle in jail prepares them for their lives in the other scenes of the urban culture nomad.

226

Our aim has been to discover the ways in which men in this culture categorize, code, and define their own experiences. Our interest has been to discover the category system of tramps and *hustling* is another to be added to those of identity, flops, ways to beat a drunk charge, and time. In each case we have attempted to describe the social construction of reality which has been elicited from informants — the construction which is in the mind of the tramp rather than the form of reality which is in the mind of the observer. This is an idealistic goal never to be fully attained, yet it is possible to approach this ideal and the desire to do so has dictated the research strategy used in the field. It has meant that the language of tramps has been the focus of our attention and the vehicle through which we have attempted to understand their definition of reality. It has led to strategies for listening in order to discover which questions were appropriate in this culture rather than creating questions a priori and asking them without regard to their meaning to informants. It has led to an emphasis throughout the research on first discovering the terms used to categorize experience and then proceeding to elicit the meaning of these terms rather than assuming some definition more relevant to the rest of American culture. Thus, the meaning of the terms in the domain have been presented as part of an ethnographic statement which describes a part of the urban nomad culture. It contains definitions of reality constructed by members of this culture in response to their experience, passed on as part of their tradition, and learned by novices as they are taught by old-time tramps. We shall now attempt to define the many actions which are categorized by tramps as "hustling."

The verb "to hustle" is shared in many of its forms by various American subcultures, although each defines it somewhat differently. Outside of jail are men and women who become known as "hustlers," and as one informant put it, "whores are hustling, too." Tramps use this term in a wider context when they are outside of jail, but we are specifically interested in its meaning within the bucket. What does it mean when a man says, "Joe was hustling the drunk tank," or "I hustled my way out of jail?" Informants defined it as "obtaining desired ends," "anything you are doing to gain from in jail," and "any way of making it regardless of ethics."

Such translations are inaccurate and provide only an initial step in understanding the full meaning of this term. A man may be doing a favor for another in order to obtain some desired end, or he might be obeying all the rules carefully, i.e., "going by the books," in order to make his time easier, but these actions will never be considered as ways to hustle. Many examples of specific actions in jail were gathered from informants and then, for each, they were asked, "Is this a way to hustle?" A man reported, "A trusty earned some money by bumming guys getting out of jail," and subsequently indicated that the trusty was hustling but the men getting out were not. Each specific instance of an activity was classified as a kind of hustling and it was discovered that there were eleven different classes of behavior which tramps referred to as hustling. The labels for these classes of behavior make up the domain of hustling (Table 8.1) and are related to the cover term by the principle of inclusion. This taxonomy enables tramps to organize and define their own actions; hundreds of specific and unique acts are grouped together into one of these eleven categories which are in turn classified under one term. A man may appropriately say, "Joe earned money by asking kickouts for it this morning," or "Joe was bumming the kickouts," or simply, "Joe was hustling the kickouts." If a man can learn and perfect the skills needed to perform the entire range of hustling activities, he has increased his chances

TABLE 8.1 TAXONOMIC DEFINITION OF HUSTLING

Hustling										
Conning	Peddling	Kissing ass	Making a run	Taking a rake-off	Playing cards	Bumming	Running a game	Making a pay-off	Beating	Making a phone call

for doing easy time and even getting out of jail in better condition than when he came in.

Conning is a strategy used to obtain some desired end by employing a verbal deception. An inmate has opportunities to con a variety of people including inmates, bulls, the medical staff, members of the larger society, and judges. Other inmates are the most difficult persons to con since they are usually aware of the deceptions used, but this avenue of action is possible:

A tramp in the drunk tank asks a trusty to get him some Bull Durham or some candy. He intends to pay him when he returns but the trusty says he can't get it without money. He gives him some money and the trusty doesn't come back.

A man may hustle a bull by conning him in the following manner:

I was clerk and had a friend in lockup who said, "Jack, can you get me out of lockup?" So I talked to the bull and asked him if we could get this man out of lockup and told him he was a good worker. The bull got him sprung as a favor to me.

The bull may have been aware that he was being conned but will overlook it if he likes the trusty. Sometimes a person who is in lockup will plan to rabbit from the bucket and as the first step towards his escape he will attempt to be assigned as a trusty. If he is placed on the right job he may be able to escape as did the man who reported this incident:

They took me down as a trusty to the Georgetown precinct. I had this uniform but I put a T-shirt and suntans underneath and I tied the suntans around me with a mattress-cover string and buttoned the uniform up so they couldn't see the T-shirt underneath. I had my lunch and I was fixing coffee for the bulls. While they were drinking coffee I went out by the cars and took my uniform off. I had to take my shoes off before I could get out of the uniform and then I pulled my T-shirt outside so no one could see that I had tied my suntans with a string from a mattress cover. I jumped over a small wall and ran through somebody's yard. I beat those guys back down town. Luckily there was no dog in the yard there. I got picked up in a few weeks. I went back and got a jug and it was kind of cold in my room and so I went down at the waterfront and sat in the sun, and sure enough I fell asleep in the sun, rather than going back to my room, and they picked me up and took me back to jail and gave me 30 days for this drunk and 30 days for rabbiting and then I had 20 days to serve on my previous charge, so I was in for 80 days.

The medical staff are often the direct objects of attempts at conning because their professional socialization has taught them to accept, at face value, the complaints of patients more readily than the police, who tend to suspect the inmate's statements. If there is to be a therapeutic relationship between the physician and patient it must involve mutual trust, but this very confidence sets the stage for the patient to con the physician. The statement of a young college graduate may be repeated here because it shows so clearly how this type of conning goes on and how the rotation of medical personnel facilitates it:

And so for the first three or four days, he'll be collecting from the doctor because he will still be shaking. Some of them will even do push-ups or something like that before the doctor comes, just to be shaking and sweating. Rather than taking these things themselves, because they are essentially alcoholics and have gone through it cold turkey so many times, they can handle it. You build up your Bull Durham to last you as long as you can. Of course, eventually, on weekends when relief doctors come in, if you haven't seen them before, you can get even more even though you've been in for three weeks.

Conning the medical staff may be only a prelude to using other strategies: the pills may be peddled, the trip to the jail hospital may provide opportunities to steal something, or the appointment at the dentist may be used for grander purposes:

I had been on the steel after being busted. I had about 45 days to go on a 90-day sentence and I told the doctor my tooth was killing me so I couldn't eat or sleep. He sent me with a bull up to the fourteenth floor dental office in the health department. I didn't take my jacket or hat with me. The bull took me to the dental office and said he would be back in 30 minutes. I watched and when he was in the elevator I hit the stairway and ran down to the first floor. I walked out right in front of the police chief's office, and he didn't know who I was. It was raining and I didn't have a jacket but I got away and left town.

Such experiences fill the inmate with a deep sense of pride — he has so mastered the skills of his world that he can walk out a free man. The medical staff, on the other hand, when they learn of this escape, are more determined than ever to suspect any complaint which comes from one of these men. They soon develop a folklore of their own account for such behavior, including the myth that "alcoholics are pathological liars." Both the patient and the

230

medical staff are caught within a social structure that forces them to actions and conclusions which create distrust and alienation, emphasing again the futility of providing adequate medical care within such a setting.

Many people outside the jail may become the objects of a man's conning activity. Researchers, social workers, friends, relatives, and ministers have been selected at one time or another as those who might be hustled in this way:

A drunk is racked up and he calls his wife or relatives or others and they have bailed him out many times and are reluctant to do so again. He cons them into doing it by telling them that he is going to go straight this time and if they would bail him out he would really make it.

Mr. Tanner observed the men in the drunk tank:

The possessors of $20 paid their dues at the jailers' convenience and left. Others, when permitted to phone, pleaded for twenty skins — offering all sorts of inducements such as "I'll give you thirty the minute I crack my check," "Honey, Ma, buddy, get on the stick!"

Tramps know full well that outsiders perceive them as bums in need of help and they become expert at capitalizing on the sympathies of such people with their stories of hard times and good intentions.

The most sophisticated conning attempts are used with judges or other members of the court staff who have the power to release a man. Many of the strategies discussed in Chapter Five for beating a drunk charge involve conning — using an alias and making a statement are probably the most common ways a man cons the judge. If these fail to result in a suspended sentence there are still other opportunities; the friend of one informant was to be released leaving him alone to finish his sentence, and so he successfully carried out the following deception: The inmate's friend was planning to go to Wenatchee upon release where he would pick apples and he agreed to mail a letter back to the jail after his arrival in eastern Washington. The inmate, with more time to do, prepared the letter, to himself, indicating that a job was available for him in Wenatchee if he could obtain an early release from jail. He signed a fictitious name to the letter and asked yet another inmate, whose handwriting was very good, to copy it for him. The inmate knew that when his friend mailed the letter from Wenatchee the postmark would be enough to deceive the judge and possibly get him out of jail early. The letter arrived, was referred to the judge, and resulted in suspension of the balance of his sentence. Another man described a similar strategy he employed to obtain an early release for a friend:

When I got out of jail I bought a ticket to Vancouver, Washington but didn't use it. I called long distance from Tacoma to the bailiff and said, "Hello, I'm Mr. Green, a contractor from Vancouver and I have a job for a man who is up there in jail and has been an employee of mine. He's a good worker and as soon as he's ready to get out I can give him his job. I bought a ticket for him to come down to Vancouver but I wasn't able to get up to the jail when I was in Seattle today but I'm mailing it to him and he should receive it soon. I'd sure like to have him come down here to work." And so the bailiff got right on it and got the man a suspended sentence and let him out and he took the bus and left town.

Another tramp was kicked out of the bucket, cleaned himself up, went over to the courthouse, and talked to the judge himself. He pretended to be an employer and asked if there was any chance of getting a certain man out of jail since he was a good worker and he could give him a job immediately upon release. The judge was conned by this man, suspended the balance of the other man's sentence, and the two were able to leave town together — relieved to be out of jail and proud to have hustled the judge successfully.

Any man who can con a judge, or others, for that matter, does so because he has learned the cultural rules used by these people for understanding tramps. He knows that ministers, relatives, physicians, and judges have a need to help those who are less fortunate, and also a desire to see these men who are living as tramps return to a style of life which they consider more "normal." Judges, in particular, realize that repeated incarcerations do very little to induce a man to seek regular employment and be a responsible family member, but there is some solace in helping the few men who sincerely want to return to this way of life. One man wrote to the judge after being returned from the treatment center to finish his sentence in jail. He very nicely touches on all the things he knows will influence the judge such as the inadequacy of his experience at the treatment center, the system of sentencing used by the judge, and his ability to hold down a regular job:

Dear Judge: I am a returnee from the alcoholism treatment camp. The trouble first started with my snoring. They put me in separate quarters so I could get my rest and they could get theirs but the fellows thought I was too good to sleep with them. Then once they got down on me it was impossible to get along. I was lied about, criticized, etc. (i.e., how can anyone get along with a bunch of bums?) Now I am back here. If I had not committed myself (i.e., I am sincere about my drinking problem) I would have received about twenty days or less. It only seems fair that I should be released. Others with more arrests than me received shorter sentences (i.e., your system of sentencing is fair, but it doesn't include me). I have a job and am self supporting (i.e., you wouldn't want to keep a man in jail who works hard and isn't a tax burden would you?).

This man was released in a few days.

It is not only the privations associated with doing time which motivate a man to hustle in jail; the fact that he has no other means at his disposal to satisfy his wants backs him against the wall with no recourse except to hustle. Later, when he is on the street, he may be able to meet his needs by working, but he will have learned that certain deceptive strategies are equally effective and involve much less effort. There are many *means* in our culture for satisfying wants — some are legitimate and others are not. The line between these becomes blurred for a man as he repeatedly makes the bucket, and practices he once rejected are now added to his repertoire of skills to be used when the need arises. In the other scenes of this culture many occasions will arise when a skilfully constructed story will be required to circumvent a police officer, avoid being thrown out of a bar, gain assistance from friends and relatives, and get a handout from missions, social workers, or someone on the street.

Peddling is a form of interaction between two persons wherein some item of value is exchanged for money or another item of value. Sometimes a tramp will speak of trading or buying and selling, although, strictly speaking, they must be distinguished from peddling in jail. A man who sells a lockup some cigarettes is peddling them, and the relationship will be defined as peddling if he

233

initiated the sale. The man who purchases the cigarettes is making a pay-off, and this form of hustling will define the relationship if he initiated the transaction. Informants generally stated that one is peddling and the other is making a pay-off. Peddling is the form of hustling which occurs most frequently. One informant gave the following description:

A guy who works in the kitchen might make a couple sandwiches and roll them up in a piece of paper or kleenex and sneak them out. Then he watches when the guys get their commissary on Tuesday and Friday, and after they get their commissary he goes over to the tank and hollers, "Anyone want to trade cigarettes or candy for a sandwich?" And so the guys will ask him, "What kind you got?" and if he's got a meat-loaf sandwich or something they want they might trade him for cigarettes. This man is peddling sandwiches. Sometimes a man in lockup might holler at a trusty and say, "Hey, how about getting me some sandwiches? I'll pay you off in cigarettes." The man who gets the sandwiches is making a pay-off.

The constant hunger experienced by lockups provides any man with food a ready market for his wares. Perhaps the second greatest need in jail is for variety and diversion to break the routine which forms the gnawing core of hard time. Smoking helps to break the drab monotony of institutional life and food may always be traded for cigarettes, especially when the doctor stops giving pills:

So then you have to find another way. By that time you've eaten enough so you're in pretty good balance and then you can make sandwiches. Sometimes you get at night a tray which is your big meal and you can barely make a sandwich out of it using the whole tray. But in any case you can trade them for a package of Bull Durham if that's what you need. All of this is pretty common practice.

Coffee not only helps to break the routine but eases the aches from lying on the drunk tank floor and so it can be peddled for relatively large sums if the drunks have been able to smuggle money in with them. One man confessed he engaged in this rather common practice: "I was on as runner and so could hustle the drunk tank. I peddled cups of coffee to some of the drunks for 50 cents a cup."

The number of items which can be peddled in the bucket is large and includes instant coffee, tailor-made cigarettes, cards, candy bars, sandwiches, clothing, wrist watches, and even matches. A tramp in the bucket discovers that he no longer has access to even the simple amenities of life and so can only relieve the frustrations this creates by hustling. One man recalled:

Another shortage that exists in the jail is paper for rolling cigarettes. You're given Bull Durham but you're not given enough paper for an entire package of Bull Durham. Matches, also, are a big shortage, and so matches and paper become matters for trading as well as Bull Durham. Candy bars are as good as money as well as food. I have, on a number of occasions, even when I was hungry, gone without eating all of my food and thereby had a sandwich to trade for cigarettes.

Even homosexual relationships are defined by the idiom of hustling — a man "peddles his ass" to someone in jail in order to receive food and cigarettes. Some men peddle to the same inmates on a regular basis, and in such a case the trusty is "taking care of the lockup" for a price:

I used to pay off when I was in lockup, one or two packages of cigarettes a week to a man who would give me sandwiches every day for a week. It depends on who it is but you can pay by the week. A man can get busted for peddling newspapers under the doors, into one of the tanks, or magazines. Those bulls don't like to have newspapers getting all over.

Some types of hustling involve the risk that, if apprehended, one will be busted to lockup or some other place in the jail. Peddling food to men in lockup is one of the surest ways to get busted, yet men are willing to risk this in order to get what they want. Informants often told of others who had been "busted for giving another inmate a sandwich of his own food," or "peddling food to those in lockup."

Trusties have the greatest freedom to obtain things which can be peddled. They steal instant coffee, salami, and other food from the kitchen and peddle it to lockups. They may have friends visit them on the firing range and slip them items which they can use themselves or peddle. Other outside trusties can go to stores, as one man observed:

A garage man is on the outside and can go to a store and buy nickel candy bars. He brings them back into the jail and sells them for a dime. He can do this because the guys in lockup only can buy eight candy bars a week and they are all the same kind. He eats those as soon as he gets them and so wants to buy more and does so from a garage man. The garage man may get $10 by the time he gets out and also keeps himself in smokes while he is in.

"Peddling" has the same meaning in all the other scenes of this culture and it is an important way in which urban nomads survive when traveling. In American culture most people purchase what they need from business establishments where the price is set and the relationship is rather impersonal. Many individuals would hesitate to approach a stranger on the street and ask him if he would like to purchase a pair of shoes or some other used object, but tramps who have had long experience in the bucket have learned how to bargain and peddle things for money, while simultaneously losing their hesitancy to engage in this kind of behavior. The deprivations in jail provide the ideal learning situation, forcing a man to pick up the skills involved in peddling.

Kissing ass refers to a set of actions and attitudes which an inmate assumes toward the bulls and sometimes toward inmates and civilians within the jail. In order to understand this form of hustling it is necessary to see it in contrast with several other patterns of behavior used to handle the hostility aroused within the inmate. The jail staff have a great deal of power at their disposal with which to control men in jail — power based on physical coercion. Bars, locks, cells, guns, handcuffs, and fists are used to control the external behavioral responses and this kind of power evokes alienation and hostility in the inmate. The way in which one learns to handle his feelings is of utmost importance because it can lead unerringly to doing hard time. It is possible to express hatred openly toward the bulls — swearing at them, calling them names, arguing with them, threatening to go to the Civil Liberties Union over injustices received, submitting writs of habeas corpus, and constantly bucking the bulls in other ways. The man who is openly hostile and self-assertive retains a sense of integrity — he has been true to his own feelings, he has refused to become an object, he has responded as a man, and although he will suffer for his actions, he can still be proud of what he has done. Other tramps in jail will consider such a man with mixed emotions: on the one hand, he

236

commands the respect of other inmates — this person is no coward, he has guts; on the other, they consider him a fool because everyone knows he is only going to bring down the wrath of the bulls upon himself for what he does.

Some inmates barely manage to keep their hostility beneath the surface, and it may boil up in the form of silent insolence as they curse the bulls under their breath and assume facial expressions which radiate defiance. Such a person may do hard time, not from extra punishment, but from the tedious effort to control his emotions and actions; he has neither the pride which comes with open defiance nor the sense of well-being that comes from fully controlling aggressive feelings. Another group of men have solved the dilemma by exercising greater control over their feelings — they respond with a passive conformity, while retaining an inner independence of spirit. Old-time tramps are especially adept at this type of adaptation and may even be philosophical about it: the bulls have their jobs to do, some are not such bad guys after all, and if I were a bull I would probably treat tramps that way too! A man who has mastered such controlled passivity within the jail looks upon self-assertive men as fools, insolent men as novices, and those who conform too much as ass kissers. They are able to congratulate themselves on having learned to adapt so well that it doesn't bother them, and yet they still hate the system and will seek to beat it at the slightest chance. One man distinguishes this response from kissing ass: "If a bull tells me the world is square I will agree with him. That isn't ass kissing, that's going by the books."

The man who controls his anger and resentment by actively trying to curry the favor of the bulls is ass kissing — he is going to the opposite extreme of the man who openly expresses his hostility. One informant described this behavior as well as the consequences that may occur:

A trusty hangs around the bulls, talks to them even when they don't initiate it. He doesn't ignore the bulls, but hangs around with them even when there is no reason. He drinks coffee with them and sits at the same table with them. He does this so that he can get into general good standing with them in case he gets caught hustling in some other way — it is insurance against the time he is caught. He may ingratiate himself to the bulls to be able to run a game. A person who is beating the bulls may need to ass kiss in order to protect himself if suspected or caught.

Any man who informs on fellow prisoners is kissing the ass of the bulls: "A tramp casually says to one of the bulls, 'Old Fred had three extra trays at lunch today, and I only got one — I'm still hungry.'" A comment of this sort, as well as other ass kissing behavior, will be concealed from other inmates if possible, since it often alienates a man from his peers. One man described this process:

A guy pushes past several other inmates to talk to a bull and you say to him, "You ass kissing son-of-a-bitch, you pushed four guys out of the way to talk to that bull." He may retort that he was only trying to con the bull.

Some men find it easy to repress their anger and express a friendly, respectful attitude toward the police; they can usefully employ this strategy when back on the street. They will personally get to know the beat bulls, go out of their way to greet them, agree with them about the despicable behavior of other men on the street, and provide them with acceptance in a hostile world. Each act is done in the hopes that it will secure a tolerance policy from the police.

Making a run occurs often on Skid Road when several men gather in an alley or under a bridge, pool their money for a jug of wine, and send one member of the group to a bar or liquor store to purchase the beverage. If a man has no money he may still be allowed to participate in the drinking group if he will make the run. His share in the cost involves the risk of carrying the bottle back to the group when encounter with a police officer may result in a broken jug or even arrest, since the presence of a bottle makes him more visible. Incarceration in jail automatically cuts a man off from access to many resources. In examining trusty and other inmate identities we saw that men defined their place in jail with respect to the degree of restriction placed upon their movement. A man who cannot go to a store, get something from his property, obtain food from the kitchen, or gain access to some other desired item may pay another who can make a run for him. "An inmate asks an outside trusty to buy him some candy bars and gives him

238

50 cents. The trusty buys five candy bars and keeps 25 cents for himself." Making a run in jail involves risks that are similar to those encountered on the outside. A trusty returning from the garage or range will sometimes be shaken down and if he has made a run for snuff, chewing tobacco, a ball-point pen, or other hot item he may find himself busted back to the steel for trying to sell his freedom of movement in this way.

Taking a rake-off is a form of hustling in which the complexity of social relationships is increased. A tramp in the bucket can take a rake-off by learning to be sensitive to both the *needs* and *resources* of other inmates. A trusty moving between the drunk tanks, time tanks, and his own trusty tank learns to look and listen for clues on the condition of other men so he can hustle: "A trusty who can hustle the drunk tank offers to peddle a package of tailor-mades for a man in lockup for a price of 50 cents. He then sells it in the drunk tank for 75 cents." Although in one sense he is peddling the cigarettes, he is simultaneously taking a rake-off since he is performing the role of a middle man or broker. The trusty who is paid for making a run may increase his income by taking an additional cut:

A drunk or lockup asks the trusty to buy him some cigarettes and gives him 50 cents, 40 cents for the cigarettes and 10 cents for making the run. The trusty returns with a pack but takes six or seven cigarettes out and tells the man he can't get a full pack, that was all he could buy.

Several kinds of hustling must be seen not only as a means for an individual man to obtain some desired end but also as a set of economic transactions which involve social *relationships*. A man isn't just peddling, he is setting up a relationship of trust and mutual support in which both his own wants and those of another inmate are partially satisfied. One who makes a run is not just bringing a hot item to a lockup, he is establishing a relationship that transforms strangers into business partners. Although kissing ass seldom occurs between inmates, it may take place at the beginning of a relationship where an inmate wants to keep the good will of the other party. A man kisses ass or purchases good will by paying slightly above the going price for cigarettes or by refusing to

239

take a rake-off of several cigarettes. Consider for a moment the novice who has been given thirty days in jail but is not yet part of the tramp world. As he is stripped of his own identity while he is making the bucket, as his alienation grows and former social relationships shrink, and as he loses his job and becomes labeled with a jail record by former friends and relatives, he is developing new and important bonds with old-timers in the urban nomad culture. It is true that on occasion he may be scalped by another inmate and feel resentment toward those who live off another man's misery, but more often he will find that other tramps will succor him in his need. They will trade him a sandwhich for a few cigarettes when he is hungry, give him some paper to roll a cigarette when he wants to smoke, or slip him a newspaper when he becomes bored. When he gets out of the bucket with other men, a casual invitation to join them in a rendezvous on Skid Road will be difficult to turn down. It has been reported that some youths from the hippie subculture are being drawn into the world of tramps in this manner. After being arrested for possession of drugs, they are unable to bail themselves out of jail, and thus are thrown into company with urban nomads who make up the majority of inmates. After several weeks in jail they have been drawn into close relationships with these men — not simply because they are both defined as criminals by society, but because they have helped to satisfy one another's needs in a time of extreme deprivation. The hippie, upon release, moves freely between members of his own subculture and those he has met in jail.

A man in jail may attempt to hold himself aloof from other inmates — but he soon finds that he is doing hard time because he has cut himself off from access to the few resources available. Hustling capitalizes upon the needs of men who are deprived and by satisfying these needs it creates strong bonds among those who participate in the interaction. Consider the following example of taking a rake-off:

A man in lockup doesn't know the trusties and wants someone to make a run for him so he asks another lockup to get his friend (who is a trusty) to make the run and says he will give the other lockup some money. This lockup is raking off something from the economic transaction.

240

Even more important, this middle man has helped a newcomer establish a tie with a trusty, one whom he may meet again in jail or later on the street, one who may not only make a run for him in jail but will also invite him to join in sharing a jug on Skid Road. Man is a social animal who knows that the most intense anxiety comes from isolation and loneliness. Another inmate may be defined as a bum by one with few arrests, but the alienation created by the experience of incarceration draws them together as human beings who must depend on one another, forcing a redefinition of identities. Hustling not only teaches a man the skills he needs for survival in the urban nomad culture, it also paves the way to finding acceptance in that world.

Playing cards and *running a game* occur in the same primary group in jail. A man with few resources will join a card game in his tank for diversion and hope to earn some money. The four men playing poker will delegate authority to a fifth man because he has provided the cards:

A trusty or lockup has a deck of cards and supplies it to the other men to play poker. He keeps the chips which are made of another deck of cards which have been cut in various shapes to designate different amounts of money. He settles any disputes and takes a rake-off from money that is won. He gets 1¢ from each person for every 15¢ they win, 2¢ for every 25¢, 3¢ for every 40¢, and 5¢ for every 50¢.

Such small groups will also form on the outside in bars or where several men are making a flop together.

Bumming is one kind of hustling which highlights a basic difference between the values of urban nomads and other Americans. In American culture most individuals learn that self-reliance and the individual acquisition of wealth is important, and although reciprocal sharing of goods occurs in our society, it is rare because there are many opportunities for earning one's own way. It is not often that one is cast upon the resources of friends or others with nothing to offer in return. The poverty experienced in jail reduces inhibitions about asking another man for help — it is not only an acceptable form of behavior among tramps, it may be the only means of easing the pain of hard time. The acceptability associated with a minimal degree of reciprocity in American culture is generalized to a large number of items and a man in jail is soon free from restraints which previously kept him from assuming such a dependent position toward others. It becomes acceptable to bum from others and give to those who bum from you. One man reported: "I was on as a runner and hung around the guys who were getting out. I bummed them and got $18 in three weeks." A man being kicked out gives freely to those who remain because he knows he can soon be on the street and engage in a similar action, though there he will call it "panhandling."

It is possible to bum cigarettes, food, candy, and even clothing and liquor in jail:

An inmate in lockup learns that another inmate in another cell is going to be kicked out. He hollers over to the inmate in the other cell to drop off his jacket or socks to him when he is leaving.

When you get picked up you might have a bottle with you that the seal is not broken. They are supposed to give it back to you, although sometimes they don't. If a guy gets out and he is leaving he goes to the booking desk and gets his property and they may give him that bottle, and as he is leaving the jail he might pass it to a trusty or throw it in a trash can and a trusty can get it and take it back to his cell and there he can drink it.

These men who go out of jail, having shared their few remaining goods with others, return to the street with a sense of belonging to a world where human needs are met by one's peers. They may soon cut in on a drinking group to make up for the bottle that was given away or "make the sally" and get clothing to replace the items shared with another tramp. After being in jail and learning to bum, a man will never again feel threatened when he is alone on the street without a penny in his pocket for he has discovered that there is a spirit of reciprocity within the world of tramps, something which he may not have known before but which now draws him into that world, where it helps him to survive. The resources he receives from other tramps in the hour of deepest need remind him that self-reliance is not so important and that even though his self-identity has been shattered it can be rebuilt with different norms and values in this culture.

Making a pay-off has been illustrated by many of the examples given for other forms of hustling. A wide range of difficulties in jail can be alleviated by paying another inmate for goods or services.

When a man is taken to the delousing tank and realizes he is about to be stripped of his clothing which may subsequently be stolen or ruined he seeks to make a pay-off:

A new inmate goes to the delousing tank and there he is told to strip naked so his clothes can be sent to the delousing cooking place. He has a good suit which might be ruined and so he pays off the trusty in charge to let him stash his clothes in a bunk while the rest are being deloused.

Becoming a trusty is the best way to do easy time, but some men are not assigned to this role because there are no vacancies on the day they are sentenced. The trusty assigned the job of clerk knows how many new men are needed each day and informs the trusty officer who then selects from those who are given time. Once a man has been assigned to lockup he has little chance of moving out of that status to become a trusty, but the clerk is in a strategic position to be of service to such a man. Lockups have some control over their identity in the bucket if they have resources to make a pay-off: "A man in lockup pays off a clerk or other trusty to get him out of lockup on to the trusty group." The hard time caused by physical discomfort for lockups may also be reduced by making a pay-off: "A man in lockup is cold at night and wants another blanket and so asks the trusty to get him one for a fee." Letters arriving in jail do not always reach a man until he is ready to be released but, for a price, it is possible to have trusties get them from the property box. Personal appearance is always a concern to these men and they may have to hustle to be able to groom themselves properly, as one man recalled:

An inmate in lockup wants his comb from his property box and he tells the trusty, "Can you see the bull about getting my comb?" I'll give you a candy bar.

Most pay-offs are designed to make time easier, but they also partially help to restore a man's sense of personal identity. Clothes that are protected from the delousing machine and a comb acquired for personal grooming keep one from feeling and looking like a bum. Obtaining trusty status provides some control over the identity one has in jail — an identity with much greater freedom than lockup. A blanket on a cold night or an extra sandwich helps to maintain the integrity of the human body; even a letter from one's property box may maintain contact with others on the outside who support more respectable identities. Perhaps it is because of this deeper psychological value of hustling that those who cannot make pay-offs were incensed at the power of the trusties in controlling resources and services in jail. One man eloquently summed up the feelings of those who cannot make pay-offs:

When you're doing time in those tanks in the city jail, the jail is run by trusties. They run that goddamn jail. And if you're among the tramps and you ain't got no money you can be starving to death out there and you won't even get an extra heel of bread, but if you pay off them trusties, give them a candy bar, or give them cigarettes, they'll go downstairs and get your glasses out of the property box or give you food which they won't do if you're broke. They'll give you a pencil if you need one. They'll get you a letter if you need it, but without any dough, unless you pay them off, these are the biggest problems in that goddamn jail and you can't get nothin' unless you give a pay-off. They have slips that you put in for glasses that are in your property and you request them, they're in your property box, but you can't even get them then from the head trusty unless you pay him off. He makes sure he gets his cut before he gets your glasses, before you get any Bull Durham, and the price they put on them is out of this world. They get them for nothin' by stealing them from the other tanks and sell them to you for cigarettes. They have you over a barrel. If you want to keep smokin' and you want to get your glasses you have to pay off.

No amount of resentment can cause this system to change and thus, even men who despise it, find their hostility melts from the heat of their own needs and they are irresistibly drawn into making pay-offs themselves as their resources grow from bumming, peddling, or beating.

Beating is the term used to refer to any form of stealing within the bucket and is one way to gather resources if you have nothing:

An inmate in lockup is let out to go to the barber for a haircut, and on the way he ducks into the trusty tank and takes cigarettes, reading material, pills, or money which a trusty has stashed in his quarters.

Trusties have the most opportunity for beating other inmates or the staff in the jail. They can engage in this form of hustling under the pretense of providing service to the drunks:

A drunk in the drunk tank asks a trusty to make a run for him for cigarettes. The drunk gives him $10 and offers to pay him a certain amount, but the trusty takes the $10 and goes to bed instead of getting the cigarettes and change.

244

The possibility that another man will beat you for your dough in this kind of situation depends upon how well you know one another. A newcomer is drawn into establishing friendly relationships with other tramps in order to avoid the higher risk of being robbed which often takes place in more impersonal relationships.

Every man in jail, especially those without personal funds, is on the lookout for chances to steal from the jail staff even though this carries with it the risk of being busted. Failure to dispose of the stolen goods carefully may lead to the following kind of experience:

I was a hospital orderly. There was a different doctor in the jail every night and one day when the doctor left he forgot to lock up the doors to the pills. Another orderly and I beat him for goof balls, yellow jackets, and barbituates. We got loaded and the other guy started performing. We set the mattress on fire and the bulls discovered us. They shook us down for pills and threw us on the steel.

Kitchen men are in the best position to beat the bulls for food but they still must smuggle it back into the main jail area in order to turn it into cash or cigarettes. A trusty may "put concentrated coffee into little plastic containers and peddle them to the guys in the tanks; then at night they are able to make coffee from hot water." Sugar is often smuggled out of the kitchen in Bull Durham sacks to help make the food more tasty. A man must use devious strategies for getting stolen goods to his customers. One man described the following one:

A kitchen trusty makes a sandwich in the kitchen and sticks it in his sock to get by the shake-down when he returns from work. He then peddles this for pills, cigarettes or something else to men in lockup.

Beating, more than any other form of hustling, creates dependency ties among men in jail — ties which do not end when they are released from the bucket, but continue to link men together in other scenes of this culture. One man described the penalties for getting caught and his own narrow escape from being busted back to lockup because another trusty warned him in time:

Well, they can shake you down. They used to make these big sweet brownies down in the kitchen, and one of the trusties had 14 brownies on him. They are made up mostly entirely of sugar and he had them in his pants and in his sleeves and they shook him down and made him sit down right outside the elevator and eat all of them. He almost

245

got sick from that. They can shake you down when you come up from the kitchen. I know sometimes they will strip you completely naked, look between your toes and feel the bottom of your feet, and look up your ass, looking for pills or something. One time I was coming up from the kitchen and got on the elevator and the elevator guy says, "Got anything on you," and I said, "Yeah, I got a lump" — which means a sandwich. The elevator guy said, "They're shaking down bare ass up there, better get rid of it." We were already started up but he took us back down to the kitchen and we got rid of it.

Whether an inmate warns another of an impending shake-down, helps another slip something by the bulls, or stands point for one who is beating the bulls for smokes, his actions symbolically define the boundaries of two cultural worlds. Those who are alienated are learning there is safety in depending on others of your own kind — or others you are slowly coming to resemble.

Making a telephone call is a simple act performed by many men in jail, but this phrase has a very complex meaning. It is a privilege of every inmate, in one sense, but if a man cannot make a phone call the definition of this action changes slightly. A lockup may have a girl friend who doesn't know he is in jail but would be able to send him some money if she knew, and if he cannot gain access to the telephone, a trusty may make the phone call for him and the action will be considered one kind of a *favor*. Although the policy is to allow lockups to make one call per week, 45 per cent of the sample reported they had been refused permission to use the phone when they were in lockup. One man recalled: "In 1966 the officer pinned a printed sign on his shirt which read, THE ANSWER IS NO." The unpredictability of the officers on duty was described by another:

Again it depends on the bull. Some will let you call every day and some will only let you make one call a week. In 1963 a bull said I had no reason to make a phone call because I had been given time and no one could help me.

What does a tramp do when he cannot use the phone? He hustles a trusty and makes a pay-off to him if he will make the call. The trusty is making a phone-call hustle by completing the call and accepting the pay-off.

A tramp in the drunk tank or one in lockup can't make a phone call often and so he asks a trusty to make a phone call for him. The trusty pretends he can't make a phone call but says he could take a chance and stick his neck out for two dollars.

Thus, one simple phrase actually designates three distinct kinds of action: a privilege, a favor, and a hustle.

Slowly but surely the man who is doing time in jail learns the meaning of hustling. He sees other men turning their limited resources into cash, cigarettes, or something else they need. He hears others talking of making a pay-off or he is asked if he would like to peddle several of his candy bars for cigarettes. He discovers that he can engage in bumming without losing the respect of those around him or that he can beat the jail for something while another man watches for the bulls. As he adds each specific kind of hustling to his repertoire of skills for survival, he becomes more comfortable with the growing sense that he is a tramp, a member of an alienated category of men who have devised adaptive strategies for coping with their situation in life. These strategies are coded in the language forms of this culture, but one learns far more than a set of terms and the actions which they label — he learns the underlying logic and principles which organize the knowledge shared by those who live by this culture. The organizing principles for the domain of hustling were elicited from informants by means of the triadic sorting task discussed earlier and are shown in Table 8.2. They provide us with a componential definition of hustling.

Four dimensions of contrast define the terms which make up

TABLE 8.2 COMPONENTIAL DEFINITION OF
HUSTLING DOMAIN

	Restriction	Risk	Reciprocity	Resources
Conning	None	Yes	Negative	None
Peddling	None	Yes	Balanced	Goods
Kissing ass	None	No	Balanced	Services
Making a run	Drunks, Lockups	Yes	Balanced	Services
Taking a rake-off	Drunks	No	Balanced	Services
Playing cards	Drunks	No	Negative	Money
Bumming	None	No	Negative	None
Running a game	Drunks	No	Balanced	Goods and service
Making a pay-off	Drunks	Yes	Negative	None
Making a phone call	Drunks, Lockups	No	Balanced	Services

this contrast set. *Restriction* refers to the relative opportunity drunks, lockups, and trusties have to engage in each kind of hustling activity. Trusties, as we saw earlier, have the fewest restrictions on their freedom but this is only one of the reasons men are eager to become trusties; far more important is the fact that trusties have unrestricted freedom to engage in all forms of hustling. Lockups can engage in all types of hustling save making a run or a phone call while drunks can only con, peddle, kiss ass, bum, and make a pay-off. The man in the drunk tank is the only one considered before the law to be innocent, yet in nearly every way his lot is the most difficult. He has no bunk or blanket, no means for personal grooming, the greatest difficulty in contacting the outside, and very limited opportunity for hustling. The differential opportunity to hustle is a powerful force, motivating the trusties to perform their jobs satisfactorily. If you are busted back to the steel you will not only eat poor food and endure greater boredom, you will have less chance to hustle other inmates.

Each form of hustling is also defined by the relative degree of *risk* it involves; though punishment for hustling is not always predictable, there is always the possibility of being busted if a man cons, peddles, makes a run, beats, or makes a pay-off. Once an inmate has learned this dimension of contrast he is able to make a choice, weighing the intensity of his own need, the visibility of his activity, and the desirability of his present status. Old-time tramps caution newcomers to avoid some kinds of hustling until their skills have improved and encourage them to try other means which do not result in being busted. Stories of life in the drunk tank or a stand-up cell reinforce the learning process making even the most awkward novice an apt pupil.

The dimension of *reciprocity* underscores the awareness on the part of informants that each kind of hustling is an exchange relationship.[1] When the relationship is *negative*, the one who is hustling gains something, but the others in the transaction do not always receive something in return. When one inmate beats another for some cigarettes, he has gained while the other has lost. The relationship is *balanced* when all members of the transaction gain something; these gains may range from the sense of accep-

248

tance the officer feels from ass-kissing behavior on the part of a trusty to regular amounts of money gained from running a game. There is a subtle change in the relationship when two men become good friends in jail — they begin to exchange favors rather than hustling each other. Friends are defined in the tramp culture not only as persons you travel with, make a flop with, or share a jug with, but also by the kind of reciprocity that is involved in doing favors rather than hustling.

Finally, hustling is defined by the *resources* necessary to engage in each kind of activity. Bumming, beating, and conning are options to any man who has certain personality traits and skills but has no money, goods, or services. An inmate with a deck of cards is in a position to earn money by running a game while those with money are able to get what they need by making pay-offs. The man who has learned the cultural logic of hustling can quickly inventory his resources and know which forms of action are open to him.

The skills involved in hustling not only prepare a man to cope more effectively with his life in the Seattle city jail — he is now ready for incarceration in almost any jail. As a stranger in another town, a man might be arrested and given time, but he will not be a stranger for long if he knows how to hustle. He can engage in most forms of hustling in almost any jail in the country; this will immediately create new bonds of human sociability and contact, not only enabling him to meet his basic needs while in jail, but also providing a sense of belonging to a group of men who may be outcasts from society but offer him much-needed support and friendship. As pointed out earlier, socialization into the Skid Road culture or the tramp world is facilitated by the experience of incarceration:

It is in this phase that the individual may be publicly labeled a deviant through arrest, sentence, and incarceration. Incarceration throws him into intimate contact with fellow associates from skid row and intensifies his socialization into the subculture (Wallace, S. 1968:101).

But how does this experience intensify socialization while stripping away old identities and labeling the man with new ones? Making the bucket does this by motivating a man to learn, and providing the opportunity to master not only the language, but, more important, the essential skills of this culture. In the other scenes of the urban nomad culture are a wide variety of strategies which men refer to as "ways of making it." The most important elicited from informants are shown in Table 8.3 juxtaposed with the skills learned in jail, demonstrating how well a man has learned to survive in the wider culture when he has learned to adapt to the bucket. The context of action, the people and places, and even some of the terms used to label action, are different from those within the bucket — but the underlying logic or principles are much the same. When a man learns to hustle in jail he has learned about his own identity, how to take risks, what is involved in reciprocity, and what resources are needed — principles which have a close correlation with his life in the other scenes of this culture. On Skid Road he can still survive: if he needs money he can panhandle or peddle some article of clothing; if he wants a drink he can cut in on a group of men whom he met in jail; if he is stopped by a bull he can kiss his ass or con him into another period of freedom; if someone asks him to make a run he knows the meaning of that request; if he needs cigarettes he can make

TABLE 8.3 TRAMP SURVIVAL STRATEGIES

In the bucket	*Other scenes*
Hustling:	Ways of making it:
Conning	Conning
Peddling	Peddling
Kissing ass	Kissing ass
Making a run	Making a run
Taking a rake-off	Taking a rake-off
Playing cards	Gambling
Bumming	Panhandling (stemming)
Running a game	Running a game
Making a pay-off	Making a pay-off
Beating	Boosting
Making a phone call	———
Working as trusty	Working
Giving blood	Making the blood bank
———	Making the Sally
———	Making the V.A.
———	Junking
———	Pooling

the blood bank; and if he wants to work he may be able to employ a skill learned while a trusty in jail.

We have focused upon the *language* of tramps as a means to understanding their culture, and while there are certain theoretical reasons for taking this approach, it is empirically valuable because it actually describes the very men we have been discussing. As a man moves from civil society through the stages of making the bucket he acquires a vocabulary of this culture from those who have been tramps for many years. He learns, in a less structured way, the very terms and meanings which we have learned, and this learning is crucial to his socialization:

The final stages in the process of becoming a skid rower is marked by integration into the skid row community and acculturation into the subculture. As the new recruit moves into the final stage of his natural life history, he masters skid row argot. Proper use of skid row terms quickly identifies him as a genuine insider (Wallace, S. 1968:101).

From an ethnographic point of view, the man who is acquiring this culture learns first to identify specific objects and events such as flops, drunk tanks, and panhandling with the correct terms, and then goes on to learn how they are taxonomically related. Most important, as he is fully socialized into this culture he learns the underlying semantic principles of such domains as tramps, trusties, flops, time, places in the bucket, hustling, and ways of making it. When he has acquired this knowledge he is able to organize his behavior according to the culture of urban nomads.

CHAPTER NINE

*A World
of Strangers
Who Are Friends*

Each year in the United States more arrests are made for public drunkenness than for any other crime. Although these arrests are made at the discretion of the police, they express and symbolize the way our society evaluates those whose style of life does not conform to the main stream of American culture. The drunk charge covers a multitude of sins — sleeping in public places, urinating in alleys, drinking on docks, sitting in bars, begging on streets, claiming the public places of our cities as one's home. The drunk charge sweeps many into jail who are quickly released for a few dollars. The urban nomad has little money, cannot beat the drunk charge in court, and so must pay for his style of life by doing time. He is punished for the crime of poverty — he doesn't have a $20 license fee for drinking. And his punishment may reach grotesque proportions as he does a life sentence on the installment plan for living by the tramp culture.

252

This study in urban anthropology has taken us into the inner world of this subculture, a world of implicit rules and definitions which these men use to understand and organize their own experience. This has not been a complete ethnography but, instead, we have studied the relationship between tramps and institutions of law enforcement. In describing the domains of this culture from the insider's point of view we have seen how the institutions which seek to control and punish these men for living as urban nomads actually draw them into this world and keep them there. The ethnographic approach has enabled us to describe in great detail a process long recognized as part of many deviant subcultures:

It is by now a thoroughly familiar argument that many of the institutions built to inhibit deviance actually operate in such a way as to perpetuate it. For one thing, prisons, hospitals, and other agencies of control provide aid and protection for large numbers of deviant persons. But beyond this, such institutions gather marginal people into tightly segregated groups, give them an opportunity to teach one another the skills and attitudes of a deviant career, and even drive them into using these skills by reinforcing their sense of alienation from the rest of society (Erikson 1962:311).

The urban nomad culture is characterized by *mobility, alienation, poverty,* and a unique set of *survival strategies.* Some men enter this way of life by choice, others are pushed toward it by personal problems, and still others are drawn to some scenes in this culture because that is where the action is. Whatever the initial impetus, once a man moves to the edge of this world he will be thrust to its center by repeated incarceration.

Urban nomads have developed a style of life based on *mobility.* They travel from town to town, job to job, and mission to mission. They ride freight trains in circuits which cover the continent. They go from one harvest to another in broken-down automobiles. They walk the streets of the city in search of a spot job or a place to sleep. The fact that they wander continuously from place to place is not nearly so important as the fact that mobility has been internalized as part of their social identity. These men see themselves and others who are like them according to nomadic criteria. The significant features of social identity in this culture involve the extent to which one travels, how he travels, and how he lives when

253

he travels. The tramp is on a perpetual journey and the trip is more important than the destination. The wanderings of any tramp have boundaries: for some it is the world; to others it is the nation; and still others move about within a single city with only occasional forays beyond its streets. Many complex motivations lie behind their mobility, but one is predominant. The structure of our law enforcement institutions makes travel a necessity for these men. Repeated arrests mean a growing criminal record which cuts a man off from jobs and friends. With each succeeding arrest, the length of time he must serve in jail is increased. The only sure way to maintain a good record is to leave town. As the number of days hanging grows over a period of repeated arrests and a man begins to contemplate the imminent necessity of leaving town, he may be apprehended yet another time and receive a long, suspended sentence. That day in court will mark his last in *that* city for at least six months. Even the homeguard tramp who patiently does his time on each sentence will sooner or later become too valuable as a trusty, or become a marked man for some other reason, and so be driven to mobility. Others find themselves loaded on a box car and shipped out of town by the police when the harvest is over. Whereas most Americans are *drawn to* a destination when they travel, urban nomads are *pushed from* a destination by these forces. In a multitude of ways, then, the practices of the police and courts, which are intended to control and punish, actually perpetuate the core of this culture — a nomadic style of life.

Although they live in our cities, urban nomads are *alienated* from the rest of society. They are stereotyped by others as bums and common drunkards. Whether looking for a job or a place to sleep, they will move with great care and expect rejection at every turn. Rejection and alienation demand constant vigilance, attempts to become invisible, and carefully constructed definitions of those who will surely interfere with one's life. The tramps' sense of alienation may have begun with friends and kinsmen because of excessive drinking or failure to hold down a steady job, but the gap is widened dramatically when they make the bucket. They lose self-respect when labeled as "drunken bums" and "Skid Road bastards." Their jail record becomes known to employers and friends, further separating them from civil society. An identity vacuum is created within as items of personal property, symbols of their identity, disappear. As they are worked over at the call box, on the elevator, or in jail, they find that autonomy and executive command over their lives are slowly dissolving. In the grey confines of the drunk tank their communication with the outside world is cut off. They appear in court after days of waiting, are made to feel like bums, and by their very appearance lose the right to be considered innocent until proven guilty. They may even have the blood drawn from their veins before they are released from jail. Most important, as they are cut off from former jobs, families, and friends, they lose those roles which gave them respectable identities. With each repeated arrest they may have less to lose, less which binds them to the larger society. For most men the stripping process works more deeply each time until finally, the alienation has become permanent and their personal identities are thoroughly spoiled for a meaningful life anywhere except in the tramp world. And thus our institutions perform a rite of passage for these men, moving them out of the larger society and transforming their identities without providing a way for them to move back again or to alleviate the sting of rejection.

But there is another side to the alienated status of urban nomads. The forces which wrench them from one social network thrust them into another. The tramp world is especially suited for those with spoiled identities. Acceptance in that culture is based on rejection from the other and the life style which was held to be despicable has now become an asset. A nomadic way of life not only hides what others may consider to be personal failures, but it is a world of strangers who are friends. The analysis of hustling showed that tramps define their strategies for survival in jail by the criteria of reciprocity. There is a "brotherhood of the road" in this culture which is often entered while in jail. Of course liquor, which is defined in American culture as a social lubricant, is widely used by urban nomads. When strangers meet they become friends more quickly when they have had a few drinks. Aside from the physiological effects of alcohol, drinking rituals, bottle gangs, and sharing a drink with another are powerful symbols of acceptance and comradeship among those who have known the opposite from outsiders. Skid Road bars are not simply places to drink, they are institutions where strangers with spoiled identities can meet and find security in their common humanity as tramps. But even as a man finds companionship on Skid Road he is reminded of his vulnerability to the police and so, after a few months, he must move on, knowing, however, that in the next town there will be kindred souls on Skid Road who will share a jug with him, show him some good flops, and warn him of the local police practices. After thirty days in jail a tramp owes himself a drunk, not simply because he desires to gratify those impulses which have been denied while incarcerated, but because drinking and drunkenness are the prime symbols of acceptance for the man who has come through a ritual experience of alienation.

The lives of urban nomads are marked by periodic *poverty*. They work at spot jobs, make the harvest for a few months, or live off meager pension checks. Their poverty is often increased by bailing out of jail or paying off fines. When arrested they are especially vulnerable to being robbed, rolled, or clipped. Because they are bums they do not deserve property receipts. These men not only *lose* their money when they make the bucket, but their poverty becomes the major reason for doing time in jail. With each arrest their sentences are lengthened while those with money pay the same amount. Drunk drivers are often given fines which can be worked off by doing time but tramps are seldom arrested for driving while drunk and they are not fined. When a tramp repeatedly compares $20 bail with the months he does in jail he comes to realize the deep significance of his poverty. As he goes to court and sees others, who are earning money from steady jobs, released because they have steady jobs, he is again reminded that monetary considerations are primary in our system of justice. Whereas poverty may hamper a man who aspires to a middle-class way of life, except for the lack of bail money it poses little difficulty for a tramp. In fact, a nomadic way of life almost requires that one have few material possessions. As one is socialized into this world he learns that the most respected kinds of tramps are those with the fewest possessions, those who can travel "streamline" and yet survive by their wits. The lack of possessions takes on a new meaning for such a man and each time he is released from jail without a penny in his pocket he learns anew the importance of other tramps who share this world where poverty need not deter him from participating in the culture.

In order to be a successful urban nomad it is necessary to learn the *strategies for survival* in this culture. Whether panhandling, junking, boosting, or peddling, each way of making it requires learning certain skills. If a man is to be mobile he cannot depend upon a single vocation but will need a variety of ways to earn a living. If a man is alienated he will have trouble holding down a steady job even if he wants one — sooner or later the stigma of his past will color his relationships with employers and colleagues. But since the skills needed in this culture are based on different values and norms, they require deep changes in personality rather than the simple acquisition of new techniques. The self-reliance which inhibits begging by most Americans must be altered to allow for this way of earning a living; values placed upon honesty, pride of accomplishment, and the virtue of hard work must all be transformed to pave the way for junking, boosting, conning, and peddling. New risks are encountered in all these ways of making it and must be considered by those who use these strategies, but the jail setting provides the ideal situation for learning to survive in the other scenes of this culture. After months of hustling or observing others hustle in the bucket, survival as an urban nomad becomes a viable alternative to other ways of life. A man may lose a great deal when he goes to jail on a drunk charge but if he is being drawn into this culture he has also gained invaluable skills.

As these men repeatedly make the bucket and do their time, *dynamic* processes are at work to change their perception of themselves and teach them styles of living which are alien to most Americans. They acquire new identities, skills, and motivations. These men have been to school where they have been taught *who* they are, *how* they should act, and given the *desire* to do so: Skid Road bums to the outsider, tramps to the insider, and urban no-

257

mads to the anthropologist. Making the bucket affects deep and lasting changes in these men. The difference between this experience and identity change rituals in most societies, our own included, is that most schools for changing identities and teaching new roles elevate a person to a higher status — they are graduation ceremonies. The one described in this book lowers a man into a world and culture which is held in disrepute. He has not been graduated but demoted. He has not gone through a promotion ceremony but a degradation ritual.

From the outside it appears that these men simply run from confinement to freedom, from restrictions to excess. They seem to seek self-punishment by their pattern of living. Though there is some truth in these observations, they are far too simple to account for the culture of tramps. The highly sophisticated organization of behavior which we have examined is not that of burned-out, backward schizophrenics. *It is that of men adapting to a society whose structure and institutions hold no place for them.* This fact has arisen again and again as we have listened to tramps tell it like it is. How does this description of the urban nomad culture provide a basis for the *renewal* of our institutions to provide freedom, equality, and justice for tramps as well as others? Many specific changes could easily be made: property receipts given to all inmates; daily court for drunk cases; a more equitable bail system; public defenders for the poor; a new delousing process; personnel trained in rehabilitation to operate the jail; changes in the laws governing drunkenness and drinking; and a host of others. Leaders in Seattle are actively working to change many facets of this system but those who work in the law enforcement institutions are often caught in the archaic system which has developed. During 1967, the Seattle Chief of Police stated publicly:

As a public official I have no choice. Whether alcoholism is a disease or not would not affect my official position. Drunkenness is a crime. So we must enforce the law by arresting people. We know in the Police Department that probably right at this moment there are more than 200 men in the city jail serving sentences for drunkenness who have never posed any threat to the community in any fashion at all. The only person they've hurt is themselves. We also know that if these people were not arrested and jailed at frequent intervals they wouldn't live very long. We do know that there must be a better way to handle them and we do know that these people are not criminals in the sense of having deliberately selected a different than normal way of living.[1]

Civic officials in Seattle generally share this sentiment and are committed to discovering a better way. The Municipal Criminal Court has begun to provide the services of a public defender for some who are too poor to pay for an attorney. An earlier report from my research was used by the Seattle City Council and court officials to better understand this population and to make changes in the law enforcement process.[2] This court has already begun to hear cases on Saturday in order to keep men from spending unnecessary time in the drunk tank awaiting arraignment. The city council has recommended the repeal of certain laws related to public drunkenness and plans to set up a detoxification center which will serve as an alternative to the jail.[3] Many other specific changes must be made if tramps are to have equal justice, but these are beyond the scope of this book. However, this study should provide a basis for making such changes.

Institutional renewal requires more than revising local ordinances and changing the policies of police and courts. If urban institutions are to serve a multicultural constituency we must all have a deeper understanding and commitment to the American value of *freedom*. Can we create a society which will recognize the dignity of diverse culture patterns; and one which allows people the freedom to live by these cultures? Urban nomads are but one category of men for whom this question is relevant. Can we renew our institutions to include those who live by Black culture, hippie culture, Mexican-American culture, or any of the many other subcultures which constitute our pluralistic society? If we continue to make *poverty* and *life styles*, which threaten us because they are different, the basis for justice and punishment, then the urban crisis will continue. We must see these cultures from the inside, as we have done with urban nomads, then go on to *accept* the presence of such life styles. We must allow those who choose to remain outside the melting pot to do so and not allow this choice to cut them off from equal justice under the law.

This kind of freedom, built into the fabric of our institutions, will mean several things to tramps. For some men, drinking has become an obsession, a craving which cannot be explained simply as participation in a drinking culture. Some of these men experience months of intoxication, endangering their health and safety. They squeeze alcohol from shoe polish or "canned heat," mix gasoline with milk, drink hair tonic or after-shave lotion to satisfy their craving. It may be best to consider such tramps as being afflicted with a disease which requires medical and psychiatric treatment. But, does the necessity of medical treatment justify incarceration and the denial of freedom? Some diseases which are a threat to the individual and society alike and for which there is an effective treatment, such as tuberculosis, have been causes for confinement. Others, such as some types of mental illness, pose such a threat to society that confinement is required even though there is no effective treatment. But chronic public drunkenness is neither excessively threatening to society nor significantly responsive to any treatment so far devised. A recent publication of the National Center for Prevention and Control of Alcoholism states:

. . . it would appear that the prognosis for chronic psychotic and Skid Row alcoholics is poor, and that less than 10 to 12 percent can obtain substantial aid from ordinary therapy (National Institute of Mental Health 1967:37).

Although it is important to provide emergency treatment and the *opportunity* for extensive therapy, involuntary treatment of these men will rob them of their freedom without the promise of changing them. This is one of the major reasons why the Supreme Court ruled as it did in the case of *Powell v. Texas.*

Yet the medical profession cannot, and does not, tell us with any assurance that, even if the buildings, equipment, and trained personnel were made available, it could provide anything more than slightly higher-class jails for our indigent habitual inebriates. Thus we run the grave risk that nothing will be accomplished beyond the hanging of a new sign reading "hospital" — over one wing of the jailhouse (*Powell v. Texas* 1968:13).

The lives of urban nomads are surrounded by institutions which act upon them, coercing them to live by their wits, robbing them of a sense of freedom and responsibility for their own actions. Most tramps need freedom rather than assistance, respect rather than restrictions. If we grant them this kind of freedom they may drink excessively and appear on our streets in a state of intoxication. Some will need to be physically removed to detoxification centers to protect themselves or others, but does such behavior demand months and years in jail? Perhaps many of these men should be considered as terminally ill and repeated drunkenness should not result in longer jail sentences any more than repeated heart attacks. If they were given freedom to choose emergency treatment when needed and longer range rehabilitation when desired, they would be exercising responsibility over their own lives, an experience which is all too uncommon in their world. This in itself could be the first and most important step towards recovery for those who are chronic alcoholics.

Other men are drawn into this world by making the bucket on a variety of charges but they are not chronic alcoholics. Repeated incarceration leads to a more nearly permanent affiliation with the tramp world than they desire. They may then want to move back into that segment of society from which they came, but find that their changed identities, and the stigma of being a bum, keep them locked into this subculture. Rehabilitation programs for such men could act as a reverse rite of passage and enhance their freedom to *choose* their style of life. Some men may wish to alternate between the world of urban nomads and other subcultures. Programs of rehabilitation, whether for chronic alcoholics or simply for tramps who want to move to another way of life, when chosen because they are alternatives to a jail sentence, do not provide opportunity to exercise personal freedom. The choice to remain a tramp and the choice to become something else must both be live options if we are to extend freedom to these men.

Finally, there are men who, out of desire, habit, or some other reason, will always be tramps. Is American society large enough to tolerate and even welcome such diversity? Can we guarantee citizens the right to be different when this means some men will choose to be tramps? Can we allow men to drink from bottles in Skid Road alleys as well as from thermos jugs in football stadiums? Sleep in fields and under bridges as well as in camp grounds and public beaches? Beg from strangers as well as friends? Become intoxicated in full public view as well as behind the walls of expensive homes? Perhaps we have been unable to allow such freedom in our cities because, although the police chief mentioned above could testify that these men pose a threat to no one but themselves, this has not been the case. The tramp, by his way of life, appears to have rejected middle-class norms and values and this may be a greater threat than criminal violence. Perhaps this is why we have waited so long to renew our institutions — to do so would require that we accept different values and patterns of behavior as valid. Sooner or later another case will come before the Supreme Court and it will rule that a jail sentence for *public* drunkenness is cruel and unusual punishment — not simply because it *wastes* lives but because socially and psychologically it *changes* lives. That decision will be the first step in restoring freedom to urban nomads and the day may come when we will go on to recognize the creative skill and dignity in this subculture so different from our own. When that day comes we will have moved closer to destroying the separateness which now permeates our cities, closer to including all the various subcultures in our multicultural society. Institutional renewal must go on until we have a society based not on the unity of similarity, but on the acceptance of difference. Beyond our nation, living in other cultures, is a world of strangers. Recognizing the dignity of urban nomads is a small but important step to creating a world of strangers who are friends.

262

Notes

CHAPTER ONE

1. *Newsweek* Magazine, 1969:41.
2. Two analytic distinctions require clarification. Anthropologists generally study some *collectivity of human beings* and report on the *regular patterns of behavior* which are found there. A variety of terms refer to *collectivities*: "family," "community," "group," "society," etc. The primary term used to refer to *regular patterns of behavior* is "culture." The concept of culture which underlies this study will be developed more fully; briefly, it refers to the symbolic system of knowledge people use to order their behavior as members of a group. The men studied have learned some traditions which are common to most Americans, and others which are common to most Westerners. They have also learned a pattern for living which is distinct from many other Americans and Westerners — and it is this aspect of their knowledge which we refer to as a *subculture*. It is this system of symbols which will be described, in part, throughout this book. Although "subculture of urban nomads" is technically more accurate, it will be used interchangeably with "culture of urban nomads." This shorter form is not only more convenient but is used to place their style of life on a par with other behavior patterns. "Subculture" is not meant to carry any inference of inferiority as "subhuman" sometimes does — the traditional knowledge used by these men to organize their behavior shows a great deal of creative intelligence and a dignity which commands our respect.

But, in what sense are these men a group, a community, or a society? They belong to many groups or collectivities, as we shall see. In jail they are members of a cell group, a work party, or friendship clique. When they are not in jail they may participate in drinking groups, work in organizations, and travel with a few friends. Urban nomads will be referred to as a group, sometimes a minority group, but they do not form a community or collectivity in the usual sense of these terms. More particularly, they are a *category* of urban males who share a common way of life, a culture. Though we shall examine some of the groups which are formed in jail, we shall concentrate on the structure of their culture, not the structure of group relations and interaction.

3. The term "urban nomads" was first suggested to me by Walter B. Miller of the Joint Center for Urban Studies of the Massachusetts Institute of Technology and Harvard University. It seems preferable to "tramps" and "migrants" since these are local terms, whereas "nomads" may have the possibility of wider application. A more detailed discussion of the meaning of this term and why it is used to typify this subculture is presented in Chapter Three.

4. One of the most recent studies of the police, which provides another perspective on many of the issues raised here, is V*arieties of Police Behavior: The Management of Law and Order in Eight Communities* by James Q. Wilson. This book not only contains references to many other studies but complements the viewpoint presented here. In the introduction Wilson states:

> A comprehensive study of the patrol function would, ideally, examine police-citizen contacts from the perspective of all participants and from start to finish — from initial police intervention to final disposition, if any, by the courts and the correctional institutions. This study is partial in that it examines only the police, not the citizen, limits its attention to police treatment of citizens, and considers only indirectly the treatment accorded citizens by other criminal justice agencies. Only a shortage of resources precluded the larger study. There is a risk that in examining only the police one will be led wrongly or unknowingly to accept their premises and conclusions. No effort at "scientific detachment" can be strong enough to avoid this altogether, though I have tried to be on my guard. The problem is stated here so the reader can be on his guard too (1968:10).

This same problem is inherent in the present volume, although it involves accepting the premises of the citizen rather than the police.

Although it would be possible to attempt to integrate the views of the police, judges, and other professionals with those of the men studied here, such an approach has many hazards. Becker has clearly stated the point of view taken here:

> It is, of course, possible to see the situation from both sides. But it cannot be done simultaneously. That is, we cannot construct a description of a situation or process that in some way fuses the perceptions and interpretations made by both parties involved in a process of deviance. We cannot describe a "higher reality" that makes sense of both sets of views. We can describe the perspectives of the other group: the perspectives of the rule-breakers as they meet and conflict with the perspectives of those who enforce the rules, and vice versa. But we cannot understand the situation or process without giving full weight to the differences between the perspectives of the two groups involved (1963:173).

5. The concept of culture has been used in different ways by anthropologists and other social scientists and thus it is important to make clear the usage

264

followed in this book. Sturtevant has reviewed many of the studies which are based on the concept of culture used here and he states:

> It is not a new proposal that an important aspect of culture is made up of the principles by which a people classify their universe. . . . However, the explicit definition of culture as a whole in these terms, and the proposition that ethnography should be conceived of as the discovery of the "conceptual models" with which a society operates was first stated quite recently in an elegant, brief paper by Goodenough (1964:100).

We have already quoted briefly from this paper, but a longer statement may amplify the meaning of culture used here:

> A society's culture consists of whatever it is one has to know or believe in order to operate in a manner acceptable to its members, and to do so in any role that they accept for any of themselves. Culture, being what people have to learn as distinct from their biological heritage, must consist of the end product of learning: knowledge, in a most general, if relative, sense of the term. By this definition, we should note that culture is not a material phenomenon; it does not consist of things, people, behavior, or emotions. It is rather an organization of these things. It is the forms of things that people have in mind, their models for perceiving, relating, and otherwise interpreting them (Goodenough 1957:167).

Although we have aimed at developing the classification systems, conceptual models, and cognitive maps of informants, the importance of expressed behavior should not be obscured. There are differences between what people say they do and what they actually do, and such differences require further investigation. But, since the *meaning* of what people do is open to a variety of interpretations, observation of behavior often imposes the outsider's interpretation on that behavior. It is our contention that, "The great problem for a science of man is how to get from the objective world of materiality, with its infinite variability, to the subjective world of form as it exists in what, for lack of a better term, we must call the minds of our fellow men" (Goodenough 1957:173). Furthermore, the distinction between cognitive maps and expressed behavior is not entirely correct. Much of what we consider *behavior* can be empirically studied by use of verbal reports from informants. A man is engaging in behavior when he tells us how he identifies places to sleep in the city and how he feels about these places. Observations of men sleeping in these places would undoubtedly add to our knowledge, but they could never tell us what the definition of the situation is for the same men. The study of terminological systems will not reveal exhaustively what there is to know about a culture, nor will it even provide a complete description of the cognitive life of those studied, but it will certainly tap a central part of the culture and cognition of informants.

An analogy suggested by Wallace may further clarify the difference between the study of cultural behavior as followed here and that used by many other behavioral scientists:

> The work of the ethnographer, in describing the cognitive processes which have been culturally standardized in society, may perhaps best be made clear by an analogy. Let us suppose that a nonmathematician is given the task of describing a new mathematical calculus which is in active use by a group of people who have not bothered to formulate their system of calculation in a text or monograph. It has, in other words, been developing informally over the years, is currently being used in developed form, and is being taught to new users by example and by oral instruction.

The investigator is allowed to interview and observe — that is, he may ask questions during coffee breaks, watch people computing, save scraps of paper from wastebaskets, take photographs of the machines employed, talk a few times with a project director, listen to people teaching one another the right way of doing things, and make other such minimally interfering kinds of observation and inquiry. He may even be permitted — and he will certainly be well advised — to join the group as a novice and learn to use the calculus himself.

Now, as he analyzes the data collected in these various ways, he does not merely tabulate the frequencies and intercorrelations of various classes of observed behavior in order to arrive at the calculus; if he did this, he would be giving equal weight to misunderstood jokes, learners' mistakes, slips of the pen, plain sloppy work, gibberish produced by broken computers, legpulling, and competent professional operations. What he does, instead, is to infer the system of rules which these people are attempting to apply. The assurance that he is on the way to an adequate understanding of these rules will be given him by the logical completeness of the system he infers and by his ability, when using it, to produce behavior which an expert will reward by saying, in effect, "That's right; that's good; now you've got it." Sometimes, of course, a sociologist or psychologist will say to him, "But it is the behavior that is real, not this abstract system which no one actually applies perfectly and completely and which is merely the asymptote of the real curve of behaviors." To this the investigator simply replies that culture — conceived in this sense as a collection of formal calculi — is just as real as algebra, Euclidean geometry, and set theory, which are just "merely" the asymptotes of the "real" behavior of fallible students, professional mathematicians, and machines (1962:351).

6. The questions and a tabulation of responses are included in Appendix A. Although the actual sample was 101 men, some did not respond to every question so that for some questions the number of responses was less than 101. In the text, whenever this sample is referred to, the actual number of men responding to a particular question is not indicated but rather a simple percentage is given. The interested reader may discover that information by referring to Appendix A.

7. A more detailed discussion of the formal ethnographic methods used in this study, as well as research problems faced by urban anthropologists may be found in *Adaptive Strategies of Urban Nomads: The Ethnoscience of Tramp Culture* (Spradley 1970). Some authors refer to the approach used in this study as "the New Ethnography," "Ethnographic Semantics" (Colby 1966), or "Ethnoscience" (Sturtevant 1964). Anthropologists whose work has been especially helpful include Conklin 1962a, 1962b, 1964; Frake 1961, 1962; Goodenough 1956, 1957; Kay 1966; Metzger and Williams 1963, 1966; and Black and Metzger 1965.

CHAPTER THREE

1. An extensive discussion of the medical model which considers alcoholism as a disease is presented in *The Disease Concept of Alcoholism* by E. M. Jellinek (1960). Jellinek has pointed to the somewhat arbitrary nature of disease concepts, the vagueness of the alcoholism concept, and the recency of its acceptance by the medical profession as a disease. He writes:

It comes to this, that *a disease is what the medical profession recognizes as such*. The fact that they are not able to explain the nature of a condition does not constitute proof that it is not an illness. . . . As will be seen later, the analysis shows that the medical profession has officially accepted alcoholism as an illness, whether a part of the lay public likes it or not, and even if a minority of the medical profession is disinclined to accept the idea. Of course, acceptance does not equal validity and one may inquire into this latter point, particularly into the matter of the facts and ideas that are in back of the illness conception, that is, into the nature or natures of some species of alcoholism. The difficulty in this instance is that the proponents of the still somewhat vague illness conception operate with many concepts which either are not defined or are frequently used in a variety of connotations (1960:12).

In the case of alcoholism, the idea that it constitutes an illness was suggested to Alcoholics Anonymous by a physician, the late Dr. W. D. Silkworth, early in the 1930's. Behind this physician were the opinions of a fair number of American and European specialists as expressed in the course of some 60 or 70 years, although their views did not coincide with the particular conception of Silkworth, namely that alcoholism is an allergy. It cannot be said that at that time the medical profession as a whole was in agreement with the medical proponents of the disease idea, yet the number of physicians of the latter conviction was not negligible (1960:160).

Progress toward the consolidation of medical attitudes toward alcoholism took a sharp upswing when the American Medical Association in 1951 created the Subcommittee on Alcoholism, under its Committee on Chronic Diseases, which was later formed into the Committee on Alcoholism of the Council on Mental Health of the AMA. The American Psychiatric Association and the Industrial Medical Association each have committees on alcoholism. Due to the great efforts of the AMA Committee on Alcoholism and its chairman, numerous state medical societies formed committees, commissions or boards on alcoholism. This, of course, contributed significantly toward the extension of the acceptance of the illness conception of "alcoholism" by the profession. These were the preparatory steps for an official declaration by the American Medical Association on the matter of alcoholism. The text of that resolution, headed "Hospitalization of Patients with Alcoholism," is given below (*Journal of the American Medical Association*, October 20, 1956). (See Jellinek 1960:164–165 for the statement). . . . This statement was accepted and approved by the House of Delegates of the American Medical Association at the 1956 meeting in Seattle, Washington (Jellinek 1960:163–165).

2. The literature on the life style and problems of the category of men reported on in this book is vast. Since a recent study provides an extensive bibliography as well as a discussion of many of the different approaches to this population, these are not included here (Wallace, S. 1965). This author writes:

Skid row has been in existence in the United States for at least a hundred years. During this time more than one hundred and fifty empirical studies have been made on the subject of skid row and members of its population; twenty-six biographies and thirty-three autobiographies about skid rowers have been published; twenty-three major programmatic statements have been drafted; twelve histories have been written; five bibliographies have been compiled. In addition, city missionaries, overseers of the poor, mission directors, municipal lodging house administrators, and a variety of other officials have issued a plethora of annual reports,

267

each of them containing at least some reference to the destitute homeless (Wallace, S. 1965:vii–viii).

In his chapter, "Previous Answers" (pp. 125–140), Wallace reviews a number of studies and points out that many have been carried out with the assumptions contained in the popular, legal, medical, and sociological models and thus tend to reflect the outsider's point of view. One study was done in Seattle, and although its authors attempted to define the categories of men on Skid Road from their point of view, they mixed this approach with the concept of alcoholism (Jackson and Conner 1953).

Wallace's book, *Skid Row as a Way of Life* (1965), is one of the best recent studies, in which, by participant observation, he attempted to discover how this population define their own experience and to describe this way of life as a subculture. He devotes only eighteen pages to a discussion of their encounter with law enforcement agencies, and only about one paragraph to their life in jail. He states:

> The role played by the police in the life of the skid rower would not be complete without including those who work at the city jail. The usual stories were related to the research staff about police officers rolling drunks. It was hard to believe these tales because the men who told them had usually been drinking for several days before going to jail, and didn't know what day it was, let alone how much money they had had in their pockets when arrested. The author, therefore, pretended to be drunk, "passed out" on the street, and had himself arrested. Deposited along with two other drunks in the city jail, he was promptly relieved of his money by the police officers on duty, one of whom he heard to remark: "They'll never know the difference, and nobody will believe 'em anyhow" (Wallace 1965:97).

3. The ethnographic method which was used in the present study has been most fruitfully applied to the study of kinship terms. Two classic articles published in 1956 stimulated a great deal of research along these lines (Goodenough 1956; Lounsbury 1956). More recently, Conklin has discussed many of the important methodological and theoretical issues in the ethnographic study of kinship in his article, "Ethnogenealogical Method" (1964).

4. See Willard Walker's "Taxonomic Structure and the Pursuit of Meaning" (1965) for a discussion of types of meaning, the importance of generic terms, and the function of taxonomic structures in human societies. He states:

> It is in all likelihood a fact that all natural languages have in their lexicons a number of generic terms. The essential characteristic of a generic term is that its reference category be divisible into two or more subcategories which are, themselves, highly codable (1965:268). The members of a speech community necessarily share a common core of highly codable reference categories, since this is prerequisite to any sort of communication. But hierarchically structured taxonomies are not essential since, even without them, the speakers of a language might communicate anything which they were capable of imagining. The apparent universality of hierarchical taxonomies in language is clearly due to the enormous increase in efficiency of communication which they provide. With the invention of the generic term, man was for the first time permitted to suspend temporarily irrelevant discriminations; and, also for the first time, he could indicate a large reference category without listing its many subdivisions. He could, in other words, refer to *pines* as *trees*, if their pineness was irrelevant. He could also indicate trees without an exhaustive list of *pines*, *oaks*, etc., etc. The hierarchical taxonomy, in a word, per-

268

mits the speaker to refocus his hearer's attention to any degree of abstraction provided by the various levels of the hierarchy. This refinement is quite possibly unique for human communication systems (1965:271).

5. The study of folk taxonomies has become an important part of much ethnoscience or ethnographic research. Several theoretical problems are pointed out here and elsewhere in the text, but those interested in related discussions of these problems may see Berlin, Breedlove, and Raven 1968; Conklin 1962a, 1962b, 1964; Fowler and Leland 1967; Frake 1961, 1962; Kay 1966; and Walker 1965.

The most important theoretical discussion of folk taxonomies is probably Conklin's "Lexicographical Treatment of Folk Taxonomies" (1962a). He notes that language groups objects into categories and *names* them and suggests the term *segregate* for such named categories. "In discussing different systems of classifying segments of the natural and social environment, the neutral term *segregate* serves as a label for any terminologically distinguished (i.e., conventionally named) grouping of objects" (1962a:121). He goes on to define folk taxonomy: "A system of monolexemically-labeled folk segregates related by hierarchic inclusion is a *folk taxonomy*; segregates included in such a classification are known as *folk taxa*" (1962a:128). At least two problems with this definition of a folk taxonomy require comment.

First, Berlin, et al. (1968), have presented evidence from their studies of Tzeltal plant taxonomies that *unlabeled taxa* do occur. These authors note that others have been interested in unnamed categories and that Keesing (1966) has questioned one of the "most fundamental assumptions of ethnoscience" when he wrote: "If we insist that the descriptive units of an ethnography be lexically labelled, we are likely to arrive at a very limited sort of description: an ethnography of how people talk about what they do, not what they do or expect each other to do. . . . There is ample evidence that expectations and distinctions need not be directly mapped in language" (1968:290). Though the present study was directed at the named categories mapped by the language of informants, nonlinguistic data cannot be ignored, and indeed, though not elaborately discussed, it was utilized throughout the research.

Second, it seems important to expand the definition of folk taxonomies, not only to include *unlabeled taxa* but labeled taxa which are *multilexemic*. It seems to this writer that the criterion noted above that folk taxonomies are to be made up of "monolexemically labeled folk segregates" is unduly restrictive. In the folk taxonomy labeled "tramp" are several segregate labels which are not monolexemic. Conklin has defined lexemes:

> It is convenient to refer to these elementary lexical units as *lexemes*, although other terms have been suggested. So far as lexemic status is concerned, the morphosyntactic or assumed etymological relations of a particular linguistic form are incidental; what is essential is that its meaning cannot be deduced from its grammatical structure. Single morphemes are necessarily lexemes, but for polymorphemic constructions the decision depends on meaning and use (implying an analysis of the constraints imposed by the semantic structure, and the specification of relevant immediate contexts) (1962a:121).

Although "tramp" and "airedale" are single lexemes, i.e., their meaning cannot be deduced from their grammatical structure, "construction tramp," "working stiff," and "professional nose diver" are not monolexemic. We could contrast "construction tramp" with "construction foreman" or "construction engineer," gaining some understanding of its meaning from the grammatical structure of the forms. The same is true for "working stiff" and "professional nose diver." The later taxonomies in this book labeled "trusty"

269

and "flop," etc., almost all include segregate labels which are constructed from more than one lexeme. On the basis of the above definition it would be necessary to exclude many of these terms. They are included here because they were consistently used by informants to label categories of objects in their world, and used in contrast to other segregates in each domain which were monolexemic. Frake takes a similar position, if I read him correctly. He states:

> In isolating these terms no appeal has been made to analysis of their linguistic structure or their signification. *Sandwich* is a single morpheme. Some linguists, at any rate, would analyze *hot dog* and even *hamburger* as each containing two morphemes, but, since the meaning of the constructions cannot be predicted from a knowledge of the meaning of their morphological constituents, they are single "lexemes" (Goodenough 1956) or "idioms" (Hockett 1958:303–318). *Ham 'n cheese sandwich* would not, I think, qualify as a single lexeme; nevertheless it is a standard segregate label whose function in naming objects cannot be distinguished from that of forms like *hot dog*. Suppose further utterances from lunch-counter speech show that the lexically complex term *something to eat* distinguishes the same array of objects as do the single morphemes *food* and *chow*. In such a case, a choice among these three terms would perhaps say something about the social status of the lunch counter and its patrons, but it says nothing distinctive about the objects designated. As segregate labels, these three frequently-heard terms would be equivalent (Frake 1962:77–78).

Although it is argued here that folk taxonomies do sometimes include multi-lexemic labels, it is necessary to exercise great care in eliciting terms for categories, since some which are made up of more than one lexeme may *appear* to be category labels, and in a sense they are, but are not to be included in the folk taxonomy. For example, informants sometimes responded to questions about kinds of objects with such phrases as "good tramps," "trustworthy tramps," and "bad tramps." When discussing the flop taxonomy they would sometimes categorize sleeping places as "damn good flops," "flops which won't quit," and "bad flops." Exclusion of these terms was accomplished by pairing them with other terms for which there was some degree of certainty about their membership in a taxonomy, and asking informants, for example, if a "good flop" was the same kind of categorization as a "flophouse." Many problems were resolved by listening to the usage of terms in casual conversation, and though none of these approaches resolves all the problems, their number is greatly reduced. Throughout the present discussion, more technical words such as "taxa," "lexeme," and "segregate" are not included; instead most constructions which make up labels in the taxonomies presented are simply referred to as "terms."

6. This basic insight is particularly important for the theory of meaning upon which the present study is based. George Kelly (1955) developed this position into a theory of personality and a number of contemporary ethnographic studies have drawn upon this work. He states:

> A construct which implied similarity without contrast would represent just as much of a chaotic undifferentiated homogeneity as a construct which implied contrast without similarity would represent a chaotic particularized heterogeneity. The former would leave the person engulfed in a sea with no landmarks to relieve the monotony; the latter would confront him with an interminable series of kaleidoscopic changes in which nothing would ever appear familiar (1955:51).

Those interested in this approach to personality and the work of George Kelly should also see the recent book by Bannister and Mair, *The Evaluation of Personal Constructs* (1968). They summarize Kelly's theory and methods as well as reporting on recent research based on this theory of personal constructs. They quote a later paper by Kelly (1966) in which he develops the importance of contrasts in the abstraction process:

Do persons indeed do their abstracting in classical form? Apparently not. Probably the most important deviation of psychological logic from classical logic is in its use of contrasts. For example, two women with whom one is acquainted may be abstracted as similar not only because they are feminine but just as much because their femininity contrasts with the masculinity of men. Thus speaking of femininity makes psychological sense only if one also implies the masculinity with which it stands in meaningful contrast. This principle holds true for all the other abstractions with which human beings psychologically structure their world. To sum it up, then, we may say that each of us finds meaning in his life not only by identifying things for what they are, but also by noting what they are not. Moreover, in noting what they are not we clarify the alternatives that are open to us, thus establishing the psychological basis of what is most important of all — human freedom (Bannister and Mair 1968:45).

7. This distinction is drawn from Conklin, who states:

In studying semantic relationships, as among folk categories, it has often been demonstrated that likeness logically and significantly implies difference (Kelly 1955:303–5). It is also pertinent, however, to note that total contrast (complete complementary exclusion) — which logically relates such segregates as *ant* and *ship* or *cough* and *pebble* — is less important than restricted contrast within the range of a particular semantic subset . . . (1962a:127).

Kelly makes the same point, although from a different perspective:

If we choose an aspect in which A and B are similar, but in contrast to C, it is important to note that it is the same aspect of all three, A, B, and C, that forms the basis of the construct. It is not that there is one aspect of A and B that makes them similar to each other and another aspect that makes them contrasting to C. What we mean is that there is an aspect of A, B, and C which we may call z. With respect to this aspect, A and B are similar and C stands in contrast to them. . . . Let us pursue our model further. Let us suppose that there is an element O in which one is unable to construe the aspect of z. O then falls outside the range of convenience of the construct based on z. The aspect of z is irrelevant in that part of the realm occupied by O. Not so C, however. The aspect of z is quite relevant to C. It is z that enables us to differentiate between C and the two similar elements, A and B. The aspect of z performs no such service in helping us discriminate between O and the two similar elements, A and B (Kelly 1955:59–60).

This is extremely important in considering the dimensions of contrast (aspects of meaning) which enable us to discriminate among the different kinds of tramps. Whereas the home guard tramp is not mobile and all others are, this does not mean that mobility is irrelevant to this particular type of tramp. It is this aspect of meaning which enables us to discriminate this type from the others. Whenever terms or constructs are in restricted contrast, aspects of meaning are important underlying values which bind a set of terms

271

into a category. The bonds which link terms together are the ties of similarity and contrast.

8. The techniques used to elicit dimensions of contrast for this and other domains were all aimed at *discovering criteria* without suggesting to informants which criteria would be relevant. The way questions are asked often suggests to informants what is considered important to the researcher. Most of the techniques used were designed to encourage a person to make a decision about a relevant distinction before asking him what the distinction involved. For example, a set of terms would be written on cards, one term per card, and an informant would be asked to sort these into as many piles as he wanted to on the basis of some similarities or differences he felt existed among the set of cards. *After* he had sorted the cards he would be queried as to the basis for his decisions. Sometimes a *dyadic sorting* task would be used in which informants were simply asked to indicate the differences and similarities between two terms. A guessing game similar to "Twenty Questions" was also used in which informants were instructed to discover which term the researcher was thinking of from a set of terms. He was told he had only a limited number of questions and so was forced to begin with questions which would narrow the field. When framing a question, informants were selecting those dimensions of contrast they used to distinguish among members of the set, thus revealing to the researcher aspects of meaning which were significant. The triadic sorting task (Kelly 1955; Romney and D'Andrade 1964) was most effective because it was a more manageable task than sorting all the terms at once, but forced more relevant distinctions than the dyadic sorting task. It is discussed at several points in the text. Those who are interested in refinements on this task should see Bannister and Mair's discussion of the "grid method" (1968: 38–77, 136–155).

9. The term "componential analysis" is sometimes used in a more restricted manner than is done here. Some maintain that a componential definition of a set of terms is impossible without some kind of etic grid as in the study of kinship and color terms. Others restrict its meaning to a set of *necessary* and *sufficient* criterial features of referential meaning. Although the componential definitions presented in this book usually provide those features of meaning which are necessary to distinguish one term from another, they do not provide both necessary and sufficient conditions. This criterion would require information sufficient to distinguish a domain from everything else in the culture, and it is doubtful that componential analyses ever produce both necessary and sufficient definitions.

10. It would have been possible to define these eight kinds of tramps with only three dimensions of contrast by combining "mobility" and "mode of travel." The reason for including mobility as a dimension of contrast was based upon my own commitment to achieving some kind of "psychological reality" in the final description of this culture. Informants tended to distinguish between mobility and mode of travel in their performance of sorting tasks as well as in conversations. They would say, "He travels from mission to mission," but the mode of travel would not be indicated until some later context. A distinction has been made between analyses which are "psychologically valid" and those which are "structurally valid" (Wallace and Atkins 1960). The latter are sometimes referred to as "formal analyses," and though they may enable the outsider to anticipate or predict behavior, they do not necessarily reflect the way in which informants define their own behavior. Wallace and Atkins point out:

A problem for research, then, must be to develop techniques for stating and identifying those definitions which are most proximate to psychological reality. This is a formidable task. The formal methods of componential analysis, even with refinement and extension of their logico-semantic assumptions, will not yield discriminations between psychologically real and non-psychologically but social-structurally real meanings. . . . Ethnographers like Goodenough and Lounsbury obtain clues to psychological reality from observations on the cultural milieu of the terminology such as residence and marriage rules or historical changes. But the only way of achieving definite knowledge of psychological reality will be to study the semantics of individuals both before and after a formal, abstract, cultural-semantic analysis of the terms has been performed. . . . It is possible to say fairly that not only in kinship, but also in other ethnographic subjects, the degree of psychological reality achieved in ethnographic reporting is not only uneven but on the average probably rather low. Social-structural reality can be achieved; psychological reality can only be approximated. But such approximations are sorely needed (1960:78–79).

One example may be given of the manner in which componential analyses may be checked for their psychological validity. After making an analysis of the dimensions of contrast which define kinds of tramps I would try to elicit from new informants the terms for tramps by giving them the criteria. One day while the researcher was eating lunch with a man from New York, this conversation took place:

Researcher: How did you travel to Seattle?
Informant: By freight car.
Researcher: What do they call men who travel on freight cars?
Informant: Tramps.
Researcher: Are there different kinds of tramps?
Informant: Oh, yes. There's bindle stiffs, mission stiffs, box car tramps, and home guard tramps.
Researcher: Are there any other kinds?
Informant: No, that's all.
Researcher: I've heard there are some tramps who have cars and they travel that way, have you ever heard of them?
Informant: Oh, yes! They are called rubber tramps.

11. These figures are taken from the annual report of the Seattle Police Department (Seattle Police Department 1968).

12. See A Survey of the Police Department — Seattle, Washington, International Association of Chiefs of Police, Field Operations Division, 1968, for the full statement of these recommendations as well as many others which resulted from this study.

CHAPTER FOUR

1. To this statement that the terms in this taxonomy are all "classes" of flops several exceptions must be admitted. Technically, a taxonomy includes only terms which label a finite set of distinct conceptual categories. The named flophouses are specific places, not categories of flops, and the same is true for the named mission flops. They are included here to provide the reader with some idea as to the specific objects which are included in these two categories. There are still many contrasts among these sets of names and they may be analyzed in a manner similar to classes of flops. (See Appendix C for an analysis of the defining criteria for different missions named by one informant.) Many of the terms which are both level one and terminal in the taxonomy also have many specific named places included in them. Penny arcade and bucket are both common flops among tramps and it would have

273

been possible to elicit the names for many different penny arcades and jails in the same way that names for specific missions were elicited. Although such terms as *trash box* and *cotton wagon* do not have names, they are categories of places to sleep and specific members of these categories would probably have been identified by their location. Informants would refer to specific members of these categories by saying, "I slept in a trash box in back of that building on Alaska Way," or some other similar statement.

2. The literature on the use of alcohol in non-Western societies is large. See *Culture and Alcohol Use, A Bibliography of Anthropological Studies* (Popham and Yawney 1967). Lemert's study, "Alcohol and the Northwest Coast Indians" (1954) is especially pertinent here due to the large number of Indians who are arrested for drunkenness in Seattle. One of the best sources for a variety of studies is *Society, Culture and Drinking Patterns* (Pittman and Snyder 1962).

CHAPTER FIVE

1. One group of more than 200 men who went through the alcoholism treatment center reported these occupations:

TABLE N.1: OCCUPATIONS

Laborer	63	General handyman	1
Painter	13	Upholsterer	1
Farm laborer	8	Jewelry polisher	1
Salesman	8	Cement finisher	1
Carpenter	7	Packer, Mover	1
Cook, Baker	7	Barber	1
Truck driver	6	Railroad clerk	1
Home maintenance	6	Molder	1
Heavy equipment operator	6	Radiator repairman	1
Seaman	6	Linotype operator	1
Warehouseman	5	Glazer	1
Office worker	4	Machinist	1
Logger	4	Dishwasher	1
Welder	4	Meat cutter	1
Electrician	4	Manager	1
Fisherman	4	Tile setter	1
Plumber	3	Hospital orderly	1
Iron worker	3	Locksmith	1
Auto mechanic	3	Watchmaker	1
Brick mason	2	Machine operator	1
Longshoreman	2	Sawmill worker	1
Sheet metal worker	2	Male nurse	1
Newspaperman	2	Tree surgery	1
Hod carrier	2	Spring-up man	1
Body and fender	2	Coal miner	1
Waiter	2	Surveyor	1
Farmer	2	Millwright	1
Janitor	2	Plasterer	1
Dry cleaner	2	T.V. repairman	1
		Bartender	1

2. See especially Becker 1963; Bahr, n.d.; Meyerson and Mayer 1966; and Wallace, S. 1965, 1968.

3. Brim and Wheeler (1966) have discussed in detail some of the theoretical aspects of identity change and socialization processes among adults. They state:

> The adult socialization context does not have these characteristics and is not conducive to the inculcation of basic values. Adult socialization probably requires a relationship resembling that of childhood to effect equivalent changes in basic values through socialization. This relationship may occur in rare and usually noninstitutionalized instances, for example, in adult religious conversion, where the submissive relationship and highly affective interchange with a religious figure underlie the radical shift in value system. Another example is the relationship in prisoner-of-war camps. Recent research on "brainwashing" and the breakdown of resistance to enemy values shows this context to be one where the captors use their extreme power in deliberate manipulation of the whole range of affect from rejection and hate, on the one hand, to support and overt sympathy, on the other, thus bringing the prisoner into a position similar to that of a child with his parent. Goffman's analysis (1961) of the characteristic settings which are conducive to identity change, such as mental hospitals, bears on this point (1966:37).

4. The anthropological literature has many studies of rituals which have been classified as rites of passage. From a psychological point of view these rituals effect change in the identity of those who go through them. The classic study is Van Gennep's, *The Rites of Passage* (1960). See also Cohen 1964, and chapters 8 and 9 in Goodenough 1963, for a discussion of identity change.

CHAPTER SEVEN

1. This notion about the attributes of time is drawn from Leach (1961) who states:

> Of course in our own case, equipped as we are with clocks and radios and astronomical observatories, time is given a factor in our social situation; it is an essential part of our lives which we take for granted. But suppose we had no clocks and no scientific astronomy, how then should we think about time? What obvious attributes would time then seem to possess? Perhaps it is impossible to answer such a very hypothetical question, and yet, clocks apart, it seems to me that our modern English notion of time embraces at least two different kinds of experience which are logically distinct and even contradictory. Firstly, there is the notion of repetition. Whenever we think about measuring time we concern ourselves with some kind of metronome; it may be the ticking of a clock or a pulse beat or the recurrence of days or moons or annual seasons, but always there is something which repeats. Secondly, there is the notion of non-repetition. We are aware that all living things are born, grow old and die, and that this is an irreversible process. I am inclined to think that all other aspects of time, duration for example or historical sequence, are fairly simple derivatives from these two basic experiences: (a) that certain phenomena of nature repeat themselves, (b) that life change is irreversible (1961: 125).

CHAPTER EIGHT

1. The dimension of reciprocity emerged from interviews and card sorting tasks with informants but was facilitated by Sahlin's excellent article, "On

the Sociology of Primitive Exchange" (1965). He delineates three types of exchange: generalized reciprocity, balanced reciprocity, and negative reciprocity. Although generalized reciprocity does exist among urban nomads, it is not part of the process of hustling, with the possible exception of *bumming*. In the jail, when a man bums from another he is getting something for nothing and does not usually expect to make a return. Some bumming, outside the jail and even within it, could be classified as generalized reciprocity, a kind of gift-giving with an expectation that at some later date the gift will be returned. If a man bums another in jail for a cigarette, he receives it as a gift but expects to make similar offerings when he can do so. Outside the jail it would perhaps be more often considered a kind of generalized reciprocity, but even if one panhandles on the street he does not expect to make return exchanges unless he is panhandling other tramps whom he knows. Some of the discussion of this domain appeared previously in a more formal analysis (Spradley 1968b).

CHAPTER NINE

1. Statement made during the KING Radio Documentary, "Cycle of Shame," January 17, 1967. Seattle, Washington.

2. This report, "The Skid Road Alcoholic's Perception of Law Enforcement in Seattle" (Spradley 1968a), was written to provide information regarding the Seattle Skid Road alcoholic for the Seattle City Council Ad Hoc Committee Concerned with the Indigent Public Intoxicant and the Ad Hoc Committee on Alcohol, Seattle Municipal Court, Department No. 1.

3. A brief analysis of the influence of arrest and incarceration upon the program of an alcoholism treatment center and the importance of a detoxification center for rehabilitation may be found in Spradley and Jahn 1969.

Bibliography

Bahr, Howard M.
  n.d. "Drinking, Interaction, and Identification: Notes on Socialization into Skid Row," *Publication A-481*, Bureau of Applied Social Research.
Bannister, D., and J. M. M. Mair
  1968 *Evaluation of Personal Constructs*. London and New York: Academic Press.
Becker, Howard S.
  1963 *Outsiders: Studies in the Sociology of Deviancy*. New York: The Free Press.
Berlin, Brent, Dennis E. Breedlove, and Peter H. Raven
  1968 "Covert Categories and Folk Taxonomies," *American Anthropologist* 70:290–299.
Black, Mary, and Duane Metzger
  1965 "Ethnographic Description and the Study of Law," in *The Ethnography of Law* (Laura Nader, editor), *American Anthropologist* 67(6) 2:141–165.
Brim, Orville G.,Jr., and Stanton Wheeler
  1966 *Socialization After Childhood*. New York: John Wiley.
Chafetz, Morris E.
  1966 "Management of the Alcoholic Patient in an Acute Treatment Facility," in *Alcoholism* (Jack H. Mendelson, editor), pp. 127–142. International Psychiatry Clinics, Summer 1966, Vol. 3, No. 2. Boston: Little, Brown.

Cohen, Yehudi A.
1964 *The Transition from Childhood to Adolescence: Cross-cultural Studies of Initiation Ceremonies, Legal Systems, and Incest Taboos.* Chicago: Aldine.
Colby, B. N.
1966 "Ethnographic Semantics: A Preliminary Survey," *Current Anthropology* 7:3–32.
Conklin, Harold C.
1962a "Lexicographical Treatment of Folk Taxonomies," in *Problems in Lexicography* (F. W. Householder and S. Saporta, editors). *Indiana University Research Center in Anthropology, Folklore, and Linguistics Publication 21*, pp. 119–141.
1962b "Comment" (on Frake 1962). In *Anthropology and Human Behavior* (T. Gladwin and W. C. Sturtevant, editors), Washington: Anthropological Society of Washington, pp. 86–91.
1964 "Ethnogenealogical Method," in *Explorations in Cultural Anthropology* (Ward H. Goodenough, editor). New York: McGraw-Hill, pp. 25–55.
Erikson, Kai T.
1962 "Notes on the Sociology of Deviance," *Social Problems* 9:307–314.
Fowler, Catherine S., and Joy Leland
1967 "Some Northern Paiute Native Categories," *Ethnology* 6:381–404.
Frake, Charles O.
1961 "The Diagnosis of Disease Among the Subanun of Mindanao," *American Anthropologist* 63:113–132.
1962 "The Ethnographic Study of Cognitive Systems," in *Anthropology and Human Behavior* (T. Gladwin and W. C. Sturtevant, editors). Washington: Anthropological Society of Washington, pp. 72–85, 91–93.
Fraser, J. T.
1966 "The Study of Time," in *The Voices of Time* (J. T. Fraser, editor). New York: George Braziller.
Gardner, John W.
1965 *Self Renewal: The Individual and the Innovative Society.* New York: Harper and Row.
Goffman, Erving
1961 *Asylums: Essays on the Social Situation of Mental Patients and Other Inmates.* Garden City, New York: Anchor Books, Doubleday.
Goodenough, Ward H.
1956 "Componential Analysis and the Study of Meaning," *Language* 32:195:216. ·
1957 "Cultural Anthropology and Linguistics," in *Report of the Seventh Annual Round Table Meeting on Linguistics and Language Study* (P. L. Garvin, editor). Washington: Georgetown University Monograph Series on Languages and Linguistics No. 9.
1963 *Cooperation in Change.* New York: Russell Sage Foundation.
Hockett, Charles F.
1958 *A Course in Modern Linguistics.* New York: Macmillan.
International Association of Chiefs of Police
1968 *A Survey of the Police Department — Seattle, Washington.* Field Operations Division.
Jackson, Joan K., and Ralph Conner
1953 "The Skid Road Alcoholic," *Quarterly Journal of Studies on Alcohol* 14:468–486.

Jellinek, E. M.
1960   *The Disease Concept of Alcoholism*. New Haven, Connecticut: Hillhouse Press.
Kay, Paul
1966   "Comment" (on Colby 1966), *Current Anthropology* 7:20–23.
Keesing, Roger M.
1966   "Comment" (on Colby 1966), *Current Anthropology* 7:23
Kelly, George A.
1955   *The Psychology of Personal Constructs*. Vols. I and II. New York: Norton.
1966   "A Brief Introduction to Personal Construct Theory," Unpublished manuscript. Brandeis University.
Leach, E. R.
1961   *Rethinking Anthropology. London School of Economics Monographs on Social Anthropology*. London: The Athlone Press.
Lemert, Edwin M.
1954   "Alcohol and the Northwest Coast Indians," *University of California Publications in Culture and Society* 2:303–406.
Levinson, Boris M.
1957   "The Socioeconomic Status, Intelligence, and Psychometric Pattern of Native-Born White Homeless Men," *Journal of Genetic Psychology* 91:205–211.
Lounsbury, F. G.
1956   "A Semantic Analysis of the Pawnee Kinship Usage," *Language* 32:158–194.
Metzger, Duane, and Gerald E. Williams
1963   "A Formal Ethnographic Analysis of Tenejapa Ladino Weddings," *American Anthropologist* 65:1076–1101.
1966   "Some Procedures and Results in the Study of Native Categories: Tzeltal 'Firewood,' " *American Anthropologist* 68:389–407.
Myerson, D. J., and J. Mayer
1966   "Origins, Treatment and Destiny of Skid-Row Alcoholic Men," in *New England Journal of Medicine* 275:419–425.
National Institute of Mental Health
1967   *Alcohol and Alcoholism*. Public Health Service Publication No. 1640. Washington, D.C.: U.S. Government Printing Office.
Newsweek Magazine
1968   "The Forgotten Men," December 23, 1968:78.
1969   "The Cities: Waging a Battle for Survival," March 17, 1969:41.
Pittman, D. J., and C. R. Snyder, eds.
1962   *Society, Culture and Drinking Patterns*. New York: Wiley.
Popham, Robert E., and Carole D. Yawney
1967   *Culture and Alcohol Use: A Bibliography of Anthropological Studies*, 2nd ed. Ontario, Canada: Addiction Research Foundation.
Powell v. Texas
1968   Supreme Court of the United States No. 405. October Term, 1967. June 17, 1968.
President's Commission on Law Enforcement and the Administration of Justice
1967   *The Challenge of Crime in a Free Society*. Washington, D.C.: U.S. Government Printing Office.
Romney, A. K., and R. G. D'Andrade
1964   "Cognitive Aspects of English Kin Terms," in Transcultural Studies in Cognition (A. K. Romney and R. G. D'Andrade, editors), *American Anthropologist* 66(3), pt. 2:146–170.

279

Sahlins, Marshall D.
   1965   "On the Sociology of Primitive Exchange," in *The Relevance of Models for Social Anthropology*. A.S.A. Monographs 1. New York: Praeger.
Seattle Police Department
   1968   Annual Report. Seattle, Washington.
The Seattle Post-Intelligencer
   1967   (December 22, 1967) Seattle, Washington.
   1968   (August 15, 1968) Seattle, Washington.
   1969   (January 8, 1969) Seattle, Washington.
The Seattle Times
   1969   (April 16, 1969) Seattle, Washington.
Solomon, Philip
   1966   "Psychiatric Treatment of the Alcoholic Patient," in *Alcoholism* (Jack H. Mendelson, editor), pp. 159–188. International Psychiatry Clinics, Summer 1966, Vol. 3, No. 2. Boston: Little, Brown.
Spiro, Melford E.
   1958   *Children of the Kibbutz*. Cambridge, Mass.: Harvard University Press.
Spradley, James P.
   1968a   *The Skid Road Alcoholic's Perception of Law Enforcement in Seattle*. Mimeographed Research Report, Department of Psychiatry, University of Washington, Seattle, Washington.
   1968b   "A Cognitive Analysis of Tramp Behavior," *Proceedings of the 8th International Congress of Anthropological and Ethnological Sciences*. Japan, 1968. In press.
   1970   "Adaptive Strategies of Urban Nomads: The Ethnoscience of Tramp Culture," in *Urban Anthropology* (Thomas Weaver and Douglas White, editors), Human Organization Monograph 11.
————, and Mary Jahn
   1969   "Detoxification Center: Open Door or Revolving Door?" *Puget Soundings*. March 1969.
Sturtevant, William C.
   1964   "Studies in Ethnoscience," in *Transcultural Studies in Cognition* (A. K. Romney and Roy G. D'Andrade, editors), *American Anthropologist* 66(3) pt. 2:99–131.
van Gennep, Arnold
   1960   *The Rites of Passage*. Chicago: University of Chicago Press.
Walker, Willard
   1965   "Taxonomic Structure and the Pursuit of Meaning," *Southwestern Journal of Anthropology* 21:265–275.
Wallace, Anthony F. C.
   1962   "Culture and Cognition," *Science* 135:351–57.
————, and John Atkins
   1960   "The Meaning of Kinship Terms," *American Anthropologist* 62:58–80.
Wallace, Samuel E.
   1965   *Skid Row As a Way of Life*. Totowa, New Jersey: The Bedminister Press.
   1968   "The Road to Skid Row," *Social Problems* 16:92–105.
Wilson, James Q.
   1968   *Varieties of Police Behavior: The Management of Law and Order in Eight Communities*. Cambridge, Mass.: Harvard University Press.

Questionnaire

These questions were used in a questionnaire administered to 101 men who had been booked for public drunkenness in Seattle, Washington. All who participated did so voluntarily. No names were placed on the questionnaires and informants were told to respond only to questions they desired to answer. The number of men who responded to each question is given in parentheses. The numbers opposite each question indicate the different responses. In addition to the open ended questions, most of those which required a standard response of "yes" or "no" or some scaled response also requested that details be written down by those who had experienced the event presented by the question. These instructions were given on the questionnaire:

The questions below all refer to the Seattle police or city jail. Although you may have had experiences asked about in the questions in some other jail or city, answer only for Seattle city police and jail. You are to circle the answer you believe to be true, or write your comment.

1. Age: (94)

Under 25	0
25–40	6
41–50	70
over 50	18

2. Race: (97)

White	74
Negro	4
Indian	15
Mexican	2
Eskimo	2

3. Have you ever been pinched for drunk in Seattle? (101)

Yes:	99
No:	2

4. About how many times have you been pinched for drunk in Seattle? (100)

1–5	46
6–20	43
21–30	4
31–60	6
Over 60	1

5. About how many times have you been pinched for drunk in Seattle during the last five years? (100)

1–5	39
6–20	36
21–30	7
31–60	11
Over 60	7

6. If you have ever pulled time in lockup, how would you rate the amount of food you received from the jail most of the time? (98)

All you can eat	3
Enough to eat	2
Not quite enough to eat	14
Never enough	42
Starvation diet	37

7. If you have ever pulled time as trusty in the city jail, how would you rate the amount of food you received from the jail most of the time? (62)

All you can eat	1
Enough to eat	23
Not quite enough to eat	12
Never enough	24
Starvation diet	2

8. List in detail what you were usually given for breakfast, lunch, and dinner when you were in lockup.

9. When you were in lockup were you given cream and sugar for your coffee or tea? (101)

Never	99
Sometimes	2
Usually	
Most of the time	
Always	

10. Have you ever gotten out of jail early by giving blood? (96)

Yes	20
No	76

282

11. Have you ever gotten out of jail early by some other means? (97)

Yes	34
No	63

12. Have you ever been busted from trusty to lockup in the city jail? (92)

Yes	9
No	83

13. Have you ever been busted to the drunk tank? (95)

Yes	6
No	89

14. Have you ever known personally someone who was busted to the drunk tank? (95)

Yes	32
No	63

15. Do you know of anyone who has pulled time in the drunk tank at his own request? (96)

Yes	10
No	96

16. Have you ever been put in the stand-up tank in the city jail? (98)

Yes	6
No	92

17. Have you ever known of anyone else who was put in the stand-up tank? (94)

Yes	8
No	86

18. What is the longest period of time you have had to sit bare ass in a tank while your clothes were being deloused? (96)

0–½ hour	4
1 hour	13
2 hours	24
3 hours	35
4 hours	14
5 hours	6
Over 5 hours	

19. What is the largest group of men you have seen at one time sitting bare ass in the delousing tank? (94)

15–20	15
21–25	10
26–30	16
31–40	29
41–45	11
46–50	5
Over 50	8

Is this by actual count or by estimate? (82)

Actual count	35
Estimate	47

20. Have you ever had some good clothes ruined in the delousing process? (97)

Yes	45
No	52

21. Have you ever had a bull in jail give you and other prisoners the heat treatment by closing all windows and keeping the tank too warm? (94)

Yes	29
No	65

22. Have you ever had a bull in jail freeze you and other prisoners by opening all the windows and making the tank too cold? (90)

Yes	48
No	42

23. Have you ever not been allowed to eat a meal in jail as punishment? (92)

Yes	4
No	88

24. Have you personally known of other prisoners who were not allowed to eat a meal as punishment in jail? (91)

Yes	8
No	83

25. How many phone calls are you allowed to make when you are in the drunk tank waiting for court? (87)

0	8
1	74
Over 1	2
Depends	3

26. Have you ever been refused permission to make a phone call while you were in the drunk tank waiting for court? (88)

Yes	28
No	60

27. How many phone calls are you allowed to make each week when you are in lockup? (66)

0	5
1	59
Over 1	1
Depends	1

28. Have you ever been refused permission to make phone calls when you were in lockup? (85)

Yes	39
No	46

29. Have you ever had money to bail out of jail on a drunk charge and not been allowed to bail out? (93)

Yes	5
No	88

30. Have you ever had a bull do a favor for you when you were in jail? (96)

Yes	22
No	74

31. Have you ever been put on the bulls' shit list? (93)

Yes	14
No	79

32. Have you ever gone up to jail and turned yourself in without being picked up? (95)

Yes	10
No	85

33. Have you ever lost a job because you did time on a drunk charge? (95)

Yes	59
No	36

34. Have you ever lost rent you had paid on a room because you did time on a drunk charge? (92)

Many times	30
Occasionally	25
At least once	18
Never	19

35. Have you ever lost property or clothing which you had left in your room because you did time on a drunk charge? (92)

Many times	29
Occasionally	18
At least once	21
Never	24

36. Have you ever had bulls use insulting language to you personally? (87)

Many times	19
Occasionally	18
At least once	9
Never	41

37. If there are any other aspects of Seattle police or jail which you feel should be known by me, I would appreciate any additional comments.

38. Have you ever weighed yourself after pulling time to see how much weight you had lost while in jail? (99)

Yes	58
No	41

If yes, what is the most weight you have ever lost? (55)

0–5 pounds	3
6–10 pounds	4
11–15 pounds	34
Over 15 pounds	14

39. Have the Seattle police ever stopped you or picked you up, taken your money or other property, and then let you go without booking you? (96)

Yes	22
No	74

40. Have you ever personally witnessed the Seattle police rolling, clipping, or stealing from a drunk or someone picked up for drunk? (96)

Yes	32
No	64

41. Have you ever had money taken by police from your property while you were in jail? (91)

Yes	36
No	55

42. Have you ever been given a property slip as a receipt for money or property taken away from you when you were booked in jail? (98)

Yes	3
No	95

43. Do you usually sign anything when booked which shows the money or property you had? (96)

Yes	30
No	66

44. Have you ever been working as trusty and actually seen the bulls steal money from drunks who were being booked or were taking money from their property box? (93)

Yes	10
No	83

45. Have you ever had a beat cop in Seattle kick you in the ass and tell you to get off his beat? (94)

Never	62
Very seldom	7
A few times	20
Many times	5

46. Have you ever borrowed money from a Seattle bull and had to pay double back? (95)

Yes	1
No	94

47. Have you ever spent several days in the drunk tank and then pulled time but did not receive credit for the time served in the drunk tank? (95)

Yes	47
No	48

48. Have you ever been picked up for drunk on the same day you were kicked out of jail when there hadn't been enough time to get drunk? (93)

Yes	19
No	74

49. Have you ever had to leave Seattle because the cops had gotten to know you and were picking you up so often? (97)

Yes	29
No	68

50. Have you ever been told by a cop that you were being picked up because he had to fill his quota for the day? (93)

Yes	11
No	82

51. Have you ever personally witnessed someone being shaken down at a call box and clipped for his dough? (93)

Yes	25
No	68

52. Have you ever had a cop take something from you when he was shaking you down at a call box? (93)

Yes	21
No	72

53. Have you ever made a pay-off to a bull so you would not be taken in on a drunk charge? (95)

Yes	6
No	89

54. Have you ever personally witnessed someone making a pay-off to a bull so he would not be taken in for drunk? (96)

Yes	2
No	94

55. Have you ever known someone who has made a pay-off to a bull so he would not be taken in for drunk? (93)

Yes	6
No	87

56. Have you ever witnessed or known of someone, or have you personally made a pay-off to a bull to keep from being pinched for bootlegging or some other charge? (96)

Yes	13
No	83

57. Have you ever had a Seattle bull take a jug from you and pour the contents over your head or down your clothes? (95)

Yes	10
No	85

58. Have you ever had a Seattle bull break a jug you had in your pocket with his night stick? (99)

Yes	10
No	89

59. Have you ever had a bull do any of the following things to you?
   1. Hit you (78)

Yes	27
No	51

   2. Take shoes to you (73)

Yes	11
No	62

287

3. Club you (71)

Yes	15
No	56

4. Shake the hell out of you (76)

Yes	24
No	52

5. Rough you up (74)

Yes	23
No	51

6. Work you over (71)

Yes	13
No	58

7. Slam your face on something (75)

Yes	13
No	62

8. Split your head open (72)

Yes	9
No	63

9. Bounce you off his knee (72)

Yes	6
No	66

10. Drag you some place (76)

Yes	21
No	55

60. When you were sober, have you witnessed a bull do any of the following things to someone?

1. Hit someone (76)

Yes	37
No	39

2. Take shoes to someone (68)

Yes	14
No	54

3. Club someone (71)

Yes	20
No	51

4. Shake the hell out of someone (73)

Yes	28
No	45

5. Rough someone up (75)

Yes	36
No	39

6. Work someone over (70)

Yes	22
No	48

7. Slam someone's face on something (67)

Yes	12
No	55

8. Split someone's head open (65)

Yes	12
No	53

9. Bounce someone off his knee (66)

Yes	11
No	55

10. Drag someone some place (72)

Yes	29
No	43

61. Have you ever been pinched for drunk in a bar or in your own room? (96)

Yes	33
No	63

62. Have you ever been pinched for drinking in public in Seattle? (100)

Yes	72
No	28

63. Have you ever been pinched for drunk in Seattle when you had not been drinking at all? (95)

Yes	17
No	78

64. Have you ever been pinched for drunk in Seattle when you had been drinking but you were sure that you were not drunk? (97)

Yes	58
No	39

65. How do you usually plead to a drunk charge when you feel sure you were not really drunk? (93)

Guilty	87
Not guilty	6

66. Have you ever told the judge you were not guilty when you believed you were not guilty? (95)

Yes	26
No	69

67. Do you feel that the Seattle criminal court has provided you with "equal justice under the law?" (90)

Yes	32
No	58

68. About how much time, on the average, do you think it takes to try you for drunk in public (from the time the prosecutor reads your charge until you are given time or kicked out)? (88)

Less than one minute	33
2–5 minutes	33

6–30 minutes	10
Over 30	12

69. Do you feel the judges have taken enough time for you when you have gone to court on a drunk charge in Seattle? (92)

Never	20
Not usually	17
Sometimes	18
Usually	25
Always	12

70. Have you ever used a fictitious or alias name when you were booked for drunk so you could get a kickout? (100)

Yes	11
No	89

Do you know personally anyone who has done this? (99)

Yes	35
No	64

71. Have you ever appeared in court on a drunk charge and not been told what your rights were? (95)

Yes	32
No	63

72. If the court provided a free defense lawyer for you, would you make use of him? (98)

Yes	55
No	12
Sometimes	14
Don't know	17

73. If you have ever entered a plea of not guilty on a drunk charge where did you go to wait for your trial? (29)

Drunk tank	10
Holding tank	19

74. Have you ever asked to make a statement in court and not been allowed to do so in Seattle? (95)

Yes	14
No	81

75. How often have you been given breakfast before going to court on a drunk charge? (94)

Always	45
Most of the time	19
Not usually	10
Never	20

76. What do you feel is the worst thing about appearing in court on a drunk charge?

77. Have you ever personally counted the number of drunks in the drunk tank for one day (24 hours) or more? (98)

Yes	65
No	33

78. What is the longest period of time you have spent in the cement drunk tank in Seattle? (88)

1–5 days	86
6–10 days	7
Over 10	5

79. Have you ever spent one or more nights in the drunk tank when it was so crowded you could not lie down? (100)

Yes	83
No	17

In your experience, how often has this happened? (86)

Most of the time	36
About half the time	36
Not very often	9
Never	2
(weekends)	3

80. Have you been given a blanket when you are in the drunk tank? (99)

Never	96
Sometimes	2
Most of the time	
Always	1

81. How many cups are provided in the drunk tank for the drunks to get a drink of water? (99)

0 cups	5
1 cup	93
More than 1	1

82. Are the lights left on 24 hours a day in the drunk tank? (99)

Yes	94
No	5

83. When the lights are on in the drunk tank does the light make it difficult to sleep? (96)

Yes	86
No	10

84. Have you ever needed medical care when you were in the drunk tank and not gotten it? (95)

Yes	44
No	51

85. How do you feel about the medical care you have received in the jail? (93)

Very poor	56
Below average	14
About average	24
Better than average	1
Very good	2

86. What do you feel needs to be changed in the medical treatment for the prisoners?

87. Have you ever been treated badly by the nurses or doctors in jail? (94)

Yes	27
No	67

Componential Definition
of Trusty Domain

TABLE B.1 DIMENSIONS OF CONTRAST FOR
TRUSTY DOMAIN

1.0 Restricted Mobility
  1.1 Inside
  1.2 Outside

2.0 Freedom
  2.1 Live outside the jail in another part of town. Eat at restaurants, are free to go to stores and movies, and may have visitors throughout the week.
  2.2 Leave the jail each morning and return in the late afternoon. Must eat a lunch prepared in jail. Some opportunity to go to stores but items must be smuggled back into jail.
  2.3 Leave the jail in morning, return at noon to eat lunch, and then go back out until late in the afternoon.
  2.4 Leave jail in morning, return at noon to eat lunch, then go back out until late afternoon, but the place of work is in the same building as the jail.

TABLE B.1 DIMENSIONS OF CONTRAST FOR
TRUSTY DOMAIN (Concluded)

3.0 Confinement
    3.1 Leave 6th and 7th floor of public safety building and travel by elevator to the jail kitchen on first floor. Upon return at the end of the work day will often be examined for contraband.
    3.2 Remain within the bucket itself (6th and 7th floors) but have freedom to move throughout these two floors.
    3.3 Must work in a restricted area on a single floor.

4.0 Work Focus
    4.1 Guns
    4.2 Buildings
    4.3 Wheeled vehicles (cars and motorcycles)
    4.4 Boats
    4.5 Food
    4.6 People

5.0 Direct Service (provided to others)
    5.1 Bulls
    5.2 Bulls and civilians
    5.3 Bulls and trusties
    5.4 Bulls and inmates
    5.5 Court
    5.6 Bulls, inmates, and civilians

TABLE B.2 COMPONENTIAL DEFINITION OF
TRUSTY DOMAIN

| | Dimensions of Contrast | | | | |
Trusty	1.0	2.0	3.0	4.0	5.0
Ranger	1.2	2.2		4.1	5.1
Odlin's man	1.2	2.4		4.2	5.1
Garage man	1.2	2.3		4.3	5.1
Georgetown man	1.2	2.2		4.2	5.1
City Hall man	1.2	2.3		4.2	5.2
Harbor Patrol man	1.2	2.1		4.4	5.1
Wallingford man	1.2	2.1		4.2	5.1
Floor man	1.1		3.3	4.2	5.4
Clerk	1.1		3.3	4.6	5.1
Bull cook	1.1		3.3	4.2	5.3
Court usher	1.1		3.3	4.6	5.5
Hospital orderly	1.1		3.3	4.6	5.6
Blue Room man	1.1		3.3	4.5	5.1
Kitchen man	1.1		3.1	4.5	5.6
Runner	1.1		3.2	4.6	5.4
Barber	1.1		3.3	4.6	5.4

APPENDIX C

Componential Definition
of Flop Subdomains

The taxonomy of *flops* shown in Table 4.1 has a number of levels. All
the terms share at least one feature of meaning in that they are all
kinds of *flops*. The componential analysis of all terms at the highest
level of contrast (Table 4.3) provides some of the semantic principles
which define lower levels of contrast, or subdomains. Table 4.3 shows
that the terms in some subdomains show a great deal of variation on
the eight dimensions of contrast whereas others show little variation.
For example, the only thing we are able to say about *railroad flops* is
that none require *monetary resources* (1.1). *Mission flops*, on the
other hand, may be defined by one value on each of the first eight
dimensions of contrast shown in Table 4.2. Componential definitions
for five additional subdomains are provided here (Tables C.1–C.5).
The dimensions of contrast and their respective values may be found
in Table 4.2. The terms which make up the subdomain of *mission
flops* (Table C.4) all refer to specific places rather than categories with
the exception of *sally*. These terms were elicited from a single informant who had been a tramp for more than twenty years. Although
many more could have been elicited from this man, the dimensions of
contrast could probably define most additional mission flops. Although

294

the componential analysis of this subdomain was not systematically tested with other informants, they used many of these dimensions of contrast in their discussion of mission flops.

TABLE C.1 COMPONENTIAL DEFINITION OF
WEED PATCH FLOP

	Dimensions of Contrast					
Weed Patch	2.0	4.0	6.0	7.0	8.0	9.0
Pasture	2.1	4.3	6.12	7.3	8.6	9.2
Cemetery	2.1	4.3	6.2	7.3	8.6	9.3
Viaduct	2.2	4.3	6.8	7.3	8.6	9.3
Bridge	2.2	4.3	6.8	7.3	8.6	9.3
Riverbank	2.1	4.3	6.8	7.4	8.6	9.3
Field	2.1	4.3	6.12	7.3	8.6	9.2
Orchard	2.1	4.3	6.8	7.3	8.6	9.2
Between buildings	2.3	4.2	6.2, 5	7.1	8.8	9.1
Park	2.1	4.3	6.8	7.2	8.8	9.1
Sidewalk	2.2	4.3	6.12	7.3	8.6	9.1
Jungle	X	4.3	6.8	X	X	9.3
Railroad track	2.1	4.2	6.8	7.4	8.8	9.2
Alley	2.1	4.2	6.8, 9	7.2	8.8	9.1
Dump	?	4.3	6.2	7.3	8.6	9.3

TABLE C.2 COMPONENTIAL DEFINITION OF
RAILROAD FLOP

	Dimensions of Contrast							
Railroad Flop	2.0	3.0	4.0	5.0	6.0	7.0	8.0	10.0
Switchman's shanty	2.7	3.1	4.3	5.1	6.12	7.3	8.4	10.1
Conductor's quarters	2.7	3.1	4.3	5.2	6.12	7.3	8.4	10.1
Coal car	2.1	3.2	4.2	5.1	6.12	7.4	8.6	10.2
Box car	2.5	3.1	4.3	5.1	6.8	7.2	8.6	10.2
Flat car	2.1	3.1	4.2	5.1	6.8	7.2	8.8	10.2
Reefer	2.5	3.1	4.3	5.1	6.12	7.2	8.6	10.2
Piggyback	2.1	3.1	4.2	5.1	6.8	7.2	8.8	10.2
Station	2.7	3.2	4.2	5.2	6.9	7.1	8.4	10.2
Gondola	2.1	3.1	4.2	5.1	6.8	7.2	8.6	10.2
Passenger car	2.6	3.1	4.3	5.1	?	7.3	8.6	10.2
Sand house	2.7	3.1	4.3	5.1	?	7.3	8.6	10.2
Crummy	2.6	3.1	4.3	5.1	6.12	7.2	8.5	10.2

TABLE C.3 COMPONENTIAL DEFINITION OF "PLACES IN PAID FLOP"

Places in Paid Flop	Dimensions of Contrast				
	3.0	4.0	5.0	6.0	8.0
Lobby	3.3	4.3	5.2	6.4	8.4
Toilet floor	3.1	4.2	5.1	6.4, 9	8.4
Hallway	3.1	4.2	5.1	6.4, 9	8.8
Bathtub	3.1	4.2	5.1	6.4, 9	8.4
Closet	3.1	4.3	5.1	6.4	8.6

TABLE C.4 COMPONENTIAL DEFINITION OF MISSION FLOP

Mission Flop	Dimensions of Contrast				
	11.0	12.0	13.0	14.0	15.0
Sally	11.1	12.2	13.3	14.1	15.1
Dawes	11.1	12.1	13.1	14.2	15.2
Pacific Garden	11.3	12.4	13.3	14.2	15.1
Holy Cross	11.4	12.1	13.3	14.1	15.2
The Mitt	11.2	12.1	13.3	14.2	15.1
Wheelers	11.2	12.4	13.3	14.2	15.1
Toby's	11.3	12.4	13.2	14.2	15.1
Bread of Life	11.1	12.4	13.2	14.2	15.2
City	11.2	12.3	13.3	14.2	15.1
Joe's	11.3	12.3	13.2	14.2	15.1

TABLE C.5 COMPONENTIAL DEFINITION OF CAR FLOP

Car Flop	Dimensions of Contrast					
	1.0	2.0	4.0	6.0	7.0	8.0
Truck	1.1	2.5	4.3	6.11	7.1	8.6
Used car lot	1.1	2.5	4.3	6.2	7.1	8.5
Junk yard	1.1	2.5	4.3	6.2, 8	7.1	8.5
Transit bus	1.1	2.5	4.3	6.2, 8	7.1	8.6
Harvest bus	1.1	2.5	4.3	6.8	7.4	8.6
Car on street	1.1	2.5	4.2	6.5	7.2	8.6
Own car	1.3	2.6	4.3	6.8	7.2	8.1

Index

297

300